ATLAS

OF

ISLAMIC HISTORY

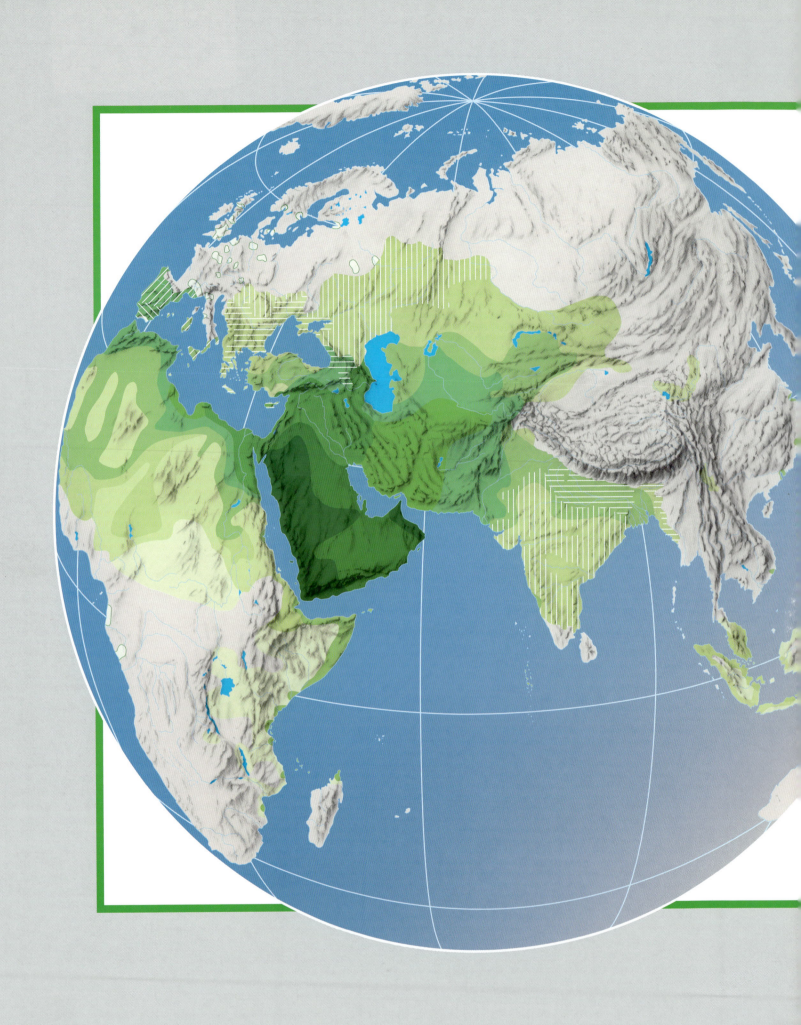

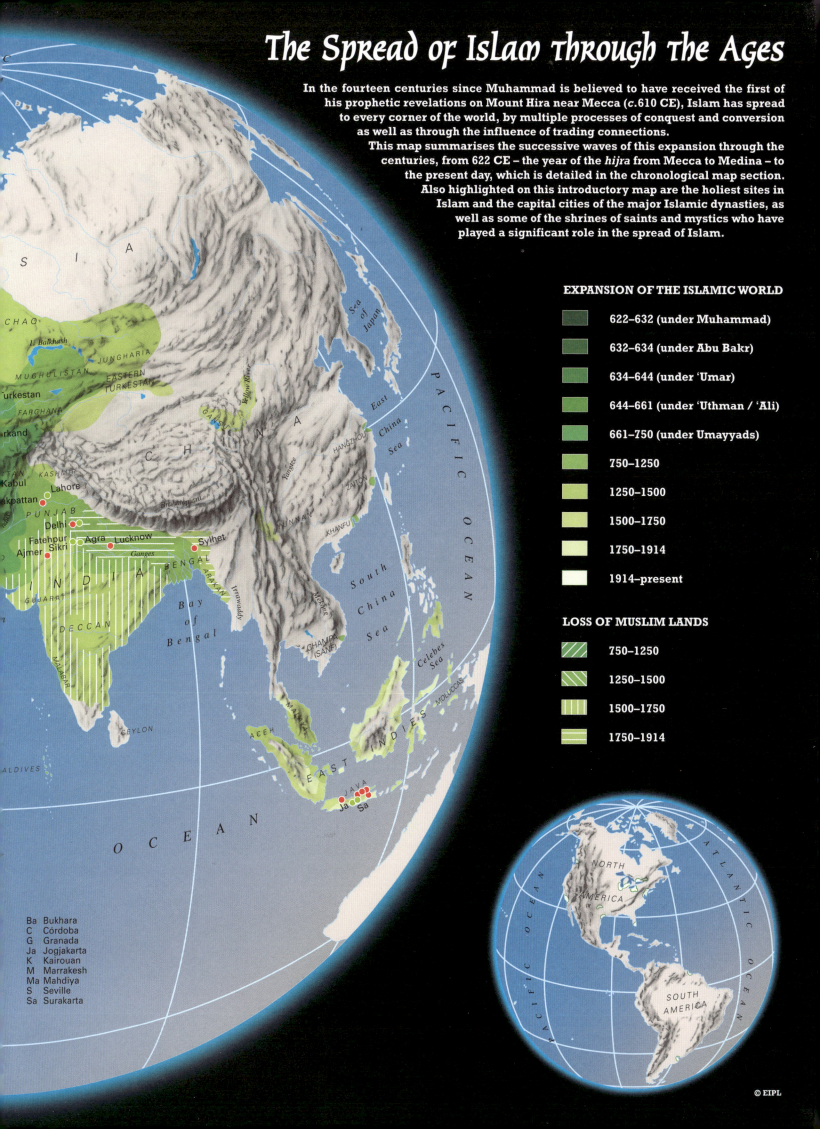

The Spread of Islam through the Ages

In the fourteen centuries since Muhammad is believed to have received the first of his prophetic revelations on Mount Hira near Mecca (*c*.610 CE), Islam has spread to every corner of the world, by multiple processes of conquest and conversion as well as through the influence of trading connections.

This map summarises the successive waves of this expansion through the centuries, from 622 CE – the year of the *hijra* from Mecca to Medina – to the present day, which is detailed in the chronological map section. Also highlighted on this introductory map are the holiest sites in Islam and the capital cities of the major Islamic dynasties, as well as some of the shrines of saints and mystics who have played a significant role in the spread of Islam.

EXPANSION OF THE ISLAMIC WORLD

- 622–632 (under Muhammad)
- 632–634 (under Abu Bakr)
- 634–644 (under 'Umar)
- 644–661 (under 'Uthman / 'Ali)
- 661–750 (under Umayyads)
- 750–1250
- 1250–1500
- 1500–1750
- 1750–1914
- 1914–present

LOSS OF MUSLIM LANDS

- 750–1250
- 1250–1500
- 1500–1750
- 1750–1914

Ba   Bukhara
C   Córdoba
G   Granada
Ja   Jogjakarta
K   Kairouan
M   Marrakesh
Ma   Mahdiya
S   Seville
Sa   Surakarta

© EIPL

ATLAS
OF
ISLAMIC HISTORY

PETER SLUGLETT

with

ANDREW CURRIE

Routledge
Taylor & Francis Group

LONDON AND NEW YORK

ATLAS
OF
ISLAMIC HISTORY

HISTORICAL DIRECTION AND NARRATIVE

Peter Sluglett
Director, Middle East Institute,
National University of Singapore

CARTOGRAPHIC DIRECTION AND DESIGN

Andrew Currie
Creative Viewpoint '*Where ideas map out*',
Glasgow, Scotland

ATLAS PRODUCTION

Ruth Coombs - *Digital mapping*
Cosmographics, Watford, England

Michael Wood - *3D hillshading imagery*
University of Aberdeen, Scotland

'**Ubayda Kohela** - *Arabic Edition adviser*
Professor of History, Cairo University

Fouad Estefan - **Georges Khoury**
Arabic Edition calligraphy and pre-press
c/o The Sayegh Group. Beirut, Lebanon

ATLAS PUBLICATION

English Edition – First published in 2014
by Routledge – Taylor & Francis Group
Milton Park, Abingdon, Oxon, OX14 4RN

Simultaneously published in USA / Canada
by Routledge – Taylor & Francis Group
270 Madison Avenue, New York, NY 10016

Arabic Edition – First published in 2014
by Egyptian International Publishing Co.
Longman (EIPL)
10a Hussein Wassef St., Dokki, Giza, 12311

Cataloguing-in-Publication Data
A record for this publication is available from the
British Library and the Library of Congress

Printed and bound in India
by Replika Press Pvt.

ISBN 978-1-138-82128-6 (hbk)
ISBN 978-1-138-82130-9 (pbk)

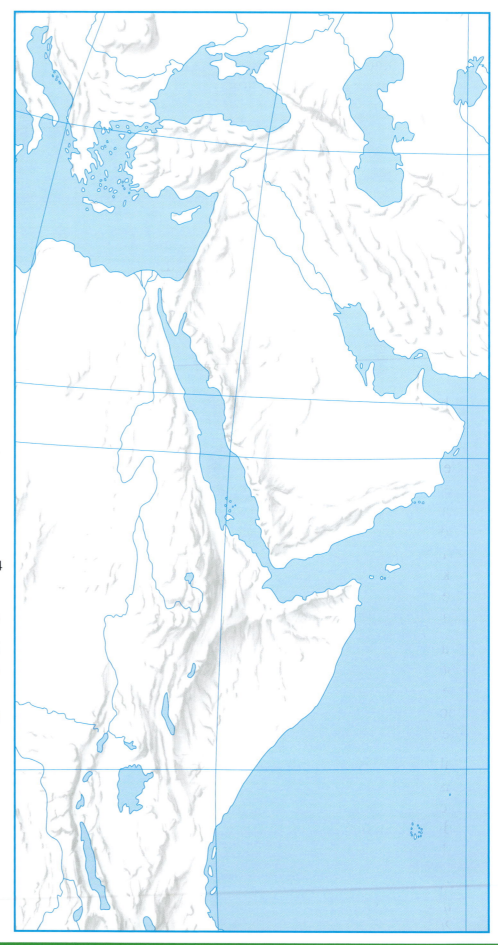

PREFACE

THIS ATLAS presents a graphic chronological history of the Islamic world in Africa, Asia and Europe until the beginning of the twentieth century. We have made use of the most recent scholarship, and of the latest internet technology and digital mapping techniques, to shed fresh light on this broad historical panorama in a visually arresting and intellectually stimulating way. Each map and its accompanying text has been thoroughly researched, scrutinised by one or more experts in particular fields of Islamic history, and duly revised according to their instructions. The breadth and scope of the Atlas has been designed to appeal not only to undergraduate and graduate students and their teachers, but also to general readers throughout the world.

This wide-ranging cartographic project, conceived from the outset for dual publication in Arabic and English, has taken many years to complete. That we have been able to bring it to fruition is entirely due to the support that we have enjoyed throughout its gestation from Librairie du Liban Publishers in Beirut. The Atlas was the brainchild of LdLP's founder, the late Khalil Sayegh, to whose memory it is dedicated, but we would also like to pay tribute to his late brother Georges who had a special passion for maps and their didactic benefits. Lastly, we must thank the current management of LdLP, under the direction of Habib and Pierre Sayegh, as well as the team at their Egyptian subsidiary EIPL, and particularly their adviser Dr 'Ubayda Kohela of Cairo University. We are also most grateful to Joe Whiting and his team at Routledge for their commitment to the publication of the Atlas in English.

We have worked on the Atlas together in a number of locations over four continents, mostly in Cairo, Glasgow, London, Salt Lake City, and Singapore. We would like to acknowledge the assistance of the staffs of the libraries of Durham University, the University of Glasgow, Harvard University and the University of Utah, and the staff of the Middle East Institute of the National University of Singapore. The sources we have used are listed in the Bibliography, but we would particularly like to salute the encyclopedic knowledge of Professor Yuri Bregel (1925–), now retired from the University of Indiana at Bloomington, whose masterpiece, *An Historical Atlas of Central Asia* (Leiden, 2003), has provided the foundation for our own coverage of a hitherto less well-known part of the world. It is also a great pleasure to acknowledge the invaluable assistance, advice and criticism, as well as the encouragement, of many colleagues and friends at various academic institutions across the world, whose names are listed in alphabetical order on the following page.

On a more personal level, we would like to thank members of our families and many friends on both sides of the Atlantic, and now on a small island off the south end of the Malay Peninsula, whose support has spurred us on, and whose polite incredulity that the project would ever be finished can now be laid to rest. In particular our spouses, Shohreh and Ruth, have put up valiantly with frequent invasions of their space, looked after us wonderfully over the years, and continue to do so.

Finally, we would like to express our gratitude to each other, for a working relationship which has lasted far longer than either of us expected when we embarked upon it, but which has been characterised by good humour, mutual respect, friendship, great enjoyment, and not least the unending excitement at the prospect of constantly discovering something new. We would like to pass this last sentiment in particular on to our readers.

Peter Sluglett ~ Andrew Currie
Singapore and Glasgow
July 2014

ATLAS ADVISERS

Gábor Ágoston - Georgetown University, Washington DC : *Ottoman Empire*

Kathryn Ebel Ágoston - George Mason University, Fairfax, Virginia : *Historical Geography of the Ottoman Empire*

Virginia Aksan - McMaster University, Hamilton, Ontario : *Ottoman Empire*

C. Edmund Bosworth - Emeritus, University of Manchester : *Medieval Islam*

Thomas E. Burman - University of Tennessee, Knoxville : *al-Andalus and the Maghrib*

Vincent Cornell - Emory University, Atlanta : *al-Andalus and the Maghrib*

Stephen Frederic Dale - The Ohio State University, Columbus : *Islamic India*

Edward J. Davies - University of Utah, Salt Lake City : *The Islamic World since 1500*

Devin A. DeWeese - Indiana University, Bloomington : *Islamic Russia and Central Asia*

Ross E. Dunn - Emeritus, San Diego State University : *Islamic Movements, 1750–1914*

Richard M. Eaton - University of Arizona, Tucson : *Mughal India*

R. Michael Feener - National University of Singapore : *Southeast Asia*

Carole Hillenbrand : University of Edinburgh : *Medieval Islam*

Peter Jackson - Emeritus, Keele University : *Delhi Sultanate*

Hugh Kennedy - School of Oriental and African Studies, University of London : *Medieval Islam*

Adeeb Khalid - Carleton College, Northfield, Minnesota : *Muslims in 19th century Russia*

Derek Latham - University of Edinburgh († 2005) : *Medieval Islam*

David Morgan - Emeritus, University of Wisconsin, Madison : *Mongols and Central Asia*

Andrew J. Newman - University of Edinburgh : *Safavid and Qajar Iran*

H. T. Norris - Emeritus, School of Oriental and African Studies, University of London : *North Africa*

Linda Northrup - University of Toronto : *Mamluks*

John Parker - School of Oriental and African Studies, University of London : *West Africa*

Timothy Parsons - Washington University in St Louis : *East Africa*

Randall L. Pouwels - Emeritus, University of Central Arkansas, Conway : *East Africa*

Madawi Al-Rasheed - King's College, University of London : *Arabia c.1700–c.1900*

David Robinson - Emeritus, Michigan State University, Lansing : *West Africa*

Francis Robinson - Royal Holloway College, University of London : *Islamic India*

Peter von Sivers - University of Utah, Salt Lake City : *Medieval Islam*

G. Rex Smith - Emeritus, University of Manchester : *Medieval Islam*

Geoff Wade - Asia Research Institute, National University of Singapore : *Early history of Islam in Southeast Asia and China*

John E. Woods - University of Chicago : *Iran and Central Asia*

ATLAS CONTENTS

Part One : Introduction

Part Two : The Maps

Part Three : Appendices

LIST OF

THE MAPS

9

GUIDE TO THE MAPS

THE MAPS IN THIS ATLAS have been specially designed to illuminate the dynamic nature of the history of Islam, bringing alive the processes of change and movement over time. The forty-five maps (including the two global images on the endpapers) are arranged in chronological order, from the Arabian Peninsula at the time of the birth of the Prophet Muhammad in the late sixth century to the entire Islamic world in the early years of the twentieth century, and beyond. Every effort has been made to group them together in regions, but this has not always been possible. Thus Maps 30 and 42 cover Islam in Southeast Asia *c.*1275–*c.*1600 and *c.*1600–*c.*1900 respectively. Each map is accompanied by a commentary that sets out the historical narrative; hence the maps and the texts complement each other.

The maps have been designed using a system of colour coding in which Muslim territory is shown consistently in various shades of green. For example, the territory of the Ottoman Empire is always shown in the same dark green (*see for example* Maps 24, 25, 31, 32, 33, 37, 38 and 39). Non-Muslim territory is shown in a variety of other colours, also used systematically throughout the Atlas. Thus in the classical period the Byzantine Empire is always indicated in purple, while in the modern period British possessions are shown in red and Russian expansion and activities are in indigo. Each map has one or more legends, or sets of keys, to the symbols specifically used, with Muslim and non-Muslim activity generally shown separately.

Also, a major feature of the maps is the use of colour-coded arrows to show the movement of ideas, peoples and armies, dated to show historical development over time. For example, on Map 3 the early expansion of Islam is indicated by a series of colour-coded arrows; the colours indicate the process under the Prophet and his immediate successors: Map 21 shows the progress of the Mongol invasions during the thirteenth century.

Another design feature denoting the gradual unfolding of events in the same region and the simultaneity of some events with others is the use of alternate diagonal colour stripes. For example, Map 27 shows the process of the *reconquista* in Granada; on Map 31 the diagonal stripes indicate the shifting power play in the eastern Anatolian / western Iranian borderlands, and the diagonal stripes on Map 35 show the decline of the Mughal Empire and the simultaneous expansion of Maratha / Hindu, Sikh and British power.

As the Muslim armies expanded, into, say, former Byzantine territory, the names of many of the principal towns were 'Islamised'. Thus on Map 1, Emesa appears as Emesa (Homs), while on Map 3 it becomes Homs. Similarly, Iconium (Konya) appears on Map 12, and remains Konya thereafter. This is explained in the Glossary, which contains all the principal variants of the geographical names.

We have followed a number of orthographic policies for the representation of place names throughout the Atlas.

- We have recognised and made use of the generally accepted English versions of place names, such as Cairo for al-Qahira, Damascus for Dimashq, Fez for Fas, Mecca for Makka, Seville for Sevilla or Ishbiliya, Kandahar for Qandahar, and so on.

- Especially for local place-names, we have tried to reflect the accepted forms of transliteration into English from the various languages involved in the coverage of the Islamic world (including Arabic, Malay, Persian, Pin-Yin, Turkish, Urdu). Macrons and microns have not been used. For reasons of space on the maps we have generally omitted the Arabic al-; hence Basra rather than al-Basra, Fustat rather than al-Fustat.

- Most North and West African names follow the French (colonial) model; hence Kairouan for al-Qayrawan, Meknès for Maknas, but in most cases an initial or medial 'w' has been substituted for 'ou'; hence Tuwat, Wargla, Walata.

- Ottoman Turkish place names on Maps 25 and 31 have been rendered according to the transliteration adopted in Donald E. Pitcher, *An Historical Geography of the Ottoman Empire from earliest times to the end of the sixteenth century*, Leiden, 1972.

- For Central Asian place names we have generally adopted the usage of Yuri Bregel, *An Historical Atlas of Central Asia*, Leiden, 2003, although we have followed common English usage for some better known places (Samarkand for Samarqand).

- Most physical geographical names (islands, lakes, mountains, rivers, seas and so on) are given in their contemporary English form (hence Tigris, not Dijla; Red Sea, not Bahr al-Qulzum).

- For personal and dynastic names we have followed a modified version of the spellings appearing in Clifford Edmund Bosworth's *New Islamic Dynasties*, 2nd edn., Edinburgh, 2004, without diacritical marks. All dynastic and regnal dates have been taken from this source.

All dates on the maps and in the texts conform to the Common Era calendar; *hijri* equivalents can be found in G.S.P Freeman-Grenville, *The Islamic and Christian calendars : AD 622–2222 (AH 1–1650) : a complete guide for converting Christian and Islamic dates and dates of festivals*, Reading, 1995.

It is worth mentioning that authorities in the same field may use different versions of the same geographical and personal names, especially in the Far East and in Central, South and Southeast Asia.

To guide the reader, the texts contain frequent cross-references to other maps in the Atlas where the material is presented either in more detail or in a different context, and as an aid to chronological continuity.

Finally, in addition to the inclusion on each map of a legend or key to the specific symbols used, a detailed and summary legend or key to the symbols and abbreviations generally used throughout the maps and texts can be found on the following page.

Map Legend
Symbols and Abbreviations

SYMBOLS used on the maps of the Atlas are fully explained here. Specific symbols are included in separate legends for each map. The depiction of relief has been purposely presented as a light 3-D hillshading background so as not to detract from the main historical data.

ABBREVIATIONS used throughout the maps and the texts of the Atlas are also defined here.

MUSLIM TERRITORIES

- Dynastic domains / other Muslim areas (in varied coded shades of green-yellow)
- Intra-Muslim territories (contested / shared over time)
- Areas of loose Muslim control

NON-MUSLIM TERRITORIES

- Empires, kingdoms and other states (in varied coded shades of blue-red)
- Non-Muslim / Muslim territories (contested / shared over time)
- Non-Muslim spheres of influence (colour coded)

OTHER LAND AND WATER FEATURES

- Non-specific land area
- Hillshading background
- Ocean / sea area
- Lake
- River
- Wadi / intermittent watercourse
- Strategic mountain pass

CITIES, TOWNS AND OTHER CENTRES

- Holy city of Mecca
- Caliphal capital
- Imperial / Provincial capital (Muslim)
- Local dynastic seat (Muslim)
- Imperial / Other capital (Non-Muslim) (colour coded)
- Other city or town
- Homeland nucleus (early Ottoman)
- Trading centre / colonial outpost (colour coded)
- Trans-Saharan 'gateway' market
- Garrison town (early Muslim)
- Centre of Islamic revival & reform (colour coded)
- Holy Islamic site (Java : wali sanga)
- Earliest evidence of Muslim presence (Southeast Asia)
- Early Muslim polity (Southeast Asia)
- Christian / Jewish settlement (in pre-Islamic Arabia)
- Important socio-economic and religious centre (in pre-Islamic Near East / Mediterranean)

MOVEMENTS OF PEOPLES AND IDEAS

- Major advances / attacks / missions (colour coded)
- Other expeditions (colour coded)
- Local raids
- Migration of peoples
- Overland caravan trade route (Primary / Secondary)
- Maritime trade route (Primary / Secondary)
- Navigable river
- Major shipping canal

SITES OF CONFLICT

- Major battle : Intra-Muslim / Other
- Sacked city (by Mongols / Timur)
- Centre of anti-colonial rebellion
- Major massacre (by Ottomans)

BOUNDARIES

- State / provincial boundary
- Territorial division (maritime)
- Other territorial sub-divisions (Muslim) (appanages, atabeg-s, successor states)
- Maximum extent of Muslim domains or spheres of trade / influence
- Russian fortification lines (Central Asia)

STYLES OF LETTERING

MAMLUKS	Dynasty / state
Qïpchaqs	Ethnic group / tribe
Isfahan	City / town
SAHEL	Geographical region
Caucasus	Mountains
Java	Island
INDIAN OCEAN	Ocean
Black Sea	Sea
Lake Balkhash	Lake
Yellow River (Huang He)	River
634	Date of advance / battle
(f.762) (1453)	Date of foundation / incorporation
(c.1496–1903)	Dates of regime power
[1819]	Date of direct colonial rule
Tropic of Cancer	Tropic
0°	Graticule reference

ABBREVIATIONS

AD	*Anno Domini* (Latin) In the year of our Lord
AH	*Anno Hegirae* (Latin) In the year of the *Hijra*
b.	born
BCE	Before the Common Era
c.	century
c.	*circa* (Latin) about
CE	Common Era
d.	died
ed. / eds.	editor / editors
edn.	edition
f.	founded
HQ	headquarters
I. / Is.	Island / Islands
J.	*Jabal* (Arabic) mountain
km	kilometres
L.	Lake
max.	maximum
Mts.	Mountains
N.B.	*Nota Bene* (Latin) note well
pp.	pages
Prot.	Protectorate
r.	reigned / ruled
St.	Saint
Sta.	*Santa* (Spanish) Saint
Str.	Strait
S/wood	Sandalwood
VOC	*Vereenigde Oostindische Compagnie* (Dutch East India Company)
Vol. / Vols.	Volume / Volumes
W.	*Wadi* (Arabic) watercourse

(Territorial Administration)

(Br.)	British
(Byz.)	Byzantine
(Du.)	Dutch
(Fr.)	French
(Ger.)	German
(It.)	Italian
(O.E.)	Ottoman
(Port.)	Portuguese
(Sp.)	Spanish
(Rus.)	Russian
(U.S.)	American

© EIPL

Map 1
The Arabian Peninsula *c.*570

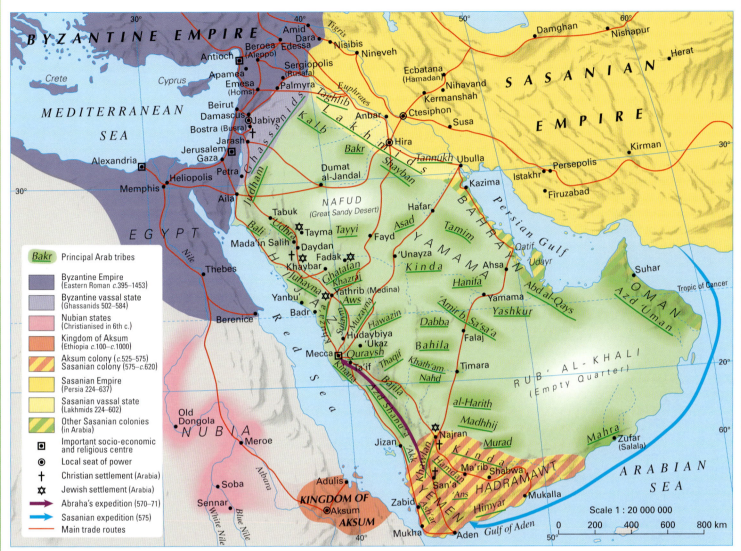

IN THE FIFTH AND SIXTH CENTURIES CE, the Arabian Peninsula gradually became more closely connected with the principal economic and political currents of the rest of the world. The Nabateans had ruled over an important trading civilisation based at Petra and Mada'in Salih between the fourth century BCE and the fourth century CE; in the first century BCE a Roman army reached Yemen, and parts of eastern Arabia were incorporated into the Persian empire in the third century CE. In the early centuries of the Christian era the authority of Yemen extended over much of central Arabia through its alliances with the tribal confederation of Kinda, until the latter's destruction in 529. In addition, there were several communities of Jews and (Nestorian) Christians in Hijaz and Yemen, while farther north there were Christian Arab tribes living on the edge of the Syrian steppe.

In the sixth century CE, outside powers again began to take an interest in the Arabian Peninsula. The Christian ruler of Aksum, in Ethiopia, conquered Yemen in the 520s, occupying the area for forty years. The last Ethiopian governor, Abraha, led an unsuccessful expedition to subdue Mecca in 570, the Year of the Elephant, traditionally designated as the year of the birth of the

Prophet Muhammad; shortly afterwards, Yemen came under Persian rule and remained so until the Islamic conquest in the 630s.

Also in the course of the sixth century, there were movements of Arab tribal populations from southern to northern and northeastern Arabia. The Fertile Crescent, on the edges of northern Arabia, formed part of the frontier between the two rival empires of the day, the Sasanian (Persian) and the Byzantine (Eastern Roman), each of which had a client or vassal state lying between itself and its rival. The Ghassanids of Jabiya were the clients of the Byzantines, and the Lakhmids of Hira those of the Sasanians.

Around 600 CE, the population of the Peninsula was divided into three main groups: the inhabitants of the small towns of the Hijaz (Mecca, Yathrib [Medina], Ta'if) and of Yemen (Ma'rib, Mukha, San'a'); the settled cultivators in the vicinity of the oases in the Hijaz, Yemen and Oman; and the nomads, the majority of the population. Relations between the groups were often tense, but they shared similar social values, and a certain symbiosis developed through interdependence on goods and services. Furthermore, they all spoke varieties of Arabic, the common formal and poetic language. The *qasida*, or ode,

with its themes of honour, hospitality, bravery, loyalty, and the transience of human life, forms the main cultural product of this period.

Almost all the inhabitants of the Peninsula claimed tribal origin, as an individual's survival depended largely on having a tribe to protect him. There were no permanent political institutions among the tribes; alliances were based partly on kinship and partly on claims of common descent, either from the northern (Qaysi) or southern (Yamani) tribal confederations. By 600 CE, Mecca was functioning as the principal socio-economic and religious centre. Its sanctuary, the Ka'ba, with its idols and tribal gods, attracted pilgrims, and the pilgrimage season was a time of tribal truce, when disputes were settled in the *haram*, or sacred enclave, of the Ka'ba, and commerce was conducted in peace. In the second half of the fifth century CE, it is believed that Hashim ibn 'Abd Manaf of Quraysh took control of the city and the shrine, and brokered a series of agreements (*i'tilaf*) with neighbouring tribes. These agreements enabled Mecca to develop into a commercial centre, although probably on a more modest scale than has traditionally been thought.

Map 2
The Near East and the Mediterranean at the Advent of Islam c.600

IN THE EARLY SEVENTH CENTURY CE the lands of the eastern and southern Mediterranean and of western Asia were divided between two vast and frequently antagonistic empires, the Byzantine, or Eastern Roman, and the Sasanian, or Persian. Well before the end of the Roman Empire in the West (around 476 CE) the increasing chaos in western Europe brought about by the invasion and settlement of Germanic, Slav and latterly Asiatic peoples had caused the centre of gravity of the Roman Empire to shift eastward. In 313 the Emperor Constantine (312–337) converted to Christianity and subsequently founded the city that bears his name on the site of the Greek city of Byzantium. Several decades later, under Theodosius (379–395), Christianity became the official religion of the Roman Empire. While western Europe continued to be overrun by invaders from the east (especially the Franks, the Goths and the Vandals), Constantine and his successors consolidated their rule in southeastern Europe, Anatolia and the eastern Mediterranean, including, for a while, Egypt and 'Greater Syria'. Some two centuries later, the Emperor Justinian (527–565) temporarily reconquered the eastern Adriatic, northern Italy, southern Spain and North Africa, and made almost the entire Mediterranean a Byzantine lake.

In matters of religion, the Byzantines rejected the primacy of the papacy, partly a consequence, and partly a cause, of the gradual dwindling of contacts between Byzantium and western Europe in the Dark Ages. This was to lead to the division of Christendom into Catholicism and Orthodoxy, although the formal breach, known as the Great Schism, did not take place until 1054. The Orthodox, or eastern, church was organised around local patriarchs loosely headed by the patriarch of Constantinople and became the state church of the Byzantine Empire, with a somewhat limited tolerance both of Judaism and of the doctrines of other churches in the area. For its part, the Catholic Church, under the direction of the popes, whose political aspirations would bring it into conflict with the rulers of the nation states that began to emerge in the high Middle Ages, remained the sole ecclesiastical authority in western Europe until the Reformation. In Egypt and the eastern Mediterranean the imposition of the Greek church and its Greek liturgy in the fifth and sixth centuries aroused a degree of opposition and resentment from local Copts, Jacobites and Nestorians, whose liturgical and literary languages were Coptic or Syriac and whose interpretation of the nature of Christ differed from that of the Greek church.

Farther east, the principal political entity was the Sasanian Empire (224–637 CE), based for most of its existence in the area that forms the modern states of Iran and Iraq. At its height in the sixth century, the Sasanian Empire extended from the Euphrates to the Indus valley, and it was involved in constant fighting with the Romans and Byzantines on its western flank. The Sasanian imperial capital was at Ctesiphon (Taj-i Khusrau), on the banks of the Tigris, just

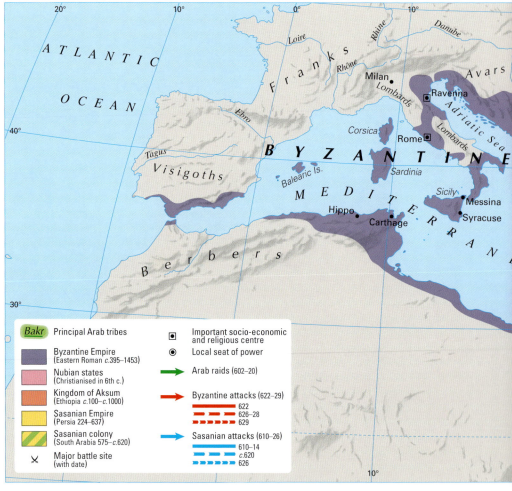

southeast of the modern city of Baghdad; its official religion, set out in the Avestan scriptures, was a modified form of Zoroastrianism, which saw life as a struggle on the part of the supreme creator (Ahura Mazda), representing life and truth, against the forces of evil and darkness, in which man would finally be judged by the extent of his commitment to one side or the other. Within the Sasanian Empire there were large Jewish and Christian (Armenian and Nestorian) communities, as well as adherents of the main heterodox offshoots of Zoroastrianism, Manichaeism and Mazdaism. On the whole the Sasanians did not require conformity in religious matters, which meant that, apart from the Manichaeans, members of the minority religions were not persecuted. Judaism, for example, flourished for most of the period of the Sasanian Empire.

Given that Muslims regard their religion as God's final message to mankind, it is important to emphasise that the apparently varied religious milieu into which Islam came, and into which it expanded beyond Arabia in the course of the seventh and eighth centuries CE, shared a number of common features. It was already largely monotheist, transcendental (believing in a higher world beyond the material one, to which the believer can aspire through faith and good works) and universalist (believing that the creator has created all men and continues to

govern their lives). In this environment, which was not always especially receptive to differences of faith, one of Islam's principal and enduring strengths would be its capacity for tolerance and assimilation.

Although the Byzantine and Sasanian Empires underwent periods of considerable prosperity in the sixth century, they became involved in a series of campaigns against each other that succeeded in greatly weakening them both. The wars intensified during the reigns of the Byzantine Heraclius (610–641) and the Sasanian Khusrau II (591–628). In 610 Khusrau attacked Constantinople; in 611–614 his armies occupied Syria, capturing Damascus and Jerusalem. In 620 Sasanian armies penetrated into Egypt, capturing Alexandria and marching as far south as Ethiopia. Heraclius gamely fought back with the aid of a huge levy from the Orthodox church, forcing the Sasanians to evacuate first Anatolia, then Armenia, Azerbaijan and Egypt. He fended off another attack on Constantinople in 626, and by 628 was laying siege to Ctesiphon. Khusrau refused to make peace, and was deposed and killed by his son, Kavad II. A period of chaos followed, caused largely by the strains of war and many years of infighting among the various claimants to the throne.

Internal weaknesses and the damage each side inflicted on the other meant that neither empire was in a position to offer effective resistance

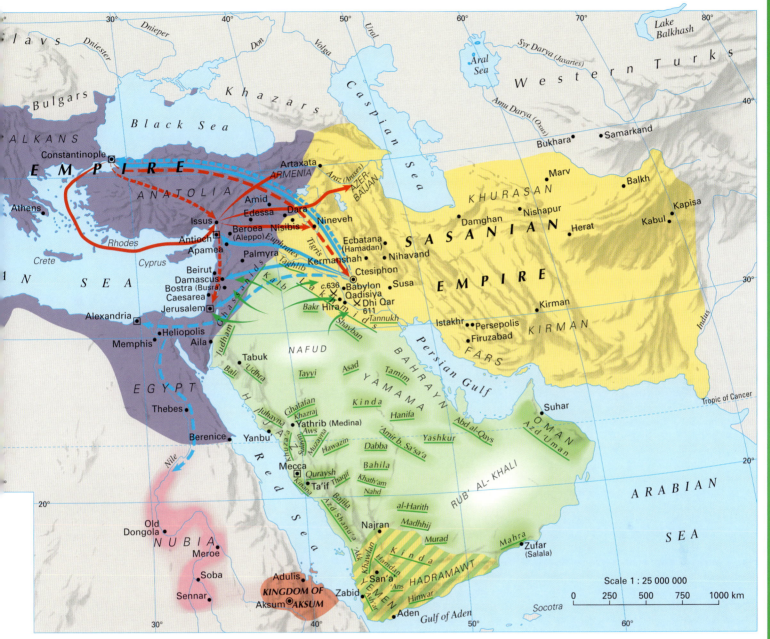

when the Arab conquests began in the second quarter of the seventh century. In the confusion following the Sasanian attacks on Syria and Palestine in 611, Arab tribal groups indulged in looting raids that penetrated to the walls of Jerusalem. Furthermore, the victory of the Arab tribes over the Sasanian armies at Dhi Qar in 611 meant the end of Sasanian control over northeastern Arabia. The Sasanian dynasty was completely extinguished within a few years, and its territories became part of the Arab domain. The last Sasanian emperor, Yazdigird III, was defeated at Qadisiya, southwest of Kufa, in 636 and eventually assassinated in 651. In contrast, although disastrously defeated by the Arabs and ultimately forced out of Egypt, North Africa and the eastern Mediterranean, the Byzantines managed to endure for far longer. Their empire persisted for many centuries in Anatolia and the Balkans, coexisting, often uneasily, with a series of Islamic dynasties in the neighbouring lands

and collapsed only in the face of constant pressure from the Ottomans in the fourteenth and fifteenth centuries (*see* Maps 22, 23 and 25).

The general tolerance shown by the Arab conquerors for the various sects and religions that they found in their new domains almost certainly served as an important factor in easing the transition from Byzantine and Sasanian to Arab rule. In the Byzantine Empire, non-Orthodox Christians had often been obliged to live on the fringes of the law. In addition, conversion to Islam was sometimes encouraged, almost always accepted, and, with relatively few exceptions, never imposed. Under early Muslim rule the 'Peoples of the Book' (monotheists with written scriptures, effectively Christians, Jews and Zoroastrians) were generally free to practise their own religion, although apostasy from Islam, as well as determined resistance to it, was almost always a capital offence.

Hence, although the majority of the population

of the region eventually converted to Islam, the process took many centuries, with the result that it was probably only in the eleventh or twelfth century CE that Muslims came to form the majority of the population of the 'Islamic world'. In addition, in the first century or so of the conquests, the Arab rulers sought to preserve a distance between members of the Arab armies (many of whom lived in specially constructed garrison towns; *see* Maps 3 and 4) and the subject populations. At this stage, because taxation was levied only on the (non-Muslim) conquered peoples, conversion to Islam was not particularly encouraged. The new rulers generally maintained the administrative and fiscal arrangements that their predecessors had put in place rather than imposing new ones. Under the early conquests, and especially where the Arabs encountered no resistance, members of the former landowning and governing elites were relatively easily incorporated into the new regime.

Map 3

The Expansion of Islam under the Prophet and the Rightly Guided Caliphs c.622–661

APART FROM THE QUR'AN, whose present form is conventionally dated to the caliphate of 'Uthman (644-56), there are no contemporary accounts either of the life of the Prophet Muhammad, the society into which he was born or the early years of the community that he founded. In addition, the Qur'an is God's revelation to mankind rather than a history of the foundation of Islam. Furthermore there is very little contemporary material on the early Islamic community in non-Muslim sources. The first record of the Prophet's life is the recension, by Ibn Hisham (d. 833), of the *Sira Rasul Allah* by Ibn Ishaq (d. 767), and this is the account that, for all the questions that it raises, serves as the main, and often the only, source of information for the origins and early years of Islam. The often repeated assertion to the effect that, of all the three great monotheistic faiths, only Islam was 'born in the clear light of history' has, therefore, little foundation in fact.

According to the traditional account, derived largely from Ibn Ishaq, the Prophet Muhammad was born in Mecca in 570 CE (the Year of the Elephant, *see* Map 1) into the clan of Hashim of the tribe of Quraysh. Muhammad's father died before he was born, and on his mother's death, when he was six, he went to live first in the household of his grandfather and later of his uncle, Abu Talib. Little is known of his early life except that as a young man he travelled as a merchant in the service of the woman he eventually married, Khadija. At this time, the people of the Arabian Peninsula were mostly animist and polytheist, worshipping the spirits of their ancestors, the moon and the stars and, in the small urban centres, various cults with a more or less elaborate pantheon of gods and goddesses. Mecca was the centre of a cult whose worship centred largely but not exclusively on Allah, Lord of the Ka'ba, a sanctuary founded by Abraham. Animal sacrifices were made there, and devotees would circumambulate the Ka'ba, invoking the name of Allah and other gods.

In 610, when he was about forty, Muhammad received the first of his prophetic revelations, which were characterised by their insistence on monotheism, God's omnipotence and guidance, and warnings of the Day of Judgment. Initially, only a few of the Prophet's closest associates (his wife, his paternal cousin 'Ali, and a few friends) accepted his divine mission, but as the community of believers gradually increased in number, other members of Quraysh became increasingly hostile, resenting the Prophet's apparent attacks on the religion of their fathers. In 617–18 a few of the early believers crossed the Red Sea and took refuge at the court of the ruler of Ethiopia, but tensions continued to rise. Especially after the deaths of his wife Khadija and his uncle Abu Talib, Muhammad's position in Mecca grew increasingly precarious. In 621, he responded to an invitation from emissaries from the agricultural settlement of Yathrib, later Medina, some 275 miles to the north, to act as

an arbitrator and mediator in the long-standing civil strife there. His migration (*hijra*) from Mecca to Medina in late June 622 marks the date on which the Muslim era begins.

In Medina, the Prophet founded what became known as the *umma*, the Islamic community, which consisted of the emigrants from Mecca (*al-Muhajirun*) and his Medinan supporters, or 'helpers' (*Ansar*). He generally succeeded in arbitrating between the various contending factions at Medina as well as laying the institutional foundations of a politico-religious community. This was buttressed by the Qur'anic revelations conventionally assigned to this period, which have formed the foundations of a corpus of Islamic civil, commercial, penal and personal law, as well as by a set of agreements (set out in the *Sira*) for regulating relations between the Medinan community, the *Ansar*, *al-Muhajirun*, and the Jews, known as the Constitutions of Medina.

One of the most pressing problems for the early Muslim community was that *al-Muhajirun* had no means of supporting themselves. This was solved by raids on caravans passing between Mecca and Ta'if, but at the Battle of Badr in 624 the Muslims made a successful attack on a more substantial caravan travelling southwards from Palestine to the Muslims' enemies at Mecca. In revenge, a Meccan force confronted the Muslims some three years later at the Battle of the Trench (*al-Khandaq*), but in spite of fierce fighting, the Muslims managed to hold their own, and the Meccans were obliged to withdraw. Further confrontations occurred through the 620s, but a peace agreement with Mecca was concluded in 628, and the Prophet entered the city in triumph, removing and destroying the idols in the Ka'ba.

Muhammad generally welcomed Arab converts, particularly, at this early stage, from members of Bedouin tribes, but the expansion of the community was also necessary for economic reasons. While still at Medina, the Prophet organised expeditions to Dumat al-Jandal (626), Mu'ta (629) and, after his return to Mecca, to Tabuk and Ayla ('Aqaba); he had dispatched an expedition to the north just before he died. While it cannot be claimed that he actually planned the conquests that took place under his successors, the Prophet seems to have understood that expansion was necessary if the nascent state was to thrive. By the time of his death, most of the tribes and inhabitants of Hijaz, Najd, Yemen and Oman had accepted Islam, made formal submission to the community at Medina and, as a sign of that submission, had begun to pay taxes (*zakat*).

The Prophet died in June 632 without having made clear arrangements for the succession. There were profound tensions within the community because of the competing claims of the different groups of which it was composed: the early Meccan converts, the Medinan *Ansar*, and those members of the aristocracy of Quraysh who had at first resisted the Prophet's message but had then come to accept it. The immediate

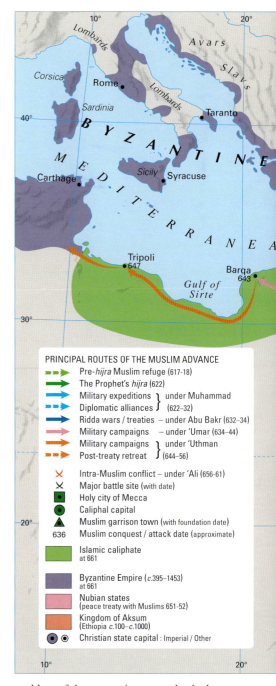

PRINCIPAL ROUTES OF THE MUSLIM ADVANCE

- Pre-*hijra* Muslim refuge (617-18)
- The Prophet's *hijra* (622)
- Military expeditions } under Muhammad
- Diplomatic alliances } (622–32)
- Ridda wars / treaties – under Abu Bakr (632–34)
- Military campaigns – under 'Umar (634–44)
- Military campaigns } under 'Uthman
- Post-treaty retreat } (644–56)
- ✕ Intra-Muslim conflict – under 'Ali (656-61)
- ✕ Major battle site (with date)
- Holy city of Mecca
- Caliphal capital
- ▲ Muslim garrison town (with foundation date)
- 636 Muslim conquest / attack date (approximate)
- Islamic caliphate at 661
- Byzantine Empire (c.395–1453) at 661
- Nubian states (peace treaty with Muslims 651-52)
- Kingdom of Aksum (Ethiopia c.100–c.1000)
- ◉ ◉ Christian state capital : Imperial / Other

problem of the succession was solved when 'Umar, one of the four closest Companions of the Prophet (who were all related to him by blood or marriage), nominated Abu Bakr, another Companion, as the successor to the Prophet (*khalifa rasul Allah*).

A major crisis facing Abu Bakr was the *ridda*, or the rejection by a significant number of Arab tribes of the authority of the new state. Following tribal custom, they had regarded whatever compacts they had entered into with the Prophet as being personal to him and thus terminated by his death. In the two years of Abu Bakr's short caliphate (632–34) he overcame this by diplomacy and armed force, effectively bringing the whole of Arabia under his control as well as beginning the conquest of Syria and Iraq. Under his successors, 'Umar (634–44) and

and 'Uthman (644–56), Arab/Muslim armies occupied Syria, Egypt, Iraq and most of what is now Iran, establishing several garrison towns. By 637, the Byzantines had lost Syria and an Arab army had entered Jerusalem. In 636 the Arabs had defeated the Sasanians at Qadisiya in southern Iraq, and in 639 they captured Edessa (modern Urfa) and much of eastern Anatolia. By 642, Arab forces had invaded Egypt, founded Fustat, taken Alexandria, and begun the conquest of North Africa. Also in the 640s, Arab armies penetrated to the Iranian plateau, took the province of Fars in 645 and reached Khurasan in 650. Meanwhile, to the south, they attempted to conquer Nubia on the upper Nile but faced fierce resistance and were obliged to conclude a peace treaty in 651–62.

While the Arab conquerers insisted on political

and fiscal submission, they generally allowed the populations whom they conquered to continue to practise their own faiths. The Qur'an says: 'Let there be no compulsion in religion: Truth stands out clear from error' (2:256). While it is conventional to refer to the armies and their conquests as 'Muslim', this appellation must be used with some caution since it cannot be assumed that 'Islam' or 'Islamic law' had yet crystallised as a fully formed religion or legal system at this stage.

Under the caliph 'Uthman, the underlying tensions within the community began to play an increasing role, largely because of his practice of favouring members of Quraysh, particularly his immediate relatives from the Banu Umayya, over the earliest Meccan converts to Islam. Eventually, in 656, he was murdered in his

home in Medina after a march on the city by discontented delegations from Kufa and Egypt. At the same time, a faction was forming around 'Uthman's successor, 'Ali (656–61), the Prophet's paternal cousin and son-in-law. Although 'Ali had not been involved in 'Uthman's murder, his position became increasingly precarious, since his supporters also came largely from a single group, the Medinan *Ansar*. A confrontation ensued at Siffin between 'Ali and a group from Quraysh led by Mu'awiya ibn Abi Sufyan, the governor of Syria, a cousin of the murdered 'Uthman. 'Ali's support began to dwindle and he was assassinated in Kufa in 661. The political centre of the state now moved from Medina to Damascus, where Mu'awiya and his descendants, the Umayyads, ruled for the next ninety years (*see* Map 4).

Map 4

The Umayyad Caliphate of Damascus 661–750

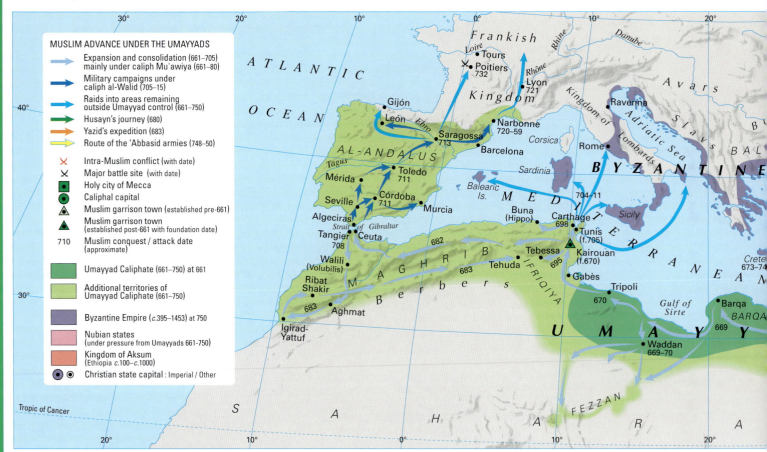

MUSLIM ADVANCE UNDER THE UMAYYADS

- Expansion and consolidation (661–705) mainly under caliph Mu'awiya (661–80)
- Military campaigns under caliph al-Walid (705–15)
- Raids into areas remaining outside Umayyad control (661–750)
- Husayn's journey (680)
- Yazid's expedition (683)
- Route of the 'Abbasid armies (748–50)

- ✕ Intra-Muslim conflict (with date)
- ✕ Major battle site (with date)
- Holy city of Mecca
- Caliphal capital
- Muslim garrison town (established pre-661)
- Muslim garrison town (established post-661 with foundation date)
- 710 Muslim conquest / attack date (approximate)

- Umayyad Caliphate (661–750) at 661
- Additional territories of Umayyad Caliphate (661–750)
- Byzantine Empire (c.395–1453) at 750
- Nubian states (under pressure from Umayyads 661-750)
- Kingdom of Aksum (Ethiopia c.100–c.1000)
- ◉ ◉ Christian state capital : Imperial / Other

THE ASSASSINATION OF 'ALI IN 661 left Mu'awiya in undisputed control of the Arab empire. Mu'awiya had been nominated governor of Syria in 641 by the caliph 'Umar and had established a strong base in Damascus. Although he was not able to resolve all the issues that had caused the Muslims to fight one another in the first place, his reign (661–80) was a period of consolidation and expansion. Sure of his base in Syria, and with a reliable ally in control of Egypt, Mu'awiya appointed a line of capable governors to the Iraqi provinces, where support for 'Ali's cause was strongest. In 671 his adopted brother, Ziyad, whom he had appointed governor of Iraq, sent a contingent of some 50,000 soldiers and their families from southern Iraq to settle in Khurasan on the northeastern frontier of the empire to create a permanent Muslim presence there.

Towards the end of his reign, Mu'awiya arranged for his son Yazid to be acclaimed as his successor, although the dynastic implications that this raised caused much discontent. Hence, on Mu'awiya's death, the main contenders for the leadership of the community once more attempted to press their claims. Husayn, the son of 'Ali, left Medina in an attempt to rally supporters in Kufa but was intercepted near Karbala' by Ziyad's son, 'Ubaydullah. Husayn and his party were subsequently killed in circumstances whose annual commemorations have remained potent symbols of the 'Alid cause.

While Husayn's failure pre-empted a pro-'Alid revolt in Iraq, Yazid found himself faced with

a serious revolt in the Hijaz, where Ibn Zubayr, the son of a Companion of the Prophet who had been a major figure in the opposition to both 'Uthman and 'Ali, proclaimed Yazid's succession unlawful and set himself up as caliph in Mecca. Accordingly, Yazid sent a force to the Hijaz, Medina was attacked, and the caliph's troops marched on to Mecca and were actually sacking the Ka'ba when it was heard that Yazid had died in Damascus. His son and successor, Mu'awiya II, died a few weeks later, and a major crisis seemed to be threatening, especially as a sizeable body of 'Syrians', particularly those from the tribal faction known generically as Qays, showed that they were prepared to abandon the Umayyad family for Ibn Zubayr.

The crisis was resolved by the resourcefulness of 'Ubaydullah ibn Ziyad, who rushed back to Damascus from Basra and persuaded the leader of the Yamani tribal faction in Syria to continue supporting the Umayyads. Between them they threw their weight behind the elderly Marwan ibn al-Hakam, a nephew of the caliph 'Uthman. In 684 a major battle took place at Marj Rahit, north of Damascus, at which the Yamani supporters of Marwan defeated the Qaysi supporters of Ibn Zubayr. A superficial reconciliation between the two factions was effected, but their continuing rivalry was to be an important factor in the Umayyads' eventual downfall.

Marwan died shortly after his accession and was succeeded smoothly by his son 'Abd al-Malik (685–705). After defeating his rival, Ibn Zubayr, and the Byzantines in the eastern

Mediterranean, 'Abd al-Malik began to consolidate his own power, setting up a centralised chancery and a mint. Arabic became the language of administration of the empire, gradually replacing Coptic, Persian and Greek. In 691, 'Abd al-Malik built the shrine of the Dome of the Rock in Jerusalem, partly as a place of pilgrimage, since Ibn Zubayr still occupied Mecca, partly, perhaps, to rival the Church of the Holy Sepulchre, and partly to symbolise the triumph of the Islamic faith. Its inscriptions emphasise the unity of God and specifically denounce the Trinity and the divinity of Jesus. Of fundamental importance for the development of Islamic civilization, it is the earliest work of Islamic architecture still retaining most of its original structure.

Although Islam was pre-eminently the religion of the Arabs, and the Qur'an had been revealed in Arabic, the conquests rapidly brought the new religion to peoples who were not Arab by birth. When non-Arabs converted to Islam, they became, in practice if not in theory, second-class Muslims, since they were still taxed as if they had not converted. In addition, taxes varied substantially from region to region in accordance with local practice before the conquests. At some stage of Umayyad rule this was changed, by making taxation on land uniform irrespective of the religion of the owner. Non-Muslims continued to pay jizya, the poll tax, but all paid kharaj, the land tax.

Under al-Walid (705–15) the caliphate expanded very greatly. By the end of the seventh

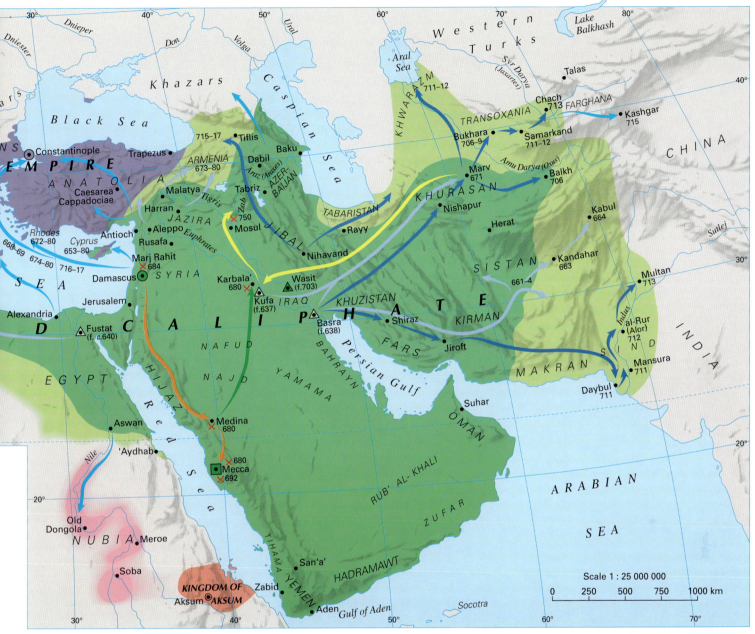

century, the Umayyads had expelled the Byzantines from the North African coastal towns, and by 708–09, despite initial resistance to Arab rule, most of the Berber tribes had accepted Islam, and much of the Maghrib was in Muslim hands. In 711, the distinguished Berber general, Tariq ibn Zayid, led an Umayyad force of some 7,000 new converts across the Strait and past the Rock that bears his name (Gibraltar, *Jabal Tariq*, the Mount of Tariq). Within five years, most of the Iberian Peninsula was incorporated into the Umayyad Caliphate as *al-Andalus*; the Muslims also raided into France until checked by Charles Martel near Poitiers in 732. The Balearic Islands, Sardinia, Sicily and other Byzantine enclaves in Italy were also raided between 704 and 711, and Constantinople was besieged unsuccessfully by a large Muslim force in 717–18.

At the same time, Muslim armies had penetrated to Khurasan and Transoxania (705–15) and to Farghana and the Indus Valley (708–13). Muslim

rule was permanently established in Central Asia; Samarkand and Bukhara became provincial capitals, and Sind and northwestern India were absorbed into the Umayyad Caliphate. However, even this rapid wave of expansion and a period of relative stability under the caliph Hisham (724–43) could not check rising discontent. By the time of Hisham's death there was profound strife between the Qaysi and Yamani factions in Syria, a Berber rebellion had been raging in North Africa for three years, and there were no Umayyad troops west of Kairouan. In addition, three of Hisham's nephews succeeded each other in less than two years. Eventually Marwan ibn Muhammad, a member of another branch of the Umayyad family, took over the caliphate in December 744 with the support of the Qaysi faction. The major threat to the dynasty, however, and the one that eventually overthrew it, was a rising in Khurasan that aimed to replace the 'usurpers of Damascus' with a descendant of the Prophet.

By the early 740s the Khurasani Muslims had transferred their loyalty from the Umayyads to the 'Abbasids, the descendants of Muhammad's paternal uncle, 'Abbas; the Umayyads, it will be remembered, were not related to the house of the Prophet. In 747, Abu Muslim, the leader of the 'Abbasid mission (*da'wa*) in Khurasan, had assembled an army that he led westwards from Marv to Iraq. After his troops arrived in Kufa in October 749, Abu Muslim gave public allegiance to Abu'l-'Abbas, whom he declared the first 'Abbasid caliph. Eventually the forces of Marwan and Abu Muslim joined battle on the banks of the River Zab near Mosul; Marwan was defeated and fled to Egypt where he was killed a few months later. The caliphal seat moved from Damascus to Iraq, and Baghdad, founded in 762 by the caliph al-Mansur, became the centre of an Islamic rather than an Arab empire (*see* Map 5). The 'Abbasid Caliphate would survive many vicissitudes until its overthrow by the Mongols in 1258 (*see* Map 21).

Map 5

Islam and Christendom under Harun al-Rashid (786–809) and Charlemagne (768–814)

THIS MAP SHOWS THE ISLAMIC AND CHRISTIAN worlds around 800, the year in which Charlemagne, the ruler of a precariously united Germanic and Roman Europe, was crowned Holy Roman Emperor by the pope in Rome. Charlemagne's grandfather, Charles Martel, who had stopped the Muslim armies near Poitiers in 732, was the son of a Merovingian court official; his father, Pippin III, King of the Franks (751–68), was the founder of the Carolingian dynasty. Pippin's two sons each inherited a share of the Frankish kingdom, and on his brother's death in 771 Charlemagne became ruler of much of continental western Europe; at their greatest extent his domains ran from Barcelona in the west to the Elbe in the east. His coronation in Rome symbolised the beginning of Europe's long recovery from the Dark Ages, during which the Roman Empire in the West had been destroyed by incursions of nomadic 'barbarians' from the Eurasian steppe. Muslim raids from *al-Andalus* and North Africa and Viking raids from Scandinavia in the ninth century meant, however, that it was not until the tenth and eleventh centuries that western Europe north of the Alps and the Pyrenees began to experience a relatively uninterrupted period of stability, economic growth and the expansion of cities and of trade (*see* Map 19).

The late eighth and early ninth centuries were a period of considerable insecurity in the Byzantine Empire, where the controversy over whether or not it was permissible to venerate icons caused deep internal divisions. In addition, a succession of weak rulers coincided with constant if not particularly effective attacks from Muslims in the east and with more pressing threats from the Avars and the Bulgars in the northwest. By 780 the Byzantine Empire had shrunk to less than a third of the size it had been in its heyday under Justinian (527–65); many provincial cities had been raided and pillaged, and trade and prosperity had declined. The Byzantine emperor Constantine VI succeeded his father at the age of ten in 780; in 797, he was blinded by supporters of his ambitious mother, Irene, the former regent, who succeeded him as ruler. In an effort to reunite the West and the East, Charlemagne proposed marriage to Irene, but she was deposed in 802 before the messengers bearing the offer had arrived in Constantinople. In spite of these internal rivalries and religious controversies, which lasted until the end of the ninth century, the Byzantine Empire experienced something of a revival, and eventually managed to hold out against the Muslims in Anatolia until the Seljuk invasions in the eleventh century (*see* Map 12). In addition, Byzantium was given a new lease of life by the gradual conversion of both Bulgaria and Russia to Orthodox Christianity, beginning in the late ninth century.

At the beginning of the ninth century, Baghdad and Constantinople were among the largest cities in the world. Baghdad, with about half a million inhabitants, was probably only

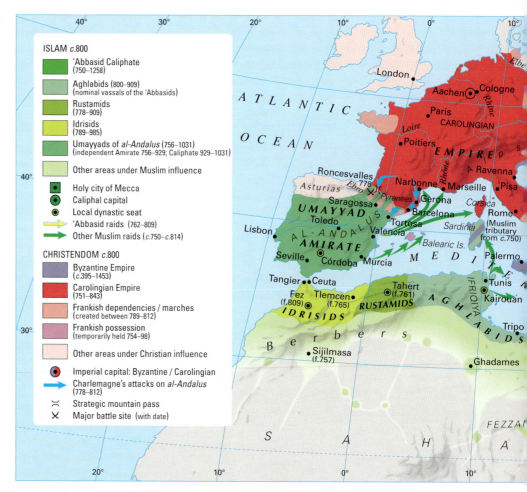

surpassed in size by the T'ang city of Chang-an (Xi'an) in China. Constantinople, founded in the fourth century on the ancient site of Byzantium, was certainly the largest city in Europe, with some 200,000 inhabitants, but it had not expanded beyond its original walls. In contrast, Aachen, Charlemagne's capital, was a town of about 5,000 inhabitants.

The construction of Baghdad, a new permanent capital on what was essentially a new site, was undertaken by al-Mansur (754–75), the brother of the first 'Abbasid caliph, al-Saffah (750–54). It marked the definitive shift of the centre of gravity of the caliphate to Iraq, the richest province of the Muslim empire, both in agriculture and in trade. Among possible alternatives, Khurasan, where the 'Abbasid *da'wa* had originated, was rather remote, and parts of it long remained rebellious; in 'Greater Syria', many still identified with the Umayyads, while Iraq had a long tradition of loyalty to the family of the Prophet, membership of which formed the bedrock of the 'Abbasid claim to legitimacy. The move also paved the way for the ascent of a new elite in which Muslims of Iranian and Turkic origin became prominent and powerful figures alongside Arab Muslims, largely doing away with the Arab 'caste supremacy' characteristic of the Umayyads. The pace of conversion to Islam was still relatively slow: perhaps only 30 to 35 per cent of the population of the former Sasanian Empire had become Muslim by the mid-ninth century.

Zoroastrianism in particular persisted for a long time, especially in settled rural areas.

The second caliph, al-Mansur, played a vital role in the establishment of the dynasty in its early years by removing or defeating potential claimants, including Abu Muslim, who had actually brought the 'Abbasids to power. He also succeeded, at least for the time being, in containing another important body of legitimist claimants, the descendants of 'Ali, who regarded the 'Abbasids as usurpers since 'Ali's family was much more closely related to the Prophet. This practice was taken further by al-Mansur's son, al-Mahdi (775–85), who tried to reunite the two branches of the family by showing special favour to the 'Alids.

The late eighth and ninth centuries marked the apogee of 'Abbasid power, although the remoter parts of the Islamic world had already begun to break up into smaller political units. *al-Andalus* and North Africa were ruled by local dynasties (a branch of the Umayyad family in *al-Andalus* and the Rustamids, Idrisids and Aghlabids in North Africa) and were never fully integrated into the 'Abbasid polity. Two important features of state administration at this time were, first, the insistence that the provinces, especially those closer ones (Iraq, Egypt, Syria, western Iran and Khuzistan), should remit part of their taxes to the central treasury, and, second, that the appointment of judges (*qadis*) was exclusively reserved to the central state.

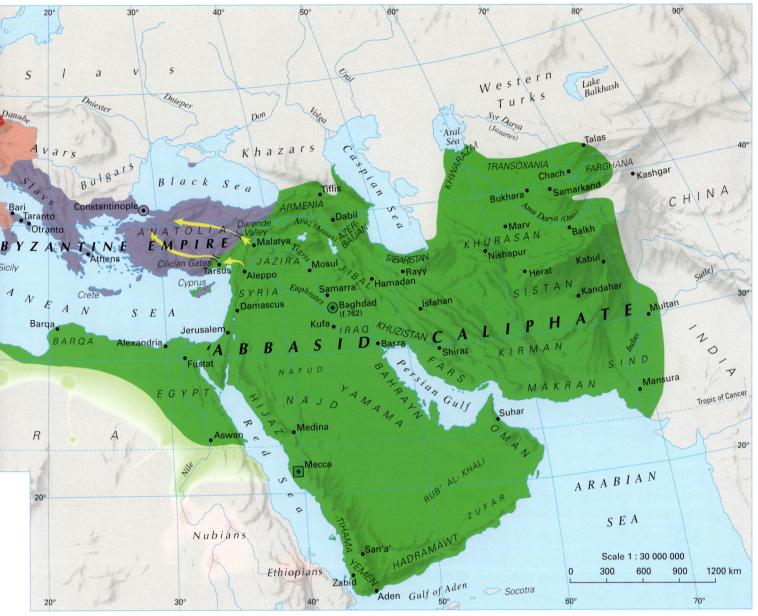

By the time of the early 'Abbasids, elements of an imperial bureaucracy, in the sense of a chancery (*diwan al-rasa'il*), an exchequer (*diwan al-kharaj*) and other departments of state with large staffs of clerks (*kuttab*), had begun to emerge. Many of the new officials were of Iranian origin; the Barmakids, from a family of Buddhist princes from Balkh, were among the first 'ministers' (*wazir*) and held important positions over several generations. Court life and ceremonial became increasingly complex, and court servants, particularly the chamberlain (*hajib*) and other senior bureaucrats, became influential figures in the administration of the caliphate. They often formed a court party, which ranged itself against elements in the army, which, in the early 'Abbasid period, was largely composed of Arabs whose ancestors had settled in Khurasan.

In common with most other Islamic dynasties, however, and for reasons that are not entirely clear, one key institutional issue was never

formalised by the 'Abbasids, namely a system of legitimate succession. This gave considerable scope for faction-forming around rival potential candidates within the family, and in the face of attacks on the dynasty from a variety of 'Alid claimants over the centuries, it always remained a fundamental structural weakness of the 'Abbasid state.

al-Mahdi died suddenly in 785; his son al-Hadi succeeded him but died just over a year later. In broad terms, al-Hadi had been supported by the army, and his successor, his brother Harun, who took the title of al-Rashid, by the court party. Like many 'Abbasids who followed him, al-Rashid tried to settle the succession by laying out the responsibilities and spheres of influence to be enjoyed by each of his two sons, but opposing factions within the court soon put paid to these arrangements.

The reign of al-Rashid has often been described as a golden age, perhaps because of its relative peacefulness when compared with

the discord that followed his death and perhaps also because he left a substantial surplus in the treasury. The 'Abbasids maintained diplomatic relations with the Byzantines, although these became increasingly strained with the constant raids into Byzantine territory in the first decade of the ninth century. The Carolingians were more distant from Baghdad, and their main contacts with the Islamic world were the Umayyads of *al-Andalus*, with whom they exchanged raids across the Pyrenean marches. On a more formal level it appears that there was some correspondence, and gifts, between al-Rashid and Charlemagne in 797, 801 and 807. While it would be many centuries before more regular trading and diplomatic relations were established with the states on the northern shores of the Mediterranean, the central Islamic lands enjoyed substantial commercial prosperity both from seaborne trade across the Indian Ocean and from overland caravan trade along the Silk Road (*see* Maps 19 and 20).

Map 6

The Eastern 'Abbasid Caliphate at the Height of its Power 750–c.820

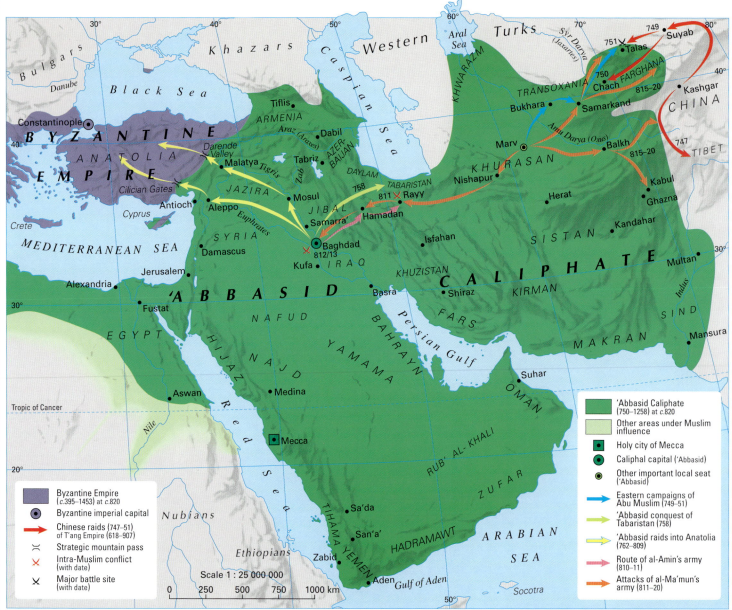

FOR THE FIRST SEVENTY YEARS of their dynasty, the 'Abbasids enjoyed undisputed mastery over the eastern part of their domains. In 751, Muslim and Chinese armies met at Talas, on the northeastern edge of Transoxania. Although victorious, the Muslims did not pursue their advantage beyond Farghana, which remained the eastern frontier of the Islamic world until late in the tenth century (*see* Map 9).

In spite of constant political upheavals, the early ninth century was one of the most brilliant periods of Islamic civilisation. Muslim scholars began to exploit the heritage of the Hellenistic world, especially Greek philosophy and science. Here a vital role was played by the caliph al-Ma'mun (813–33), who created a *scriptorium* for Greek, Sanskrit, Pahlavi and Syriac manuscripts in Baghdad, the Bayt al-Hikma, which provided facilities for the study and translation of the texts. Greek philosophy made major, if often controversial, contributions to Islamic theology (*kalam*).

In an attempt to secure the succession, al-Rashid had directed that the caliphate should

pass to his older son, al-Amin, and then to his second son, al-Ma'mun. When his father died in 809, al-Amin feared that his brother would challenge his rule, and eventually sent an army against him, which was defeated near Rayy in 811 by al-Ma'mun's general, Tahir. In 812 Tahir laid siege to Baghdad, and al-Amin was killed trying to surrender. Having had himself proclaimed *imam*, a religious title adopted by all subsequent 'Abbasid caliphs, al-Ma'mun returned to the capital only in 819. The intervening years were a period of great confusion, with a rival caliph being briefly recognised in Baghdad, and Egypt and Greater Syria slipping away from central government control.

The caliphate of al-Ma'mun was remarkable for several reasons, particularly for his attempts to turn the office into a religious as well as a political institution. First, he proclaimed 'Ali ibn Musa (al-Rida, the eighth imam of the Ja'fari Shi'is and a descendant of 'Ali) as his successor. This was most unpopular, and when al-Ma'mun left Khurasan, 'Ali was murdered and buried at

Mashhad in Khurasan where his shrine is still an important pilgrimage centre. Second, al-Ma'mun tried to impose the doctrine of Mu'tazilism, which emphasised free will and individual responsibility, holding that God had created the Qur'an (i.e. that it was not co-eternal with Him). As well as advocating that the caliphate should pass to the worthiest member of the Prophet's family, the doctrine implied that the imam/caliph could reinterpret divine revelation to accommodate the changing needs of the Muslim community. This would have turned the caliphate into a theocracy and was roundly opposed by the 'traditionists', who held that both the Qu'ran and the *sunna*, the sum of the reported practices of the Prophet as collected in the *hadith*, or 'tradition literature', were immutable and thus not open to human interpretation. Mu'tazilism was abandoned in the 850s, after which religious authority passed to the *'ulama'* the reciters and interpreters of the Qur'an and the *sunna*, thus creating a *de facto* separation between religion and state.

Map 7

The Emergence of Local Dynasties in the Eastern 'Abbasid Caliphate c.820–c.908

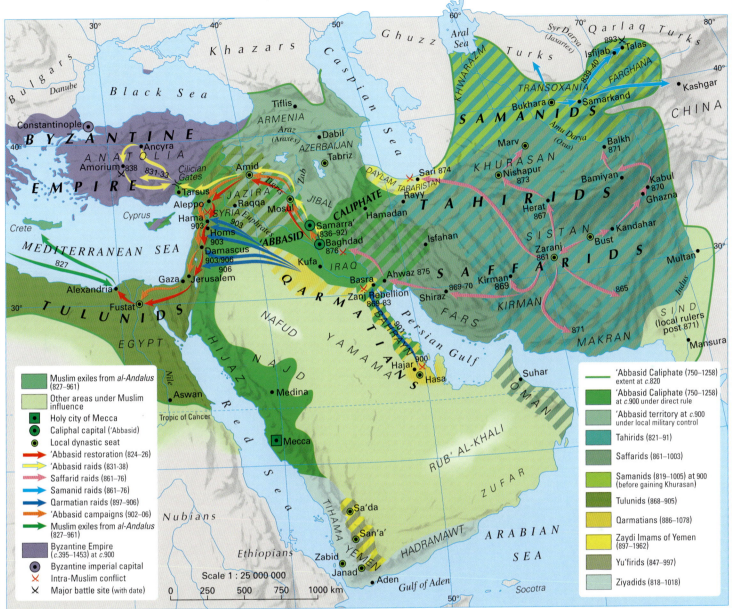

Legend (left):
- Muslim exiles from *al-Andalus* (827–961)
- Other areas under Muslim influence
- ⊙ Holy city of Mecca
- ⊙ Caliphal capital ('Abbasid)
- ⊙ Local dynastic seat
- → 'Abbasid restoration (824–26)
- → 'Abbasid raids (831–38)
- → Saffarid raids (861–76)
- → Samanid raids (861–76)
- → Qarmatian raids (897–906)
- → 'Abbasid campaigns (902–06)
- → Muslim exiles from *al-Andalus* (827–961)
- Byzantine Empire (*c.*395–1453) at *c.*900
- ⊙ Byzantine imperial capital
- ✕ Intra-Muslim conflict
- ✕ Major battle site (with date)

Scale 1 : 25 000 000
0 250 500 750 1000 km

Legend (right):
- 'Abbasid Caliphate (750–1258) extent at *c.*820
- 'Abbasid Caliphate (750–1258) at *c.*900 under direct rule
- 'Abbasid territory at *c.*900 under local military control
- Tahirids (821–91)
- Saffarids (861–1003)
- Samanids (819–1005) at 900 (before gaining Khurasan)
- Tulunids (868–905)
- Qarmatians (886–1078)
- Zaydi Imams of Yemen (897–1962)
- Yu'firids (847–997)
- Ziyadids (818–1018)

DURING THE NINTH CENTURY, much of the eastern 'Abbasid empire came under the rule of a number of local dynasties, despite the fiction generally maintained in Baghdad that supreme caliphal authority was still functioning. A number of would-be rulers seem to have decided that the best way of serving their political ambitions was to secure their power base in notional partnership with the caliph in Baghdad. Thus, al-Ma'mun's general, Tahir, and his descendants ruled eastern and northeastern Iran from Nishapur between 820 and 873. Tahir himself had begun to assert his independence from Baghdad, and al-Ma'mun was obliged to let Tahir's son Talha succeed him, although Talha and his successors were to remit regular tribute to Baghdad. In 873, their capital, Nishapur, fell to a warlord of a rather different order, Ya'qub ibn Layth al-Saffar of Sistan (861–79). Ya'qub attacked Baghdad unsuccessfully in 876, and he and his brother and successor, 'Amr, eventually ruled an area that included Sistan and Khurasan. In 900 the Saffarids were challenged in their turn by

a 'loyalist' eastern Iranian dynasty, the Samanids, supposedly descended from the Sasanian emperors; 'Amr was captured and executed by the Samanid Isma'il ibn Ahmad, whom a grateful caliph appointed governor of Khurasan (*see* Map 10).

The civil war had convinced al-Ma'mun of the importance of securing a smooth succession, and accordingly he nominated his younger brother, al-Mu'tasim (833–42), as his successor. In the process of bringing Egypt and Syria back under direct 'Abbasid rule in the 820s, al-Ma'mun had discontinued the practice of paying stipends to Arab elite families (i.e. the descendants of the original conquerors); now only al-Mu'tasim's own soldiers received payment. al-Mu'tasim himself led raids deep into Byzantine Anatolia notably a major campaign in 838.

A period of relative calm came to an end with the assassination of the caliph al-Mutawakkil in 861. Between 861 and 870 four caliphs ruled chaotically in the new capital, Samarra', which al-Mu'tasim had constructed some eighty miles north of Baghdad. The effects of this anarchy

were never entirely repaired. The caliphs gradually lost their ability to compel the provinces to send taxes to the centre, which meant that they were often unable to pay their troops. Several other provinces broke away from the centre: between 868 and 905 the governor of Egypt, Ahmad ibn Tulun, and his descendants carved out a principality for themselves in Egypt and Syria; Zaydi Shi'is founded dynasties in Yemen and the Caspian coastlands of Daylam and Tabaristan; and the Qarmatians, members of a militant and audacious Shi'i movement, based in Iraq and Bahrayn, attacked Basra in 901, and besieged Damascus twice, in 901 and 903. The caliphate survived under al-Mu'tamid (870–92) largely because of his energetic brother, al-Muwaffaq, who managed to defeat a slave revolt that had ravaged southern Iraq for fourteen years. After the court returned to Baghdad from Samarra' in the mid-890s, the dynasty's fortunes enjoyed a brief revival under al-Mu'tadid (892–902) and his son, al-Muqtafi (902–08), who restored 'Abbasid control over Egypt and Syria.

Map 8

The Development of Muslim Rule in North Africa and Spain c.800–c.950

THE MUSLIM CONQUEST OF NORTH AFRICA had begun with expeditions from Egypt to Barqa and Tripoli in the 640s (*see* Map 3) and continued in 670 with the foundation of the garrison town of Kairouan from where Arab and Berber armies gradually spread westwards through the Maghrib, eventually crossing to Spain (*see* Map 4). In 800, Harun al-Rashid conferred the province of Ifriqiya on the son of an Arab commander in the 'Abbasid army, Ibrahim ibn Aghlab, in return for an annual tribute (*see* Map 5). The Aghlabids ruled more or less independently until the Fatimid conquest in 909, initiating an Arab occupation of Sicily that was to last more than 250 years and raiding Corsica, Sardinia and southern Italy.

Especially in the early years of the conquests, when leadership was confined to the Arab warrior caste, the egalitarian Ibadi or Khariji movement gained many adherents among the Berbers. 'Abd al-Rahman ibn Rustam founded a principality at Tahert in modern Algeria in 761; he and his descendants were recognised as leaders by all the North African Ibadi communities but, like the Aghlabids, were destroyed by the Fatimids in 909.

Idris ibn 'Abdullah, the founder of the Idrisid dynasty of Morocco, was a great-grandson of 'Ali ibn Abi Talib and had fled the Hijaz after a failed revolt against the 'Abbasids in 786. In 808 his son, Idris II (803–28) built the city of Fez, which developed into a major centre of Islamic learning in the ninth and tenth centuries. The *shurafa'*,

or male descendants of the Prophet through his grandsons Hasan and Husayn, have continued to play a central role in Moroccan history. In the 910s, the Idrisids were obliged to accept a Fatimid governor, and the dynasty came to an end in 985, when Morocco became incorporated into the Fatimid empire. Meanwhile in Sijilmasa on the Saharan fringes of Morocco, the Midrarids, another Berber dynasty, came to power around 800, nominally as 'Abbasid vassals until 909 when they switched their allegiance to the Fatimids.

In 711 Tariq ibn Ziyad began the conquest of *al-Andalus* by defeating the Visigothic king Roderick (*see* Map 4). He soon captured Córdoba (which became the Muslim capital) and then Toledo; in 713 another army, led by Musa ibn Nusayr, took Seville and Mérida. The early conquests coincided with a period of dynastic upheaval in Spain; most resistance collapsed with the defeat of the monarchy, but the Muslim invaders also offered generous surrender terms. Many Visigothic aristocrats converted to Islam and thus retained their lands and positions of authority.

Although *al-Andalus* was nominally a province of the Umayyad and 'Abbasid caliphates, it is doubtful whether any tribute was remitted to the centre after about 720. By the late ninth century most of the population (Arabs, Berbers and native Iberians) spoke Arabic; many Christians and Jews had converted to Islam (*Muwalladun*), perhaps because of the heavy fiscal obligations

that had been put upon them. Seville and Córdoba developed into rich commercial centres, with splendid buildings and sumptuous courts, where the rulers patronised musicians, poets and scholars.

Three major rulers, each with long reigns, were the principal architects of this prosperity. The first was the founder of the Umayyad dynasty, 'Abd al-Rahman I (756–88), the second, 'Abd al-Rahman II (822–52), and finally 'Abd al-Rahman III al-Nasir (912–61). The latter came to power following a profound crisis in the late ninth century brought on by a combination of local rebellion, family intrigue and mass conversion to Islam, with its corollary, the diminution of the tax base. 'Abd al-Rahman III's reign marked the revival, and perhaps the zenith, of Muslim power in Spain, which extended as far north as the Duero river, to the Pyrenean marches, and beyond Tortosa on the Mediterranean coast. In 929, after restoring his authority in the south, and after having largely halted attacks from Christian states of the north by leading a number of decisive counter raids, 'Abd al-Rahman took the titles of caliph and *Amir al-Mu'minin*, Commander of the Faithful. This coincided with a major crisis in the 'Abbasid state in Baghdad (*see* Map 10), and also with the struggle between the Umayyads and the Fatimids for control of the gold route through North Africa (*see* Map 20).

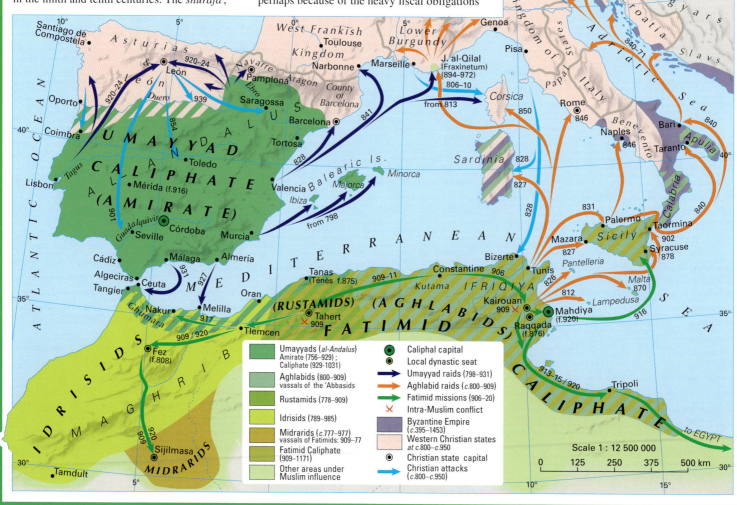

Map 9

The Ghaznavids and the Early Muslim Conquest of India 977–1099

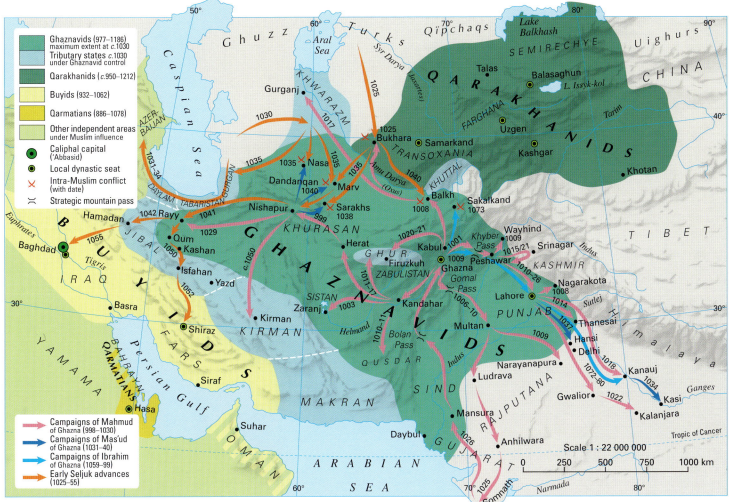

IN THE COURSE OF THE TENTH CENTURY, the 'Abbasid empire largely disintegrated and was replaced by Arab and Berber dynasties in the west and Turkic dynasties in the east. Two rival caliphates were declared in Cairo and Córdoba, and a Shi'i dynasty, the Buyids, ruled Baghdad in the name of the 'Abbasid caliphs. In 875 the caliph al-Mu'tamid had given the Samanid Nasr I ibn Ahmad (864–92) the governorship of Transoxania (*see* Map 7). In 900 Nasr's brother and successor, Isma'il, from his capital at Bukhara, defeated the Saffarids and was rewarded with control of Khurasan, while under Nasr II (914–43) the amirate extended west to Tabaristan, east to Farghana, north to Khwarazm, and south to Sistan (*see* Map 10). The Samanids' prosperity was linked to their control of the slave trade and to their location astride the east-west Silk Road from the Far East to Baghdad and the north-south route (for furs and amber) from Russia to the Punjab.

The Samanids were Persians; their successors, the Qarakhanids (992–1212) in Farghana and Transoxania, and the Ghaznavids (977–1186) in Khurasan, Zabulistan, and northwestern India, were Turks, like so many of the subsequent rulers of these areas. The Qarakhanids converted to Islam c.950, captured Bukhara in 999 and swiftly took over the former Samanid domains north of the Amu Darya, while the Ghaznavids took the lands to the south. The Qarakhanid 'state' was a loose federation, with branches ruling simultaneously

(and rarely harmoniously) in Balasaghun, Kashgar, Samarkand, and Uzgen, while the Ghaznavids set up a Perso-Islamic centralised state.

Following an unsuccessful *coup d'état* in 962, a Turkish commander of the Samanid army in Khurasan established himself in the fortress of Ghazna in Zabulistan. He and his successors ruled the region nominally on behalf of the Samanids until Sebüktigin (977–97) and his son Mahmud (997–1030) took over and set up the Ghaznavid dynasty. Under Mahmud, the Punjab became a major focus of Muslim settlement. The Umayyads had already reached the area in the eighth century, but Mahmud's campaigns were pivotal in the Islamisation of India and in the concomitant reduction of Hindu power. In 1018–22 he penetrated down the Ganges plain, and in 1025–26 he destroyed the temple of Shiva at Somnath in Gujarat, bringing back huge quantities of plunder to Ghazna. Some of the Ghaznavids' wealth was used to endow an impressively cultured court that patronised (and sometimes kidnapped) scholars and literary figures such as the poet Firdawsi (c.942–1020), the author of the Persian national epic, the *Shah-nama*, and al-Biruni (973–c.1050), historian and natural scientist, one of the great intellectuals of medieval Islam.

One of the keys to the Ghaznavids' success was their cordial relations with the 'Abbasid caliphs. Thus, in 1008, when the struggle over Khurasan between the Qarakhanids and the Ghaznavids

was resolved at Balkh in favour of the latter, Mahmud was invested with the province by the caliph al-Qadir, in whose name the Friday prayer was recited in the mosques and from whom he received the title of *Wali Amir al-Mu'minin*, Friend of the Commander of the Faithful. Another important factor was the Ghaznavids' profession of Sunni orthodoxy at a time when Shi'ism was in the ascendant after the foundation of the Fatimid Caliphate and the rise of the Buyids. After his father's death in 1030, Mas'ud ibn Mahmud (1031–40) asked the caliph al-Qa'im to grant him a long list of territories in Iran, Afghanistan and India.

However, the Ghaznavids were soon challenged by the Seljuks, another nomadic Turkic confederation pushed westwards by other steppe nomads. They entered the Islamic world as auxiliary soldiers, converting to Islam in the 990s. In 1038 they took Nishapur and in 1040 defeated Mas'ud of Ghazna at Dandanqan near Marv; this led to his deposition and also to the permanent loss of the Ghaznavids' Iranian provinces. The Seljuks were to assume the Ghaznavids' mantle as defenders of Sunni orthodoxy; in 1055, Tughrïl entered Baghdad and freed the 'Abbasid caliph from the Shi'i Buyids (*see* Maps 11 and 12). Although forced out of Iran, the Ghaznavids, especially during the reign of Ibrahim ibn Mas'ud (1059–99), continued to prosper in Zabulistan, Qusdar, Makran, Sind and particularly in the Punjab (*see* Map 12) which they held until their fall in 1186 (*see* Map 16).

Map 10
The Decline of the 'Abbasid Caliphate and the Rise of the Fatimids c.900–c.1000

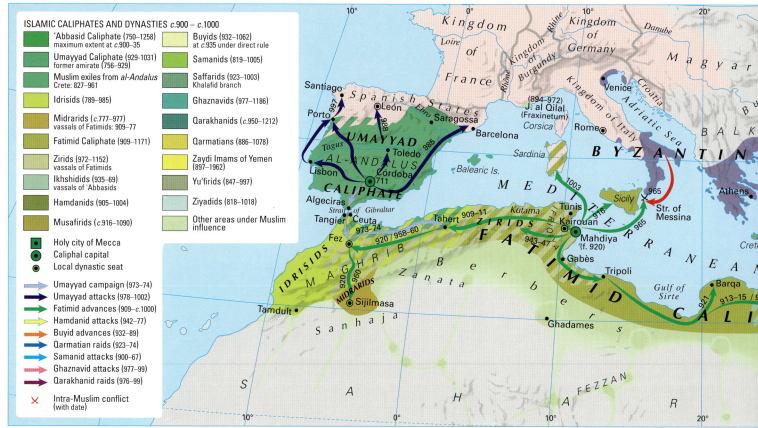

ISLAMIC CALIPHATES AND DYNASTIES c.900 – c.1000

- 'Abbasid Caliphate (750–1258) maximum extent at c.900–35
- Umayyad Caliphate (929–1031) former amirate (756–929)
- Muslim exiles from al-Andalus Crete: 827–961
- Idrisids (789–985)
- Midrarids (c.777–977) vassals of Fatimids: 909–77
- Fatimid Caliphate (909–1171)
- Zirids (972–1152) vassals of Fatimids
- Ikhshidids (935–69) vassals of 'Abbasids
- Hamdanids (905–1004)
- Musafirids (c.916–1090)
- Buyids (932–1062) at c.935 under direct rule
- Samanids (819–1005)
- Saffarids (923–1003) Khalafid branch
- Ghaznavids (977–1186)
- Qarakhanids (c.950–1212)
- Qarmatians (886–1078)
- Zaydi Imams of Yemen (897–1962)
- Yu'firids (847–997)
- Ziyadids (818–1018)
- Other areas under Muslim influence

- Holy city of Mecca
- Caliphal capital
- Local dynastic seat

- Umayyad campaign (973–74)
- Umayyad attacks (978–1002)
- Fatimid advances (909–c.1000)
- Hamdanid attacks (942–77)
- Buyid advances (932–89)
- Qarmatian raids (923–74)
- Samanid attacks (900–67)
- Ghaznavid attacks (977–99)
- Qarakhanid raids (976–99)
- ✕ Intra-Muslim conflict (with date)

THE TENTH CENTURY saw the confinement of direct 'Abbasid authority to southern Iraq and the immediate environs of Baghdad. The unity of the Islamic world had already begun to dissolve in the ninth century (see Map 7), but the process took on new dimensions in the tenth with the appearance of two additional caliphates, that of the Umayyads in al-Andalus (Spain) and of the Fatimids, first in Ifriqiya (Tunisia) and then in Egypt. In addition, a powerful Shi'i dynasty, the Hamdanids, ruled in Mosul and the Jazira until 979, and in Aleppo between 944 and 1004, and began to take on a revived Byzantine Empire. In the northeastern part of the Islamic world, the Samanids expanded into Khurasan after overcoming the Saffarids in 900 and then briefly into Sistan (911–23), although a collateral branch of the Saffarids regained local control in Sistan between 923 and 1003. In the late tenth century the Ghaznavids began to consolidate their rule over Zabulistan (southeastern Afghanistan) while the Qarakhanids emerged as a new Muslim force in the far north (see Map 9). Further west, the Buyids occupied Baghdad in 945 and took control over the caliphate until 1055. Of all these events, the rise of the Fatimids represented the most serious potential challenge to the 'Abbasid Caliphate, since their doctrine questioned its very legitimacy. In fact, as the Fatimids never penetrated permanently beyond Syria and their claims were not widely accepted, the challenge eventually foundered.

Late in 909, after a campaign fought on his behalf by a Kutama Berber army, which defeated the Aghlabids of Ifriqiya, the Isma'ili Shi'i leader 'Ubaydallah, emerged from hiding and was proclaimed *Mahdi*, Rightly-Guided One or Awaited Saviour, and *Amir al-Mu'minin*, Commander of the Faithful. The rise of the Fatimids reflects the arrival of a form of Islamic messianism influenced by Hellenistic gnostic speculation, which did not require the observation of 'outward' religious obligations (such as prayer or fasting). It would be led by a *Mahdi* who possessed special knowledge of the inner sense of the faith and would challenge the legitimacy of the 'Abbasids, whom the Isma'ilis considered had wrongly appropriated the 'true' Shi'i revolution in 750. At the same time, the Isma'ilis sought to take authority in Islam out of the hands of the jurists and confer it on a single Imam, who would be a descendant of Muhammad ibn Isma'il, the grandson of the sixth Imam, Ja'far al-Sadiq (d. 765), which the *Mahdi* claimed to be. The Imam would restore the original religion of Adam and the angels, thus evoking a paradisiacal (rather than a Meccan/Medinan) golden age. The validity of 'Ubaydallah's claim is impossible to corroborate, hovering as it does on the borderline between history and legend, and of course it was denied by many of his contemporaries.

In any event, 'Ubaydallah set about expanding his caliphate, initially with missions (*da'wa*) in North Africa (see Map 8) but soon making raids, albeit unsuccessful, on Egypt, his prime target, in 913–15 and 920. However for the next fifty years, Berber rebellions and Umayyad ambitions in the Maghrib obliged the Fatimids to turn their attention westwards. After the fall of Sijilmasa and Fez in 958–60, the Fatimids seem to have felt sufficiently confident to entrust their North African domains to their loyal vassals, the Zirids.

'Ubaydallah's goal was realised in 969 with the conquest of Egypt from the Ikhshidids, vassals of the 'Abbasids, and the foundation of Cairo under his great-grandson al-Mu'izz (see Map 11).

In contrast, the 'resumption' by 'Abd al-Rahman III of the caliphal title of his forbears in 929 did not signify any new doctrinal claim. The Umayyad amirs of Córdoba (since 756) had largely ignored the 'Abbasid caliphs in Baghdad, partly because the latter had been responsible for their overthrow, partly because they were so far away, and partly because the main challenges faced by the amirate were from within Spain itself. It is not entirely clear what prompted 'Abd al-Rahman to make his claim at the time. Perhaps the assumption of caliphal status would enable the Umayyads to be considered by the Byzantines (and others) as in some sense on a par with the 'Abbasids, and now the Fatimids, who had declared their caliphate only twenty years earlier. In asserting his new status in letters to his governors, 'Abd al-Rahman declared quite simply: 'We have decided that the *da'wa* should be to us as Commander of the Faithful and that letters emanating from us or coming to us should be [headed] in this manner.' While evidently posing a challenge to 'Abbasid legitimacy, the declaration seems to have had little or no practical consequences for relations between Córdoba and Baghdad.

During the early tenth century the 'Abbasid Caliphate was in profound disarray with its *de facto* authority reduced to parts of Iraq and Fars. The reign of al-Muqtadir (908–32), who succeeded at the age of thirteen, was marked by constant insecurity: there were fifteen changes of *wazir* and

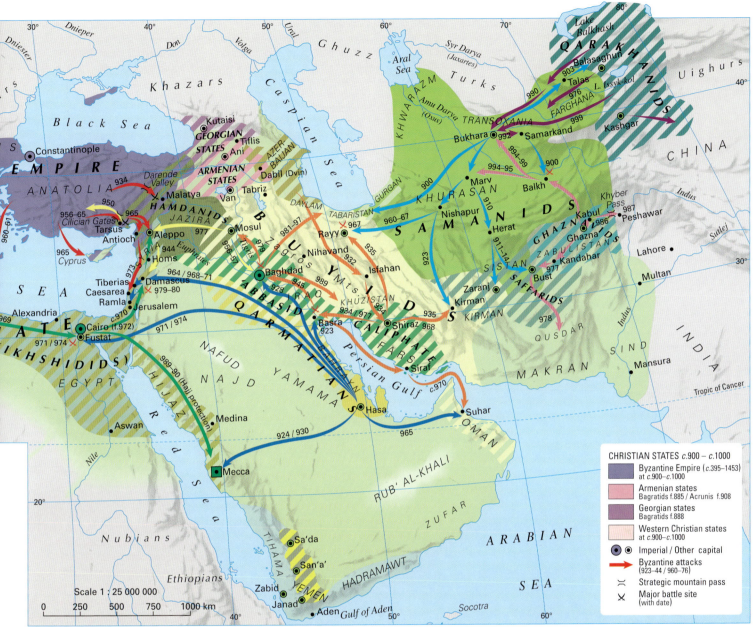

CHRISTIAN STATES c.900 – c.1000

	Byzantine Empire (c.395–1453) at c.900–c.1000
	Armenian states Bagratids f.885 / Acrunis f.908
	Georgian states Bagratids f.888
	Western Christian states at c.900–c.1000
⊙ ◉	Imperial / Other capital
→	Byzantine attacks (923–44 / 960–76)
⋊	Strategic mountain pass
✕	Major battle site (with date)

five *coups d'état*. Both under al-Muqtadir and his son al-Radi (934–40), affairs of state were largely controlled by the head of the Turkish palace guard, to whom al-Radi gave the title *Amir al-Umara'*, Prince of the Princes. Contemporary chroniclers paint a grim picture of the chaotic atmosphere in Baghdad, a city given over to famine, the depredations of the warring factions within the Turkish guard, and attacks on trade and pilgrim caravans by the (anti-Fatimid) Qarmatian Shi'is of Bahrayn. This turmoil continued under the successors of al-Muqtadir: the treasury was empty, the troops could not be paid, and five military commanders in turn seized the caliphate from the other between 936 and 945.

Around this time 'Iran' (in the broad sense of the territories between the Zagros Mountains in the west, Zabulistan in the east and Transoxania in the northeast) began to emerge as a more or less coherent entity. For a considerable time, the medieval Islamic world became divided *de facto* into an 'Arab' west and an 'Iranian' east, in

which none of the competing powers on either side of the divide could maintain more than temporary supremacy over the other.

Ahmad ibn Buya, who took Baghdad in 945, was one of a group of brothers who had served in the tribal armies of the rulers of Daylam on the southwestern shore of the Caspian. In the power vacuum of the early tenth century they gained control of most of southern and western Iran, and eventually forced their way into Baghdad and the rest of southern Iraq. Initially, each of the brothers ruled a separate region (Rayy, Shiraz and Baghdad) more or less independently, but a temporary unification of the three areas was achieved under 'Adud al-Dawla (977–83). Initially, Ahmad ibn Buya seems to have thought of getting rid of the caliph in Baghdad, but soon realised that his control of the office was a fairly straightforward means of legitimating his own position as *Amir al-Umara'*. The Buyids took over the land-holdings of the caliphate to pay their followers, captured Basra and initially enjoyed

fairly cordial relations with the Qarmatians (whom they managed to persuade to return the Black Stone, which the latter had captured from the Ka'ba in 930) before defeating them and putting an end to their influence in 986.

It is difficult to be sure of the sectarian loyalty of the individual Buyid rulers. While most of the people of tenth-century Daylam were Zaydi Shi'is, several of the Buyids clearly identified themselves with Ja'fari or Twelver Shi'ism. As can be inferred from their attitude to the caliphate, however, the Buyids made a distinction between their own personal beliefs and the 'official religion' of the state under their control. On the other hand, Shi'is (as well as Christians and Jews) were allowed to profess their faith and gain promotion to high positions in the bureaucracy. In addition, Buyid rulers gave generously to the Shi'i holy places in Iraq. Almost inevitably, after the Sunni Seljuks seized power in 1055, the position of the Shi'is and the non-Muslim minorities declined again (*see* Map 12).

Map 11
The Fatimid Caliphate and the Buyid State 969–1062

BY THE LATE TENTH CENTURY, SHI'ISM seemed in the ascendant everywhere: the Buyids were promoting Twelver Shi'ism in Baghdad, the Hamdanids, also Twelver Shi'is, were in control of northern Syria and the Jazira, while the Fatimids ruled Egypt, most of North Africa and the Hijaz. In addition, partly perhaps in response to the more coherent formulation of Isma'ili Shi'ism under the Fatimids, Twelver Shi'ism began to develop a more defined doctrinal form, especially in terms of jurisprudence and of collections of *hadith*, as well as in the establishment of annual ceremonies commemorating both the Prophet's nomination of 'Ali at Ghadir Khumm and of the martyrdom of Husayn. As far as the Buyids were concerned, the fact that Twelver Shi'ism focused on a 'Hidden Imam' meant that the sect posed no obvious threat to their temporal authority. However, while many of the ruling dynasties of the Islamic world were Shi'i or at least sympathetic to Shi'ism, the movement made little headway in the cities, except in Kufa and Qum, and was largely confined to the southern Caspian coastlands, northeastern Iran and Transoxania, northern Syria and Iraq. Thus, whatever the inclinations of their rulers, most of the people of the major cities (such as Isfahan, Damascus and Cairo, and even Baghdad, apart from a few traditionally Shi'i suburbs in the south of the city) continued to follow Sunni Islam.

It has already been suggested (*see* Map 10) that the Fatimids (as Isma'ilis) posed the most serious political and doctrinal challenge to Sunni Islam. The political challenge became more acute with

the Fatimid conquest of Egypt and the foundation of their new caliphal capital, Cairo (*al-Qahira*, 'the Victorious'), in 972. During the long reign of al-Mustansir (1036–94) the Fatimids expanded into Syria, holding Aleppo for a brief period and even capturing Baghdad temporarily in 1059. Also at this time, with devastating consequences, the Fatimids sent Hilal and Sulaym tribesmen from Egypt to quell a rebellion in North Africa initiated by their former vassals, the Zirids and their western branch, the Hammadids (*see* Map 14), who had transferred their allegiance to the 'Abbasids in 1041. Isma'ili *da'i*-s, missionaries, trained at the al-Azhar college in Cairo, penetrated as far as Yemen and Sind.

For much of the eleventh century, trade with Europe and India flourished and Egypt and North Africa enjoyed considerable prosperity. The great monuments of Fatimid architecture still form an important feature of the urban landscape of the region. Although the Fatimid dynasty continued to rule in Cairo until its overthrow by Salah al-Din in 1171 (*see* Map 17), its authority would begin to decline with the dispute over the succession which followed the death of al-Mustansir in 1094.

In the latter part of his reign, 'Adud al-Dawla (d. 983) created a Buyid 'empire', uniting the family's possessions in Fars, Khuzistan, Kirman and southern Iraq, an arrangement that lasted until the death of his son, Baha' al-Dawla (989–1012). According to one source, 'Adud al-Dawla attempted to consolidate his family's position by trying to

marry his daughter to the 'Abbasid caliph al-Ta'i'. In 1029, Rayy, one of the independent Buyid kingdoms, was conquered by the Ghaznavids, after which the confederacy began to fall apart as a result of internal rivalries and pressures from the Seljuks, who eventually took Baghdad in 1055. Buyid power held out for a little longer in Fars, where it came to an end in 1062. Following the practices of so many other local dynasties since the mid-ninth century, the Buyids relied extensively on Turkish slave soldiers, whose commanders often became sufficiently powerful to determine the dynastic succession of their nominal overlords.

In contrast to the prosperity that accompanied Fatimid rule, the Buyid period was marked by economic recession, caused partly by declining productivity because of silting and inadequate drainage, partly by a series of major floods on the Mesopotamian plain, but also as a result of new and punitive taxes imposed by various rulers. On the other hand, the Buyids presided over something of a cultural renaissance, perhaps as a consequence of their generally tolerant attitude to both Muslims and the non-Muslim minorities. 'Adud al-Dawla opened a famous hospital in Baghdad that attracted medical practitioners from all over the Islamic world, and during the tenth and eleventh centuries the Buyids supported poets, philologists and historians, both in Baghdad and at their other courts in Shiraz and Rayy.

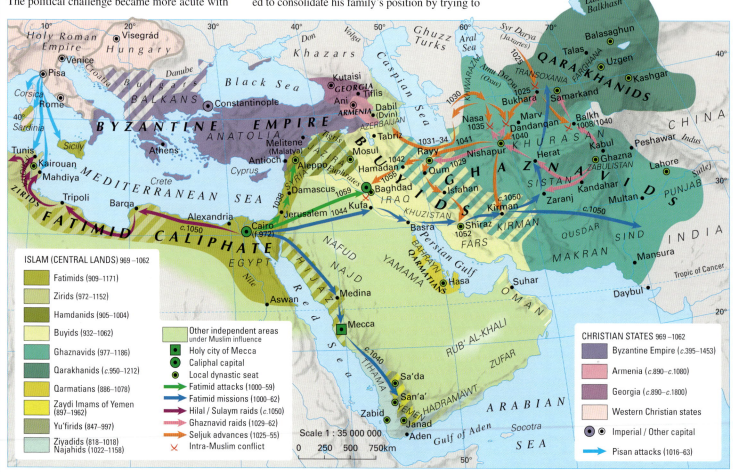

ISLAM (CENTRAL LANDS) 969–1062
- Fatimids (909–1171)
- Zirids (972–1152)
- Hamdanids (905–1004)
- Buyids (932–1062)
- Ghaznavids (977–1186)
- Qarakhanids (c.950–1212)
- Qarmatians (886–1078)
- Zaydi Imams of Yemen (897–1962)
- Yu'firids (847–997)
- Ziyadids (818–1018) Najahids (1022–1158)
- Other independent areas under Muslim influence
- Holy city of Mecca
- Caliphal capital
- Local dynastic seat
- Fatimid attacks (1000–59)
- Fatimid missions (1000–62)
- Hilal / Sulaym raids (c.1050)
- Ghaznavid raids (1029–62)
- Seljuk advances (1025–55)
- Intra-Muslim conflict

Scale 1 : 35 000 000
0 250 500 750km

CHRISTIAN STATES 969–1062
- Byzantine Empire (c.395–1453)
- Armenia (c.890–c.1080)
- Georgia (c.890–c.1800)
- Western Christian states
- Imperial / Other capital
- Pisan attacks (1016–63)

Map 12

The Consolidation of Seljuk Power from 1040 to the Death of Malik Shah in 1092

Legend (top-left):
- ■ Holy city of Mecca
- ● Caliphal capital
- ◉ Local dynastic seat

SELJUK 'EMPIRE' c.1092
- Great Seljuks (1040–1194)
- Seljuk branches
  Kirman (1048–c.1188)
  Syria (1078–1117)
  Rum (1092–1307)
- Other Seljuks & Turks
  Anatolian beg-s (c.1025–c.1100)
- Seljuk tributary enclaves
  Kakuyids of Yazd (c.1051–1141)
  Shaddadids of Ani (1072–1174)
- Qarakhanids (c.950–1212)
  vassals of Seljuks from 1089

- → Early Seljuk advances (c.1040–63)
- → Campaigns : Alp Arslan (1063–72)
- → Campaigns : Malik Shah (1072–92)
- → Migrations of Turks (c.1025–92)
- ✕ Intra-Muslim conflict (with date)

Scale 1 : 25 000 000
0   250   500   750 km

OTHER POWERS c.1092
- Fatimids (909–1171)
- Ghaznavids (977–1186)
- Zaydi Imams of Yemen (897–1962)
- Najahids (1022–1158)
- Sulayhids (1047–1135) vassals of Fatimids
- Other independent areas under Muslim control
- Byzantine Empire (c.395–1453)
- Georgia (c.890–c.1800)
- Cilician Armenia (c.1080–1375)
- ◉ ● Imperial / Other capital
- ✕ Major battle site (with date)

ALTHOUGH SOLDIERS OF TURKIC ORIGIN had long played a major role in Muslim armies, most of them were slaves, acquired in wars or in raids across the frontiers of the *Dar al-Islam*. In contrast, the Seljuks were Turkmen tribal nomads from the Central Asian steppes whose leaders had converted to Islam and migrated into Transoxania and Khwarazm in the early eleventh century, rapidly imposing their rule over a large part of the Islamic world. The Seljuk conquest, which was consolidated by the seizure of Khurasan after the defeat of Mas'ud of Ghazna at Dandanqan in 1040 (*see* Map 9), initiated a period of 'Turkish' rule over Iran that lasted at least until the rise of the more 'Persian' Safavids (although they were in fact also of Turkic origin) at the beginning of the sixteenth century.

In 1055 forces led by Tughrïl Beg (1040–63) entered Baghdad and restored it to Sunni rule. In return, the 'Abbasid caliph granted Tughrïl the titles of *sultan*, literally authority, and *Malik al-Mashriq w'al-Maghrib,* King of the East and the West.

Some four years later, Tughrïl and his nephew Alp Arslan defeated a Fatimid attack on the city. Alp Arslan (1063–72) succeeded his uncle; he and his son, Malik Shah (1072–92), were perhaps the most distinguished of the Seljuk rulers. They both had the good fortune to be served by the same Persian *wazir,* (chief) minister, Nizam al-Mulk, who established the pattern of a Persian-Islamic monarchy supported by a bureaucracy and a Turkish slave army that long outlasted the Seljuk dynasty.

The Seljuks, whose armies were generally larger than any of their predecessors, elaborated the system of land grants already known as *iqta',* a term that covered a wide range of fiscal arrangements. It proved a reasonably effective method of provincial government and was also the principal means of providing military manpower, thus relieving the state of financing a standing army.

Alp Arslan's principal ambition, the subjugation of the Fatimids, remained unfulfilled, although he and Malik Shah did manage to subdue their vassals in Aleppo and the Jazira. Alp Arslan's campaigns against Armenia and the Byzantine Empire were more successful: he took Ani in 1064 and won a stunning victory over the Byzantines at Manzikert near Lake Van in 1071, at which the Emperor Romanus Diogenes was captured. Although the Byzantine Empire survived for another four centuries, it was only ever able to exercise intermittent control of central and eastern Anatolia for a brief period under Manuel Comnenus (1143–80).

In 1081, following civil war in the Byzantine Empire for which Turkish assistance was sought, the Seljuks established their authority over most of Anatolia, penetrating as far as Nicaea (İznik). This, together with several other decisive campaigns, including the humiliation of the Qarakhanids in 1089, saw the Seljuks reach the zenith of their power, for soon after the death of Malik Shah in 1092 the dynasty would divide into a number of branches. The most significant of these was the sultanate of Rum, later based on the central Anatolian city of Konya (*see* Map 17), where Seljuk rule continued until it fell to the Mongols in 1307 (*see* Map 21).

Map 13
The End of the Umayyad Caliphate and the Rule of the *Muluk al-Tawa'if* c.1000–1086

Legend (Christian Spain c.1000–86):
- Spanish Christian states
- ⊙ Christian state capital
- Other Western Christian state
- → Campaigns of Alfonso VI of León & Castile (1083–86)
- × Major battle site (with date)

Legend (Muslim AL-ANDALUS c.1000–86):
- → Umayyad campaigns of al-Mansur (985–1002)
- Northern extent of Muslim al-Andalus c.1030
- ▯ Ta'ifa kingdoms } at c.1030
- • City state / Seat } at c.1030
- *1066* Date of annexation by larger ta'ifa kingdoms
- Ta'ifa kingdoms } at c.1086
- ⊙ Capital city } at c.1086
- Berber principalities (in North Africa)
- → Early Almoravid advances (c.1050–86)
- Northern extent of Muslim al-Andalus c.1086

Scale 1 : 6 500 000

THE REIGNS OF 'ABD AL-RAHMAN III, his successors, al-Hakam II (961–76) and Hisham II (976–1009: 1010–13), marked the apogee of Umayyad power in *al-Andalus*. For most of the reign of Hisham (who was only fifteen when he succeeded his father), real power lay in the hands of the court chamberlain (*hajib*) Muhammad b. Abi 'Amir al-Mansur (d. 1002). On the one hand, al-Mansur expanded *al-Andalus* to its farthest extent, leading numerous expeditions across the Duero and the Ebro on which he was often joined by Christian allies. His forces sacked Barcelona in 985 and Santiago de Compostela in 997, and gradually consolidated the Umayyad position in North Africa. On the other, al-Mansur was largely responsible for the downfall of the Umayyad dynasty because of his almost exclusive reliance on imported Berber and Slav (*Saqaliba*) troops and officials. By 1031, more than twenty years of internecine warfare between the various 'foreign' groups and the

local population had brought about the demise of the caliphate and thus the end of centralised authority in *al-Andalus*.

The Umayyad Caliphate was replaced by a large number of local states, whose rulers were known as the *Muluk al-Tawa'if* or 'Party Kings' (from *ta'ifa*, pl. *tawa'if*, party or faction). Some of the states (for instance Toledo and Badajoz) were quite extensive, while others consisted only of a principal city and its immediate hinterland. Many of the rulers were local notables whom the Umayyads had appointed as governors, and who had seized power for themselves at various times before the fall of the dynasty; others were set up by opportunists fleeing the chaos in Córdoba. Although the larger *ta'ifa* kingdoms, especially the 'Abbadids of Seville, subsequently expanded at the expense of their neighbours, none of them seems to have considered that its interests would be best served by the restoration of the caliphate.

By the latter part of the eleventh century, in consequence of the disarray caused by the rivalries among the *ta'ifa* kingdoms, the Christian north

had made considerable progress in its now explicit objective to reconquer the Muslim south. Finding themselves in need of allies, the *ta'ifa* rulers looked to North Africa for help. This was to come from a group of Berber warriors who had converted to Islam in the 1040s, taking the name *al-Murabitun*, 'the frontier warriors', latinised to Almoravids. They acquired a large army, founded a capital at Marrakesh and conquered Fez, Tlemcen, Tangier and Ceuta. The first contacts between the *ta'ifa* rulers and the Almoravids took place in the early 1080s, but it soon became clear that seeking their aid was not without its own risks. They were extreme and puritanical, and could not easily countenance either the religious laxity of the *ta'ifa* rulers or their habit of buying off their Christian neighbours with tribute in gold (*parias*). But by 1085 Alfonso VI of León and Castile (1065–1109) had taken Toledo, and by 1086 he had raided as far south as Aledo in Murcia and Tarifa in Málaga. In that year the Almoravids proclaimed a *jihad* against the Christians, crossed the Strait of Gibraltar with a large army, and defeated Alfonso's forces at the battle of Zallaqa/Sagrajas (*see* Map 14).

Map 14

Northwest Africa and Spain under the Almoravids c.1050–c.1130

BY THE EARLY TWELFTH CENTURY most of the *ta'ifa* kingdoms in *al-Andalus* had come under Almoravid rule; in 1110, Saragossa was also taken, although it was permanently recaptured in 1118 by Alfonso of Aragon, 'El Batallador' (1104–34). The Almoravids were an alliance of Sanhaja Berbers from the Guddala, Lamtuna and Massufa tribes, which formed in the 1040s in the area that is now Mauritania and Western Sahara. They adopted a strict form of Maliki Sunnism, and through a combination of religious fervour and military enterprise expanded their territory in two directions: southwards and then southeastwards through Awdaghust and Timbuktu; and northwards, first to Morocco and then to Spain. Traders between Sijilmasa and Awdaghust brought gold from the south and textiles and salt from the north and centre of the Sahara (*see* Maps 19 and 20). In addition, Islam travelled southwards along the trans-Saharan trade routes. Hence by the mid-eleventh century many of the Berber tribes of this remote region were at least nominally Muslim, and Islam has continued to be the prevailing faith of the peoples of the Sahel to this day (*see* Map 15).

Some time during the 1050s the Almoravids adopted the name by which they are now known (*see* Map 13) and moved gradually northwards, easily taking the major towns in Morocco where they also earned the nickname *al-mutalaththimun*, 'the veiled ones', because of their habit of covering their faces to protect against sand and wind. In 1061 Yusuf ibn Tashufin took charge of the Almoravids' northward expansion, and in the following year he set up his new capital at Marrakesh, financing its administration through his control of the trans-Saharan salt and gold trade. By 1075 Ibn Tashufin had extended Almoravid control over most of Morocco.

At much the same time, Alfonso VI of León and Castile (1065–1109) had begun his seemingly inexorable progress southwards (*see* Map 13). It is not entirely clear which of the *ta'ifa* kings invited the Almoravids to come to their aid, but a Berber army under the command of Ibn Tashufin landed at Algeciras in July 1086, and went on to defeat Alfonso at Zallaqa in October. Anxious to protect his base in North Africa, Ibn Tashufin returned soon afterwards to Morocco with most of the army. Over the next few years Alfonso kept up the pressure on *al-Andalus*, gaining control of the strategically important fortress at Aledo.

After the failure of an expedition to recapture Aledo, Ibn Tashufin seems to have come to the conclusion that little would be served by continuing to cooperate with the *ta'ifa* kings (one of whom, al-Mu'tamid of Seville, actually joined forces with Alfonso). The Almoravids seized Granada in 1090, and by the end of 1091 had taken Córdoba, Seville, Aledo and Almería, and the Kingdom of Badajoz some three years later. Over the next few years Valencia went backwards and forwards between a puppet Muslim ruler controlled by El Cid, a Castilian force, and Almoravid occupation in 1102. Apart from this, the Almoravids had not recovered any of the lands captured by Alfonso VI by the time of Ibn Tashufin's death in 1107.

The swift collapse of the *ta'ifa* kingdoms was partly due to internal and intra-*ta'ifa* rivalries, partly to pressure from the Christian north, but also to the fact that they often preferred to pay tribute to their Christian neighbours rather than to hire soldiers who might subsequently turn against them. In addition, although most of the sources are written from the Almoravid point of view, they generally agree that the invaders showed respect to the Andalusian *'ulama'* and that they were welcomed by most of the population, who had long suffered from the ineffectiveness and rapacity of the *ta'ifa* rulers, while the Almoravids were well known for their simple lifestyle. The new rulers called themselves *Amir al-Mu'minin*, Commander of the Faithful, while acknowledging the spiritual authority of the 'Abbasid Caliphate, at least on their gold coinage.

Ibn Tashufin was succeeded as ruler by his son, 'Ali (1107–42), who spent most of his time in Marrakesh. 'Ali's brother Tamim ruled *al-Andalus* from Granada, which now became its effective capital. On a rare visit to *al-Andalus* in 1109 'Ali attempted to recapture Toledo, but the city withstood a long siege. The Almoravids confined themselves to the cities of *al-Andalus*; there was no large-scale immigration from Africa. The Berber tribesmen who formed the core of the army were generally a disciplined force, easily identifiable by their veiled faces. Their power base was tightly controlled, and there were few instances of intra-elite rivalry or feuding.

However, with the loss of Saragossa to Aragon in 1118, Almoravid power began to decline, and by the 1120s and 1130s the Christian armies were making incursions deep into *al-Andalus*. By the mid-twelfth century the Almoravids were faced with another movement of Islamic renewal, led by the Berber Almohads from southern Morocco, followers of Ibn Tumart (d. 1130), who overthrew the last Almoravid in Marrakesh in 1147 and soon turned their attention to Spain (*see* Map 26).

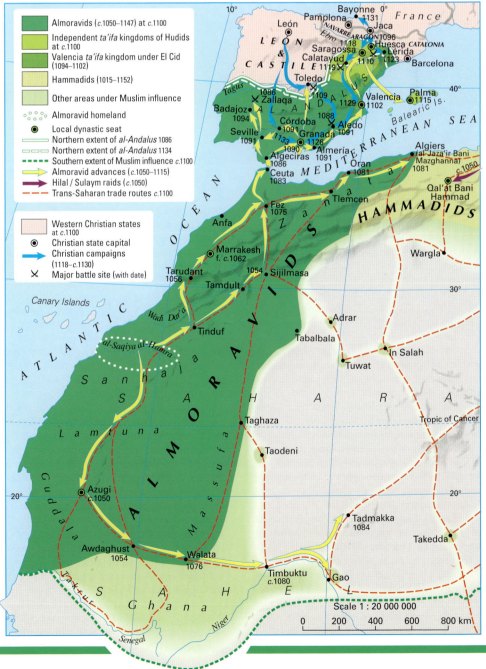

Map 15

The Diffusion of Islam in West Africa c.1000–c.1500

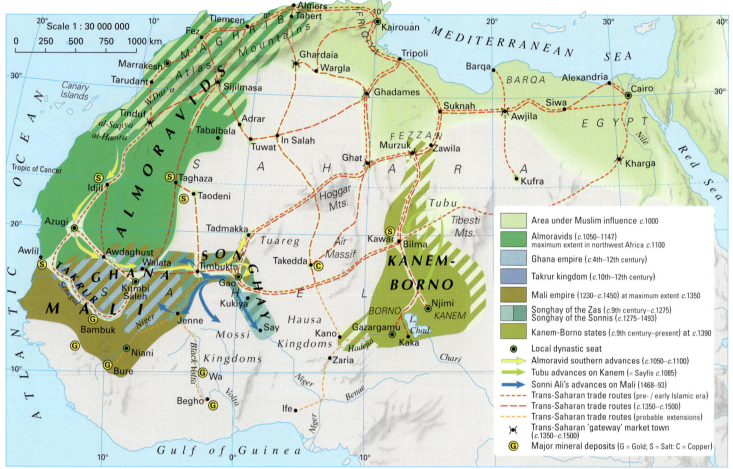

ALTHOUGH MUSLIM MERCHANTS from southern Ifriqiya and the Maghrib had founded mosques in towns along the Niger as early as the beginning of the ninth century, the more sustained Islamisation of West Africa began with the Berber Almoravids (c.1050–1147), who originated in what is now Mauritania and swiftly expanded in two directions: northwards to Morocco and southwards through Azugi, Awdaghust, Walata and Timbuktu to Tadmakka and Gao (see Map 14). The Almoravids followed the Maliki legal school of Sunni Islam dominant in North Africa, and implanted it in the regions under their control. Other Islamic influences came through trade from Egypt, along ancient caravan routes across the Sahara by way of the Hoggar Mountains and the Aïr Massif to the 'Niger Bend' (Gao to Jenne), as well as through the Tibesti Mountains to Lake Chad and beyond. Muslim traders in the gateway cities on the northern edge of the Sahara came to constitute a 'trading diaspora' which also served as an important channel for the spread of Islam (see Maps 19 and 20).

In 1067 the geographer al-Bakri described the situation of Islam in three states, Gao, Ghana and Takrur. In Gao, the king had accepted Islam while the commoners remained overwhelmingly idol-worshippers; in Ghana, the centre of the gold trade, the capital at Kumbi Saleh had a Muslim and a non-Muslim quarter; many traders and court bureaucrats were Muslims while the king was a non-Muslim; in Takrur, the king was a devout Muslim who practised *jihad* against his non-Muslim neighbours.

Between the early thirteenth and the mid-fifteenth century the most powerful Muslim state in the region was the Mali Empire, which at its height, around 1350, extended from the Atlantic coast to Gao on the Niger Bend. One of the early kings, Mansur Ulli (1255–70) is credited with setting up the first large-scale commercial links between the region and Egypt in the course of a pilgrimage to Mecca in the late 1260s. Perhaps Mali's most famous ruler was Mansa Musa (1312–37) whose lavish pilgrimage to Mecca and visit to Egypt in 1324 (on which he was apparently accompanied by a vast retinue that included eighty camels laden with gold) has been described by the chronicler al-'Umari. Mansa Musa also appears on an early European map of West Africa, the Catalan Map of 1375, where he is depicted as lord of the entire Sahara. On a visit to the region during the reign of Musa's brother Mansa Sulayman (1341–60), the renowned Moroccan traveller Ibn Batuta gave a vivid picture of the royal court and of 'Muslim life', although he was critical of the way in which non-Islamic customs continued and were tolerated. While many rulers in this region themselves converted to Islam, they often quietly maintained animist customs, or at least permitted others to observe them, a practice that seems to have continued at least into the eighteenth century.

In the late fifteenth century the Mali Empire was gradually eclipsed by the rise of the Songhay state, originally founded in the ninth century by the Za dynasty from Kukiya, but now based in Gao on the Niger Bend. The Songhay king, Sonni 'Ali (1464–92), who was only nominally Muslim, annexed Timbuktu and Jenne to the Songhay state, and his military commander and successor, 'Askiya Muhammad Ture (1493–1528), kept his capital at Gao, although Timbuktu maintained its reputation as a major centre of Islamic learning. 'Askiya Muhammad made the pilgrimage to Mecca in 1496–97, where Sharif 'Abbas invested him as 'ruler of Takrur'. The dynasty lasted until it was overthrown by an expedition from Morocco mounted by Sultan Ahmad in 1591 (see Map 33).

The other major state in the region was Kanem-Borno, which spanned much of what is now north-eastern Nigeria and eastern Chad. Islam entered the region from the north, through Fezzan and Tubu; the first Muslim ruler of Kanem was Mai Hume (1075–86), but pagan practices continued until the mid-thirteenth century. Kanem's prosperity was heavily dependent on the trans-Saharan trade, and it declined in the mid-fourteenth century because of the insecurity of the route and widespread political instability in North Africa. By 1390 the Sayfi dynasty of Kanem had moved to Borno; 'Ali Gaji (1470–1503), who took the title of *Amir al-Mu'minin*, restored the power of the dynasty and founded a new capital at Gazargamu, where his successors ruled until the nineteenth century.

By the end of the fifteenth century, while still not forming a majority of the population, Muslim communities were present in most parts of the Sahel, the sub-Saharan belt of savanna stretching across West Africa. Their presence was conspicuous in all the major towns and in many villages along the trade routes running north-south and east-west.

Map 16

New Muslim Dynasties in Iran, Central Asia and India *c.1092–c.1206*

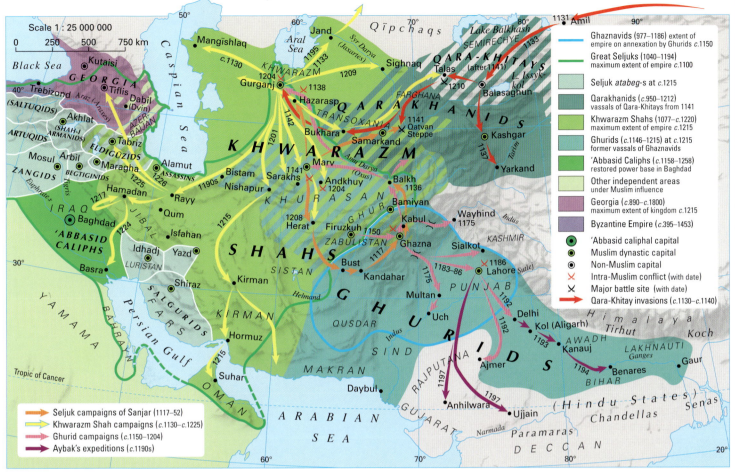

Scale 1 : 25 000 000

Legend:
- Ghaznavids (977–1186) extent of empire on annexation by Ghurids *c.*1150
- Great Seljuks (1040–1194) maximum extent of empire *c.*1100
- Seljuk *atabeg*-s at *c.*1215
- Qarakhanids (*c.*950–1212) vassals of Qara-Khitays from 1141
- Khwarazm Shahs (1077–*c.*1220) maximum extent of empire *c.*1215
- Ghurids (*c.*1146–1215) at *c.*1215 former vassals of Ghaznavids
- 'Abbasid Caliphs (*c.*1158–1258) restored power base in Baghdad
- Other independent areas under Muslim influence
- Georgia (*c.*890–*c.*1800) maximum extent of kingdom *c.*1215
- Byzantine Empire (*c.*395–1453)
- 'Abbasid caliphal capital
- Muslim dynastic capital
- Non-Muslim capital
- Intra-Muslim conflict (with date)
- Major battle site (with date)
- Qara-Khitay invasions (*c.*1130–*c.*1140)

- Seljuk campaigns of Sanjar (1117–52)
- Khwarazm Shah campaigns (*c.*1130–*c.*1225)
- Ghurid campaigns (*c.*1150–1204)
- Aybak's expeditions (*c.*1190s)

I N THE CENTURY BEFORE THE CATACLYSM of the Mongol invasions, a succession of major upheavals affected large parts of the eastern Islamic world. These included the eclipse of the Fatimid Caliphate, the collapse of the Great Seljuks in Iraq and Iran, the subjugation of the Qarakhanids by the Qara-Khitays from Mongolia, the meteoric rise and speedy fall of the Khwarazm Shahs, the replacement of the Ghaznavids by the Ghurids in Zabulistan, and the latter's conquest of northern India, which would lead to the foundation of the Delhi Sultanate in 1206.

Under Malik Shah (1072–92), the Great Seljuk sultanate reached its furthest extent (*see* Map 12), but after his death the tendency towards decentralisation and division characteristic of the Turkish practice of 'family sovereignty' seems to have reasserted itself. The sultanate gradually split into an eastern part with its capital at Marv, which enjoyed a degree of stability during the long reign of Malik Shah's son Sanjar (1097–1157), and a weaker western part, based in Iraq, where nine sultans ruled between 1118 and 1194. Sanjar campaigned in Transoxania, where he established his authority over the eastern and western Qarakhanids; in 1117 he seized Ghazna and placed the Ghaznavid Bahram Shah (1117–52) on the throne as his vassal.

In the middle of his reign, Sanjar turned his attention to Khwarazm which had been ruled by Ghaznavid governors in the first half of the eleventh century and subsequently by Seljuk appointees. One of these, 'Ala' al-Din Atsïz Khwarazm Shah (1127–56), rebelled against Sanjar, taking Marv and

Sarakhs in the early 1140s, and this action, which coincided with a crushing battle on the Qatvan Steppe resulting in the conquest of Transoxania by the non-Muslim Qara-Khitays, put an end to Seljuk rule in northeastern Iran. In 1194, at the behest of the 'Abbasid caliph al-Nasir (1180–1225), the Khwarazm Shah Tekesh defeated the last 'western' Great Seljuk, Tughrïl III. By the early 1200s the Khwarazm Shahs, having recaptured Transoxania from the Qarakhanids, had also triumphed in their long struggle with the Ghurids for hegemony in Khurasan and Zabulistan, and were able to expand across the whole of Iran. However, the foundations of their power were weak, and their territories were quickly overrun by Chingiz Khan in the 1220s (*see* Map 21).

An important consequence of the Seljuk capture of Baghdad in 1055 had been the liberation of the caliphs from Shi'i (Buyid) control. However, the Buyids were not the only 'Shi'i threat'. The Fatimid Caliphate in Cairo lasted until 1171, and in 1090, Hasan-i Sabbah, an Isma'ili from Qum, established himself with his followers, 'the Assassins', in the fortress of Alamut in the Elburz Mountains. Hasan has often been credited with the murder of the *wazir* Nizam al-Mulk in 1092; in 1095 he launched a series of deadly attacks on Seljuk officials. He and his followers went on to support the claims of Nizar ibn al-Mustansir (d.1095; *see* Map 11) and his descendants to be the rightful Fatimid caliphs, with the result that he was opposed both by the Seljuks and by the 'other' Fatimids. The dispute

over the Fatimid succession caused a permanent schism within Isma'ilism, between the adherents of Must'ali, whose descendants are the Bohras of Bombay and Gujarat, and the followers of his brother Nizar, whose descendants acknowledge the authority of the Agha Khan.

Although the Ghaznavids (*see* Map 9) had already lost much of their territory to the Seljuks by the mid-eleventh century, they continued to control much of Zabulistan and the Punjab. The dynasty became tributary to the Seljuk ruler Sanjar in 1117, and in 1150, 'Ala' al-Din Husayn, a scion of a princely family from Ghur, the mountainous region east of Herat, sacked Ghazna in an episode whose ferocity earned him the soubriquet *Jahan Suz*, 'World Burner'. His nephew Mu'izz al-Din Muhammad Ghuri (1173–1206) drove the Ghaznavids out of Zabulistan in 1173, obliging them to take refuge in Lahore, the 'capital' of their Indian territories, on which Mu'izz al-Din began to cast an envious eye. He captured the Isma'ili stronghold of Multan in 1175, and Lahore in 1186, and defeated a major Hindu alliance in 1192, continuing to campaign in northwestern India and in Khurasan against the Khwarazm Shahs until his death in 1206. In his absence from India, his general Aybak governed the conquered territories in the Punjab and the Gangetic plain; on Mu'izz al-Din's death Aybak established himself as ruler in Lahore, and on his own death four years later, his subordinate Iltutmish set himself up as ruler, founding the Delhi Sultanate, the first 'independent Muslim power' in India (*see* Map 28).

Map 17
Fatimids, Seljuks and Zangids 1092–c.1170

THE END OF THE ELEVENTH CENTURY and the first half of the twelfth was a time of considerable disarray for the Muslims of Egypt and Syria. The Fatimids of Egypt seemed set on a path of irreversible decline, while the Great Seljuks, who had effectively chased the Fatimids out of Syria and Palestine by about 1080, gradually shifted their focus further east towards Iran, Afghanistan and Transoxania, leaving behind them an unsettled domain of semi-independent *atabeg*-s and principalities in the west. However, a third major regional power, the Seljuks of Rum, although generally unsuccessful in its attempts to gain a foothold in Georgia, had taken control of much of Anatolia (including Cilicia and Antioch) by the early 1080s and would split away from the Great Seljuks after the death of Malik Shah in 1092 (*see* Map 12).

The Seljuks of Rum had penetrated as far west as Nicaea (İznik), but a combination of the Byzantine revival under Alexius Comnenus and the arrival of the armies of the First Crusade obliged them to retreat to Konya, where they established a permanent capital in 1116. By 1174 they had defeated and absorbed their principal Muslim rivals, the Turcoman Danishmendids, who had controlled the northern route across Anatolia from their base at Sivas for much of the twelfth century. As well as fighting the Armenians in Cilicia and the crusaders in Edessa, the Seljuks of Rum also managed to hold the Byzantines at bay, especially after defeating Manuel Comnenus at Myriokephalon in 1176 – a battle at least as significant as that at Manzikert a century earlier (*see* Map 12), since it marked the beginning of the transformation of 'Byzantine Anatolia' into 'Muslim Turkey'.

The Seljuk conquest of Baghdad in 1055 had restored 'Sunni orthodoxy', although the 'Abbasid caliph continued to be a cipher, retaining the sole, though exclusive, prerogative of legitimating the rule of the (Seljuk) sultan. The Fatimid Caliphate had already begun to falter after the death of al-Hakim (996–1021); a long period of chaos and uncertainty came to an end in 1073, when the caliph al-Mustansir (1036–94) managed to persuade the governor of Acre, Badr al-Jamali, who was of Armenian descent, to bring his army to Egypt to restore order. Later, after the establishment of the Latin Kingdom of Jerusalem in 1099, which was followed by a crushing defeat of the Fatimid army, the Fatimids withdrew to Egypt. Nevertheless they made determined efforts to keep control of the port cities of Syria and Palestine, in which they were successful until the capture of Ascalon by Baldwin III of Jerusalem in 1153. During this period, while continuing their *da'wa* elsewhere in the Islamic world, especially in Yemen, and maintaining control over Mecca and Medina, the Fatimids gradually abandoned any insistence on the exclusive employment of Isma'ilis in the high offices of state in Egypt.

At the end of the eleventh century, even before the death of Malik Shah (1072–92), his vassals and descendants had begun to fight each other for control of northern Syria, the Jazira and northern Iraq. In the 1070s, Atsïz, a Turkmen warlord,

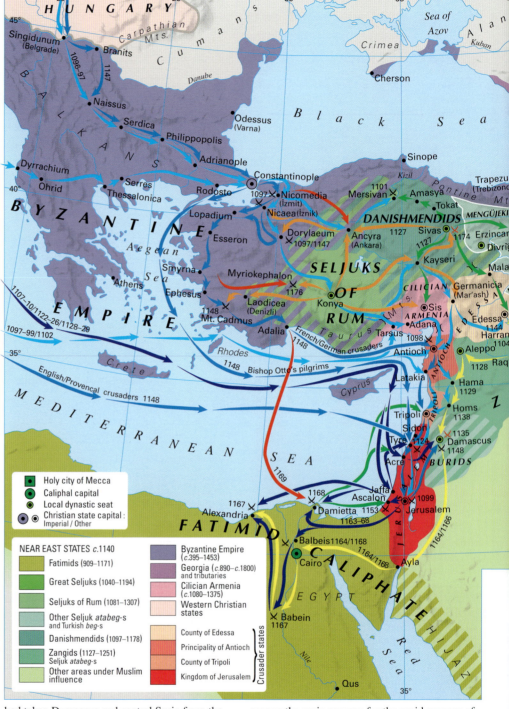

had taken Damascus and central Syria from the Fatimids in Malik Shah's name. In 1078, Atsïz was murdered by Malik Shah's brother Tutush (1078–95), whose own sons subsequently fought each other for control of Aleppo and Damascus.

Malik Shah and his chief minister Nizam al-Mulk died within a few weeks of one another in 1092, to be followed, only two years later, by the Fatimid caliph al-Mustansir after a reign of some sixty years, and the 'Abbasid caliph al-Muqtadi (1075–94). The resulting disunity, weakness and lack of experience among their successors in the Muslim political leadership (though almost certainly not perceived or conceptualised as such by their Western European contemporaries) were

among the main reasons for the rapid success of the First Crusade, whose armies would arrive in the region in the late summer of 1097.

The proclamation of the First Crusade by Pope Urban II at the Council of Clermont in November 1095 called for a holy war to recapture Jerusalem from the Muslims. By the late summer and autumn of 1096, the Pope had succeeded in rallying substantial numbers of the faithful. 'The armies of the Franks', an estimated 40,000 mounted knights and foot-soldiers, led by notables from Lorraine, Normandy, Provence and southern Italy, assembled in various parts of Europe and would arrive in Constantinople between November 1096 and the spring of 1097. Given

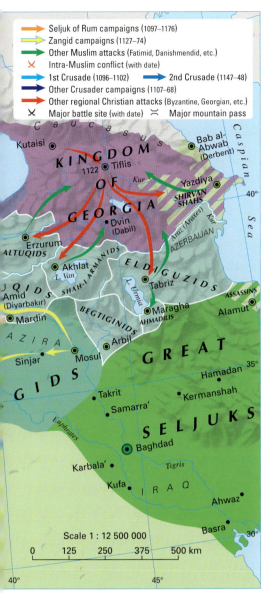

Legend:
- Seljuk of Rum campaigns (1097–1176)
- Zangid campaigns (1127–74)
- Other Muslim attacks (Fatimid, Danishmendid, etc.)
- Intra-Muslim conflict (with date)
- 1st Crusade (1096–1102)
- 2nd Crusade (1147–48)
- Other Crusader campaigns (1107–68)
- Other regional Christian attacks (Byzantine, Georgian, etc.)
- Major battle site (with date)
- Major mountain pass

Scale 1 : 12 500 000
0 125 250 375 500 km

Hijaz–Yemen (at half main map scale)

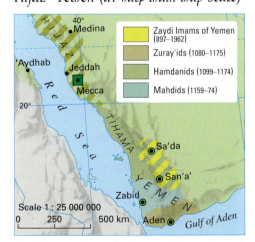

- Zaydi Imams of Yemen (897–1962)
- Zuray'ids (1080–1175)
- Hamdanids (1099–1174)
- Mahdids (1159–74)

Scale 1 : 25 000 000
0 250 500 km

their large numbers, the absence of a coordinated command, and the fact that the various armies had to be fed and accommodated at considerable local expense, it was hardly surprising that relations among the various leaders, and with the Emperor Alexius, quickly became strained.

Eventually, the crusaders left Constantinople and captured Nicaea (İznik) in June 1097.

Antioch, with its impressive fortifications and substantial garrison, lay astride the route to the Holy Land; the city had been taken from the Byzantines by the Seljuks of Rum in 1084, but by the time the crusaders arrived (and indeed long afterwards), control over northern Syria was being hotly contested by different Seljuk factions. The crusaders besieged Antioch between October 1097 and July 1098; during this time they received assurances of neutrality from the Fatimid *wazir* al-Afdal (the son of Badr al-Jamali) and also profited from the constant and deadly quarrels between the nephews of Malik Shah. After the fall of Antioch the crusaders proceeded to march on Jerusalem, which they captured in July 1099, meting out great brutality to its inhabitants.

Over the next decade the various crusader leaders established four small principalities at Antioch, Edessa, Jerusalem and Tripoli; this was to be the fullest extent of the 'crusading states'. In these cities, and in the various smaller towns which the crusaders conquered, the Muslim and Jewish inhabitants faced a number of possible fates: they were either obliged to 'convert or die', or were enslaved, or were exiled, or were allowed to stay. In Antioch and Sidon, for example, the local cultivators (both Muslims and Christians) were actively encouraged to stay: on the other hand, the recapture of Jerusalem by Salah al-Din al-Ayyubi (Saladin) in 1187 apparently led to the release of some 20,000 Muslim captives.

In essence, the crusades were a series of military campaigns whose general objective (although only temporarily realised) was to bring the Holy Places of Christendom under (Western) Christian protection. The crusading movement took place at much the same time as the Christian *reconquista* of Spain, and indeed, 'on their way' to the Holy Land in 1147, some of the northern Europeans who had joined the Second Crusade found themselves 'assisting' King Afonso Enrique of Portugal to capture Lisbon from the Muslims (*see* Map 26). Some near-contemporary Muslim writers, notably the jurist al-Sulami (d. 1106) in his *Kitab al-Jihad* and the historian Ibn al-Athir (1160–1233), were able to make the connection between events in Sicily, Spain and the Levant. However, the long-term fortunes of the three movements would go in diametrically opposite directions. Sicily was fully under Norman rule by 1091; in the mid-thirteenth century, Granada was all that was left of Muslim *al-Andalus*, while in the east, the crusades essentially came to an end with the fall of Acre to the Mamluks in May 1291 (*see* Map 22). Of course, relatively few Western Europeans ever took up permanent residence in the crusading states, while many of the southern cities of *al-Andalus* received substantial numbers of Christian settlers from the north.

After considerable prompting, the Great Seljuk Sultan Muhammad (1105–18), a younger son of Malik Shah, eventually declared a somewhat half-hearted *jihad* against the crusaders. In

1115 one of his armies was defeated by a force composed of an alliance between the crusaders and the Seljukid rulers of Aleppo and Damascus, and after this he sent no further expeditions against 'the Franks' (*al-Ifranj* in contemporary Arabic sources). The latter remained virtually unchallenged until Muhammad's successor Mahmud (1118–31) appointed 'Imad al-Din Zangi, the son of one of his grandfather Malik Shah's generals, governor of Mosul and guardian of his two sons. Zangi (1127–46) and his son Nur al-Din (1147–74) expanded their rule westwards into Syria and northwards into Anatolia and Kurdistan: in the process, Zangi became ruler of Aleppo in 1128, Hama in 1130 and Homs in 1138. At this stage Damascus was ruled by the Burids (1104–54), who were Seljuk 'appointees' like Zangi, but whose intrigues with the Fatimids and the crusaders made it difficult for him to dislodge them. 'Imad al-Din Zangi's major achievement was to recapture Edessa from the Franks in 1144, making him the first Muslim leader to begin to turn back the Christian tide.

The fall of Edessa prompted Pope Eugenius III to call for the Second Crusade. In contrast with the First Crusade some fifty years earlier, the leadership this time was of a very different order. Some contingents were led by European monarchs, including Louis VII of France, and Conrad III of Germany. In June 1148 a meeting of crusader leaders and local notables, presided over by Baldwin III of Jerusalem, took what turned out to be the strategically unwise decision to besiege Damascus, which they soon abandoned in disarray on the news of Nur al-Din's southward advance. In 1153 Baldwin captured the port of Ascalon from the Fatimids, and the people of Damascus, feeling the need for a strong protector against both crusaders and Fatimids, allowed Nur al-Din to enter the city in 1154, enabling him to unite 'Muslim Syria' under a single ruler.

For nearly ten years there was an uneasy stalemate between Jerusalem and Damascus, and a period of great confusion in Egypt, which was paying tribute to the Latin kingdom. When this was withheld, in 1163, Amalric, Baldwin III's successor, made an unsuccessful attempt to occupy Cairo, the Fatimid capital. At this point Shirkuh, one of Nur al-Din's Kurdish generals, persuaded his overlord to send an expedition to Egypt, which he led inconclusively in 1164. In response, the Egyptian *wazir* Shawar sought the help of the Franks; once again, Nur al-Din acceded to Shirkuh's request for an invasion of Egypt, during which Shirkuh's young nephew, Salah al-Din, was installed as governor of Alexandria. Eventually, in 1168, the Franks were forced to withdraw, and a year later, after his uncle's death, Salah al-Din became commander of Nur al-Din's troops in Egypt, and *wazir* to the Fatimid caliph al-'Adid (1160–71). On the latter's death, Salah al-Din, founder of the Ayyubids, proclaimed himself governor of Egypt (*see* Map 18). In 1174, Nur al-Din died in Damascus on his way to Egypt, apparently intending to punish Salah al-Din for having the temerity to remit insufficient taxes to Damascus.

© EIPL

Map 18

Salah al-Dın and the Rıse oꜰ the Ayyubıds c.1170–1250

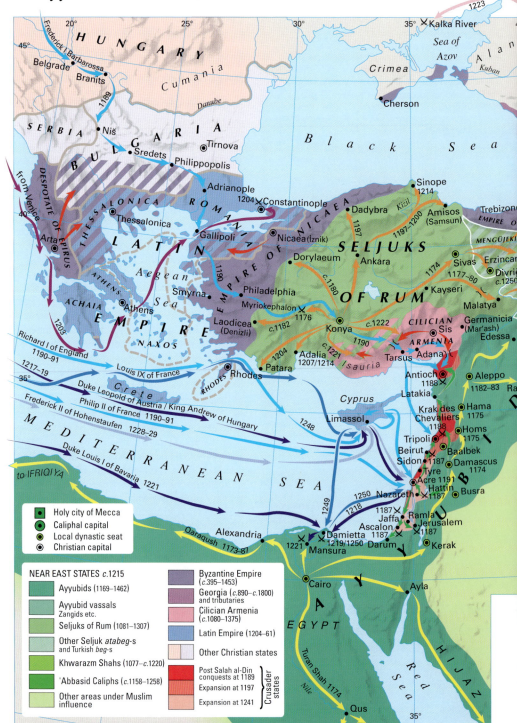

LIKE MANY OF THE 'PROVINCIAL RULERS' of the Near East in the twelfth century, Salah al-Din and his uncle Shirkuh were 'Turks' (in their case Turkicised Kurds) in the service of their local military commanders. Shirkuh and his brother Najm al-Din Ayyub were recruited into Zangi's army in Mosul in the late 1130s, around the time of the birth of Najm al-Din's son Salah al-Din. The brothers continued to serve Zangi and his son Nur al-Din (*see* Map 17) and by the time he was about thirty, Salah al-Din (1169–93) had become ruler of Egypt, and the founder of the sprawling dynasty which bears his father's patronymic. At its height in the 1180s, various members of the family ruled in Egypt, Damascus, Aleppo, Homs, Hama, Amid (Diyarbakır) and Yemen, but, some sixty years after its founder's death, the 'Ayyubid empire' fell victim to the familiar combination of family quarrels and ambitious subordinate military leaders, as well as to the more specific threat posed by the Mongols (*see* Maps 21 and 22).

Salah al-Din had virtually done away with the Isma'ili religious establishment in Cairo even before the death of the last Fatimid caliph al-'Adid (1160–71), and he had also installed his Syrian army in place of the Fatimid cavalry. He continued to act as the standard bearer of the restoration of Sunni Islam by ordering, in September 1171, that the *khutba* or Friday sermon in the mosques should be pronounced in the name of the 'Abbasid caliph in Baghdad. In the late 1170s he began to build the Cairo citadel, probably influenced by similar structures in the Syrian cities with which he was familiar.

Like his Fatimid predecessors and Mamluk successors, Salah al-Din made sure that he controlled the Hijaz and the Holy Cities, and sent his brother Turanshah on expeditions to both Upper Egypt and Yemen to secure the eastern and western coasts of the Red Sea (*see* Map Inset). Turanshah became ruler of Yemen between 1174 and his death in 1181, taking the title of al-Malik al-Mu'adhdham; the descendants of his brother al-Malik al-'Aziz Tughtigin (1181–97) ruled the region until 1229, when the last of them left Yemen for Syria, nominating Nur al-Din Rasuli as regent. Since the Ayyubids did not in fact return, the Rasulids, who claimed descent from the pre-Islamic south Arabian nobility but were almost certainly from a Turkic family which had entered 'Abbasid service under the Seljuks, ruled most of Yemen (beginning with the Tihama and the southern highlands, but eventually controlling an area stretching as far east as Zufar in southern Oman) until they were ousted by the Tahirids in 1454.

Salah al-Din's position was strengthened by the death of the Zangid ruler, Nur al-Din, in May 1174, followed two months later by that of Amalric of Jerusalem, and the fact that the heirs of both rulers were minors. In December 1174, claiming to be acting on behalf of the young al-Salih Isma'il ibn Nur al-Din (who was nominal ruler of Damascus and Aleppo between 1174 and his death in 1181), Salah al-Din laid siege to Aleppo,

where al-Salih Isma'il's followers had taken him. Salah al-Din was obliged to lift the siege in the spring of 1175 because of a crusader attack on his forces outside Homs. Once he had repulsed them, he declared himself sultan of Egypt and Syria in May 1175, with the approval of the 'Abbasid caliph in Baghdad, who gave him the title of *Mujaddid al-Dawla li-Amir al-Mu'minin* (Renewer of the State for the Commander of the Faithful). It took him a further eight years to subdue all the other Zangid commanders and consolidate his hold over Syria.

In 1180 Salah al-Din came to an agreement with the Rum Seljuk sultan Qilij Arslan II (1156–92) under which he took control of the

great citadel of Hisn Kayfa in the Jazira. By 1186 he had gained control of Egypt, Yemen, the Hijaz, Greater Syria, Northern Iraq, and, through the efforts of one of his Mamluks, Qaraqush, the North African coast as far west as southern Ifriqiya. The crusaders had become increasingly isolated since Qilij Arslan's defeat of the Byzantines at Myriokephalon in 1176, which had deprived them of their only significant regional ally. In addition, in marked contrast with the situation a century earlier, they were now confronted with a united Muslim front. In July 1187, at the battle of Hattin near Lake Tiberias, Salah al-Din defeated the combined army of the Frankish states, and went on to capture Acre and Nazareth,

NEAR EAST STATES c.1215

⊙●	Holy city of Mecca			
⊙	Caliphal capital			
⊙	Local dynastic seat			
◉	Christian capital			

■	Ayyubids (1169–1462)	■ Byzantine Empire (c.395–1453)
■	Ayyubid vassals Zangids etc.	■ Georgia (c.890–c.1800) and tributaries
■	Seljuks of Rum (1081–1307)	■ Cilician Armenia (c.1080–1375)
■	Other Seljuk *atabeg*-s and Turkish *beg*-s	■ Latin Empire (1204–61)
■	Khwarazm Shahs (1077–c.1220)	■ Other Christian states
■	'Abbasid Caliphs (c.1158–1258)	■ Post Salah al-Din conquests at 1189
■	Other areas under Muslim influence	■ Expansion at 1197
		■ Expansion at 1241 (Crusader states)

Hijaz–Yemen (at half main map scale)

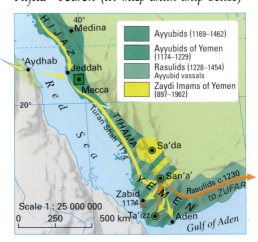

before entering Jerusalem at the beginning of October, an event that was certainly the climax of his career. In the course of 1187 and 1188 he captured some fifty crusader castles, only encountering major resistance at the strategically significant fortifications of Tyre, Tripoli and Antioch.

The arrival in Europe of the news of Salah al-Din's capture of Jerusalem occasioned the immediate preaching of the Third Crusade. Like the Second Crusade, it attracted the participation of several major European rulers: first Henry II of England and then (after his death in 1189) his son Richard I; Philip II of France; the German Emperor Frederick Barbarossa (who drowned in a river in southeastern Turkey in 1190 on his way to the Holy Land), as well as the rulers of Sicily and Austria. Political differences and personal conflicts among them ensured that the expedition's objectives were often blurred.

Acre surrendered to the crusaders in July 1191; Philip returned to France, but Richard and his army spent the next sixteen months in Palestine. In September 1192 Richard concluded an agreement with Salah al-Din that allowed the Franks to visit Jerusalem and left them in control of the coastal area between Acre and Jaffa.

In 1197 a German crusade recaptured Beirut and Sidon, although Jerusalem and most of the interior remained in Muslim hands. Hence at the end of the century, the Franks controlled the coastal towns and their hinterlands between Ascalon and Tortosa, the castle of Krak des Chevaliers (within the County of Tripoli) and the Principality of Antioch.

After the death of Salah al-Din in 1193 his territories were ruled by his successors until they were overthrown in their turn at various times between 1250 and 1260 by members of their Mamluk praetorian guard (see Map 22). Three of these rulers, Salah al-Din's brother al-'Adil (1200–18), the latter's son al-Kamil (1218–38) and al-Kamil's son al-Salih Ayyub (1240–49) acted as paramount sultans, but other members of the dynasty made treaties with various Frankish rulers or actually fought alongside them against their Ayyubid rivals. Such flagrant breaches of the conventions of ideal conduct occasioned great dismay on the part of contemporary chroniclers, who looked back with longing to the 'good old days' of jihad.

One of the consequences of the fiasco of the Fourth Crusade, which was intended to attack Egypt but instead was diverted by its Venetian paymasters to capturing and taking control of Constantinople in 1204, was that few new crusaders arrived in the Kingdom of Jerusalem, and the number of troops there declined substantially. In 1204, al-'Adil concluded a peace treaty with Amalric II for eight years (1197–1205), under which he ceded Beirut, Jaffa, Ramla and Sidon to Amalric; in 1210, al-'Adil asked for the treaty to be renewed, and after some hesitation another five-year truce was accepted, to last until July 1217. Questions of disputed succession, or long regencies, or struggles among competing claimants bedevilled the politics of the crusader states in the first half of the thirteenth century. Seemingly endless confusion and intrigue meant that western European ardour for crusading expeditions to the East became somewhat dimmed, especially because of the far more spectacular

progress being made in Spain, as exemplified by the resounding victory of Alfonso VIII of Castile over the Almohads at Las Navas de Tolosa in 1212 (see Map 26).

The Fifth Crusade, preached by Pope Innocent III in 1213, began as another attempt to recapture Jerusalem from the Muslims, and contingents from Austria, Hungary and northern Europe landed at Acre at the end of 1217. Little progress was made, and by the spring of 1218, the various leaders had decided on an attack on Egypt, arriving at the mouth of the Nile in May. The crusaders succeeded in capturing an island near Damietta and subsequently the Chain Tower, a crucial fortification on the Nile. They went on to take Damietta in November 1219; even before this, the Ayyubid Sultan al-Kamil was so shaken by their presence that he offered them a thirty-year truce and the return of almost all the territories of the Kingdom of Jerusalem in exchange for the evacuation of Egypt. However, the crusaders were unable to agree amongst themselves; the Ayyubids rallied, and by the end of September 1221 the crusaders were obliged to leave Egypt. Some seven years later, al-Kamil sent an embassy to the Emperor Frederick II Hohenstaufen (1212–50), whose wife Yolanda was the heiress of the Latin Kingdom, offering him a modified version of the truce held out to the crusaders in 1219. These negotiations were concluded in February 1229; a month later, Frederick, who had been excommunicated by the papacy in 1227 for his constant prevarication over actually going on crusade, appeared wearing his crown in the Church of the Holy Sepulchre. The city was handed over to the Franks for ten years, much to the consternation of al-Kamil's Muslim contemporaries.

In 1249, at the end of the Ayyubid period, the King of France, Louis IX (1226–70) set off on a crusade to Egypt, taking Damietta in June. al-Salih Ayyub offered to trade Jerusalem for Damietta, but Louis, who thought it was his duty to defeat the 'infidels' rather than treat with them, refused. Reinforcements arrived, and by November the crusaders seemed well positioned to march on Cairo; at the end of the month, al-Salih died, with his son Turanshah away in the Jazira. But by April 1250 the Egyptians had rallied, the Franks had imperilled themselves through various strategic miscalculations, and their army was ravaged by disease. Eventually they were obliged to surrender, and Louis was taken prisoner. A month later, after paying an enormous ransom, he left for Acre, where he stayed for four years.

By the mid-1250s, the fortunes of the crusading states seemed to have revived; for a while it seemed that Syria might succumb to the aggression of the Mongols, but the latter's defeat at 'Ayn Jalut in 1260 at the hands of the Mamluks resulted in the Mamluks, rather than the Mongols, taking over Syria (see Maps 21 and 22). Subsequently the Mamluk sultans Baybars I, Qalawun and al-Ashraf directed constant attacks on crusader territory, culminating with the fall of Acre in 1291, which signalled the end of some two centuries of crusader presence in the East.

Map 19
Trade between the Western Islamic World and Europe c.1100–c.1300

UNTIL COMPARATIVELY RECENTLY, most Europeans believed that their continent had always been the centre of the civilised world. The thrust of much recent research has largely modified this view and suggests that European pre-eminence does not significantly antedate the scientific revolution (c.1540–c.1680) and its various technological applications in the industrial revolution (c.1770). Hence, the 'new science' bestowed no technological competitive advantage on, say, England, France or the Netherlands as against China, or the Ottoman Empire, before the end of the eighteenth century.

In terms of trade and commerce, it is evident that a complex world economic system was flourishing long before 'European hegemony'. The collapse of the Roman Empire in the fourth and fifth centuries caused a severe economic regression in Europe that lasted until around the eighth and ninth centuries, when the Muslim invasions invigorated the economies and urban life of southern Europe, and, as a result of the Muslim conquests of Western and Central Asia, commercial links were restored between Europe and the great civilisations of the east.

Hence, between the mid-eighth and the mid-ninth centuries there was a lively and continuous series of exchanges around the Mediterranean, and between the worlds of the Mediterranean and the Indian Ocean, as well as between the eastern Arab world and northwestern Europe. The latter trade was carried on by Norsemen who made the connections between Baghdad and Aachen via the Volga and the Baltic, and its buoyancy was a major factor in the 'Carolingian Renaissance'. However, this did not extend to Italy and the non-Muslim part of Spain: the Muslims raided Italy regularly between the ninth and tenth centuries (*see* Map 9) and the Italian cities only began to recover in the early eleventh century. Similarly, the commercial development of Castile and Aragon began after the end of the Umayyad Caliphate in 1031, largely as a result of the *parias* (tribute in gold) paid by the *ta'ifa* states (*see* Map 13).

In general, with the exception of gold, silver and slaves, the northern Europeans had little to offer the Muslims between the conquest of Spain in the early eighth century and the economic recovery of Italy after c.1000. Furthermore, while Charlemagne and his successors still had plenty of gold and silver, the Norman, Magyar and Muslim raids of the ninth and tenth centuries sucked much of the precious metals from France, Germany and Italy into Scandinavia, Hungary, *al-Andalus* and Ifriqiya, which explains the dearth of trade between France, Germany, Italy and the eastern Mediterranean during this period. It is no accident that trade recovered first in northern Italy, which had been relatively sheltered during these two centuries of foreign invasion.

In the beginning, much of the trade between the Islamic world and Europe was carried out by Jews. While the contrast between medieval Christian anti-Semitism and medieval Muslim tolerance has often been too crudely drawn, it is clear that, especially during the Fatimid period,

PRINCIPAL TRADING SPHERES c.1300

Maritime Republics & Trading Associations

- Muslim
- Venetian
- Genoese
- Pisan (pre-Genoese takeover in 1284)
- Catalan-Aragonese
- Angevin-Naples
- Hanseatic League
- Other Western European
- Other Eastern European

— Overland / River trade routes (Primary / Secondary)
— Maritime trade routes
Gold High value product sources

A	Almería	Me	Marseille
Aa	Ancona	Mo	Modena
As	Amastris	N	Negroponte
B	Bologna	Ne	Narbonne
Bo	Burtrinto	Nv	Nizhny Novgorod
C	Córdoba	P	Parma
Ca	Cartagena	Pe	Prague
F	Florence	S	Seville
Fa	Famagusta	Sa	Saragossa
Ft	Frankfurt	Se	Syracuse
H	Hunayn	Si	Siena
L	Lisbon	T	Tortosa
M	Málaga	Ta	Thessalonica
Ma	Mérida	V	Valona

Islam was kinder to the Jews than Byzantium or Visigothic Spain, and that, throughout the Islamic world, Jews were engaged in almost all trades and professions as well as often being in business partnerships with Muslims. There was a network of Jewish mercantile communities all over the Islamic world, and Jewish merchants were important figures at the courts of Baghdad, Cairo and Córdoba. The documents of the Cairo Geniza, mostly dating from the period between the Fatimid conquest of Egypt in 969 and the fall of the Ayyubids in 1250, reveal an intricate 'international' web of business relations, with far-flung trade partnerships based on letters of credit and other forms of commercial guarantee. By the late eleventh century, however, the Jews were gradually being excluded from maritime trade on the northern Mediterranean coasts by the rise of the Italian maritime republics. This was stimulated

by the First Crusade and led to fierce competition between Venice and its dependencies, Zara, Ragusa (Dubrovnik), Preveza, and Crete; Pisa and its dependencies, Amalfi and Palma de Mallorca; and Genoa and its dependencies, Palermo, Naples and Messina; and the expanded trading spheres of Angevin Naples and Catalonia-Aragon. By the late fourteenth century, Venice had gained maritime supremacy in the Mediterranean as a whole.

The Middle East occupied a pivotal position in medieval world trade, with its inhabitants' multi-directional commercial activities in the Mediterranean and Africa, and in the farther-flung regions of central, south and southeast Asia (*see* Map 20). Some of the crops grown for local consumption and for export were native to the Mediterranean region, such as cereals, olives and vines, while others had been transplanted from farther east, such as rice, sugar cane, citrus trees,

world, could be enslaved, it followed that slaves could only be procured from outside the *Dar al-Islam*. They were mostly imported from five areas: the Balkans, central and north-eastern Europe (including Finland and the principalities of Russia), Transoxania, Turkestan and sub-Saharan Africa (the Sahel around the Niger Bend, Kanem-Borno, and Nubia/Ethiopia). The European slaves (Arabic *Saqaliba* = Slavs) were mostly assembled in Prague and then either sent southwestwards to Spain through France, or to Egypt and Syria by sea from Venice, or from Kiev, down the Volga and along the western shore of the Caspian to Baghdad. In northern Europe the slave merchants were mostly 'Franks' or Jews from the Danube and the Rhine. The trade was quite considerable until the eleventh century, when significant numbers of Turks began to convert to Islam.

Between the eighth and eleventh centuries camels became widely used along the southern Mediterranean littoral and in the western Sahara, and Berber and Arabian horses were crossbred with indigenous Spanish and Sicilian varieties. The Islamic world accounted for most of the wool production of the early Middle Ages, and Berbers brought the system of communal pasturing and sheep-rearing (Arabic *mashta*; Spanish *mesta*) to Spain from North Africa, together with the fine-fleeced merino sheep. Gold came into the region from central and inner Asia as well as from western Africa (the upper reaches of the Senegal, Niger and Volta rivers), Nubia (Wadi 'Allaqi) and southeastern Africa (Zimbabwe).

Gold coins began to be minted in Europe in 1252, supplementing the Byzantine and Muslim coinage already in circulation. In terms of commodities travelling in the opposite direction, since there were almost no forests in the Islamic world, timber from the forests of the Alps, the Apennines and Dalmatia (for ships and for firing furnaces in the metallurgical industries) was exported through Venice. Iron came from north-central Europe, where iron ore (and the wood used in its extraction) was plentiful. Grain and salt were imported into Anatolia and farther east from northern Europe; dates were a major export to Europe from the Arab world, as were ivory and gold from sub-Saharan Africa. In Europe, the river valleys of the Rhône, Rhine, Danube, Vistula, Dvina, Dnieper and Volga were the principal north-south arteries, linking the Islamic world with the Hanseatic trade of the Baltic and North Sea lands.

Evidence of the trade routes comes from contemporary chronicles and descriptions, but also from large hoards of silver coins minted in the Muslim world, which have been found mostly in Russia, Scandinavia and the Baltic. In addition, the region (and indeed the Mediterranean basin as whole) was always at risk from insufficient rainfall and subsequent crop failure, which constantly threatened the food supply, so that bread riots, or other demonstrations against food shortages, were a perennial preoccupation of the rulers. Depending on where crop failures occurred, grain could be moved from Egypt to Syria and vice versa, or from Ifriqiya to Sicily and vice versa.

date palms, mulberry trees, cotton and indigo, all of which required the use of artificial irrigation. Large quantities of grain were exported from Egypt, both eastwards and westwards; corn was also exported from North Africa to Spain and Sicily. Olives and olive oil from Ifriqiya (modern Tunisia) were exported to Sicily, mainland Italy and Egypt. Vegetables and fruit were cultivated in 'garden suburbs' around the main cities, using techniques that had become widespread in Spain and Sicily. Cotton (Arabic *al-qutn*; Spanish *algodón*), which originated in India, spread first to northern Iraq, thence to northern Syria and eventually to Spain in the eighth century. The technique of silk production (silk is produced by silkworms, which feed on mulberry leaves) came to the West from China through the Byzantine Empire and thence to Syria and Muslim Spain. Textile manufacture (for clothing and furnishings

– carpets, tents and flags) was one of the chief industries of the Islamic world. Egypt exported all kinds of textiles to Europe, including locally produced flax interwoven with Syrian silk.

Slavery formed a particularly important item of commerce in the Islamic world. Slaves worked in mines and plantations, as servants and entertainers of all kinds in courts, in more humble domestic settings, and, of course, in the various Muslim armies, where, especially as freed slaves, they often came to wield immense power. Thus, slaves from southern Russia and the northern Caucasus, mostly of Christian origin, ruled Egypt and Syria between 1250 and 1517 (*see* Maps 22 and 23), and a dynasty descended from Turkish slaves ruled in Delhi between 1206 and 1290 (*see* Map 28). By definition, since neither Muslims nor the *dhimmi*-s, that is, the Christians, Jews and Zoroastrians living within the Islamic

Map 20

Islam and the Trade of Africa and Asia c.800–c.1300

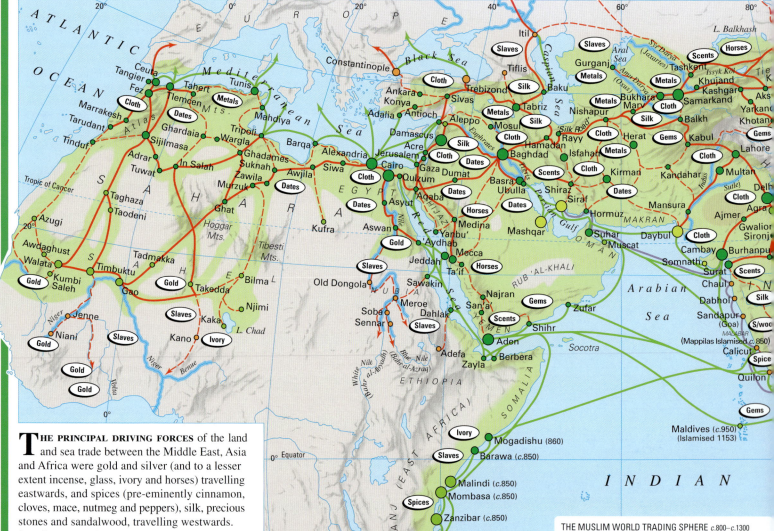

THE MUSLIM WORLD TRADING SPHERE c.800–c.1300

- Area under Muslim control or influence c.1300
- (c.800) Date of earliest Muslim trade in Indian Ocean
- ● ○ Muslim trading towns : prominent c.800–c.1300
- ● ○ Muslim trading towns : prominent after 1000
- ● ○ Muslim trading towns : declined after 1000
- ● ○ Non-Muslim trading towns : prominent c.800–c.1300
- ● ○ Non-Muslim trading towns : declined after 1000
- Principal Muslim maritime trade routes
- Principal Indian / Chinese maritime trade routes
- Principal overland caravan trade routes
- Secondary overland caravan trade routes
- Principal navigable river trade routes

THE PRINCIPAL DRIVING FORCES of the land and sea trade between the Middle East, Asia and Africa were gold and silver (and to a lesser extent incense, glass, ivory and horses) travelling eastwards, and spices (pre-eminently cinnamon, cloves, mace, nutmeg and peppers), silk, precious stones and sandalwood, travelling westwards. Jewellery, ceramics, and other luxury objects, as well as lower-value bulk goods for ballast, travelled in both directions. In addition, India had long been exporting substantial quantities of cotton cloth to East, West and Central Asia. Thus there were a lively series of exchanges both around the Mediterranean and between the worlds of the Mediterranean, the Middle East and the Indian Ocean, largely promoted by the vibrancy of the great cities of the Islamic world. Some had been in existence for many centuries, while others had been founded in the course of the Muslim conquests. The caliph al-Mansur, the founder of Baghdad in 762, is quoted as saying: 'This is the Tigris; there is no obstacle between us and China; everything on the sea can come to us on it'.

In the early Middle Ages, most of the gold going eastwards came from northern or central Europe, but when these sources gradually dried up as one of the consequences of the Muslim, Magyar and Norman invasions (see Map 19), Africa became the principal source of supply. In North Africa, trade routes followed the coast, while there was a lively trans-Saharan trade, both north-south, from Fez and Sijilmasa to Gao and Timbuktu (founded c.1100), and southwest-north-east, from the latter two towns and Kumbi Saleh and Walata across the desert to Alexandria and

Cairo through Ghat, Zawila, Awjila and Siwa (see Map 15). Slaves and gold from sub-Saharan Africa were brought across the desert in exchange for textiles and salt; slaves and gold were also brought northwards from Zimbabwe to Egypt via the port of Sofala initially by local Muslim merchants in return for textiles, jewellery and pottery. Wadi ʿAllaqi (on the east side of the Nile, south of Aswan) was also an important source of gold. In addition, commodities from the Middle East (such as incense, pearls, sandalwood, dates and attar of roses) were all traded by land and sea to both east and west.

The expansion of trade eastwards from the

'Islamic heartlands' between the ninth and thirteenth centuries was accompanied by the diffusion of Islam into the remoter parts of Africa and Asia through the agency of Muslim merchants: to the courts of Ghana, Mali and Songhay along the middle Niger, and later with the establishment of several coastal and island Muslim states in east Africa southwards from Mogadishu (see Map 41); through the steppes and deserts of Central Asia into western China using the ancient overland caravan routes collectively known today as the 'Silk Road'; and by sea to India and the Maldives, and on to Indonesia where Islam came to Aceh around 1275. Indonesia, subsequently divided into a number of

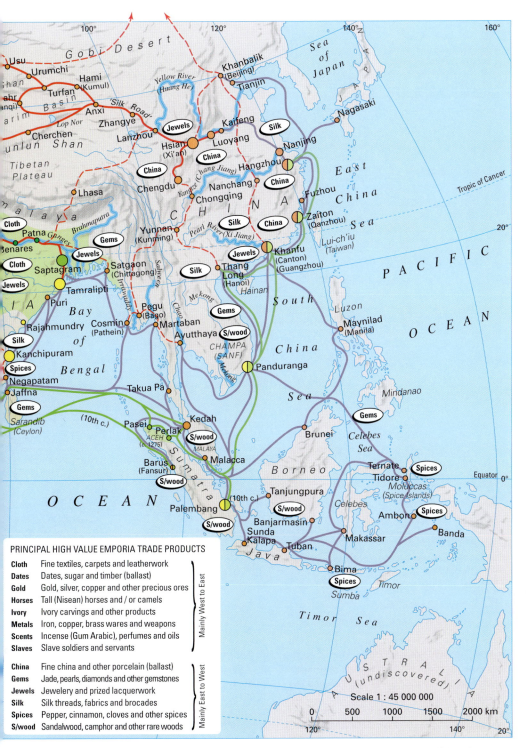

PRINCIPAL HIGH VALUE EMPORIA TRADE PRODUCTS

Cloth	Fine textiles, carpets and leatherwork	
Dates	Dates, sugar and timber (ballast)	
Gold	Gold, silver, copper and other precious ores	*Mainly West to East*
Horses	Tall (Nisean) horses and / or camels	
Ivory	Ivory carvings and other products	
Metals	Iron, copper, brass wares and weapons	
Scents	Incense (Gum Arabic), perfumes and oils	
Slaves	Slave soldiers and servants	
China	Fine china and other porcelain (ballast)	
Gems	Jade, pearls, diamonds and other gemstones	*Mainly East to West*
Jewels	Jewelery and prized lacquerwork	
Silk	Silk threads, fabrics and brocades	
Spices	Pepper, cinnamon, cloves and other spices	
S/wood	Sandalwood, camphor and other rare woods	

Scale 1 : 45 000 000

0   500   1000   1500   2000 km

A number of features differentiate the Indian Ocean from the Mediterranean. Few navigable rivers, except the Po, the Rhône and the Nile, empty into the Mediterranean, while India, eastern Asia and southeastern Africa have major river systems. Thus, most of the Indus and Ganges valleys, 2900 and 2500 kilometres long, were accessible to river transport, as were the Mekong, the Yangtze and the Yellow River, the Zambezi and Limpopo. Transporting goods along the rivers was often the only means of moving them, and in places where alternatives existed, using the river was usually cheaper than using draft animals.

In addition, the availability of river water for the cultivation of rice was especially important when the monsoons were irregular. A cereal-based largely rain-fed food culture characterised much of the Mediterranean, the Middle East, Central Asia, northern India and northwest China, while rice was the staple for tropical Asia. Like the Mediterranean, most of Asia faced constant food insecurity because of the lack of reliable rainfall, famines and wars (including the passage of large armies, for example, during the Mongol invasions) in addition to frequent seismic shocks and disastrous tidal waves.

Since there are few deep-water harbours in the Indian Ocean (and none at all on the eastern coast of India), ports were usually located either at river mouths or at some distance upriver. Even then, it was often necessary to use small craft to carry passengers and goods through the surf to the shore. Ships' commanders needed to know how to calculate latitude, to use sextants and to navigate by the stars, as well as to be familiar with the patterns of the winds. Magnetic compasses were in use in the Middle East and China by the early thirteenth century. Sailing manuals in Arabic from the mid-ninth century show sea routes between Siraf on the Persian Gulf and Khanfu on the South China Sea, describing journeys across the open Arabian Sea to the Malabar coast, and then across the Bay of Bengal to Malaya and beyond.

Given the generally flat landscape of northern India, the alluvial deposits brought downstream could cause considerable shifts in the river beds. Sometimes this resulted in cities finding themselves at great distances from the rivers on which they had been built, and this and other natural disasters could cause rapid declines in both prosperity and population. Thus the silting-up of a tributary of the Indus was one of the principal factors in Lahore's losing its status as the major trading city between the eastern Mediterranean and India in the late seventeenth century, and silting eventually caused Malacca to cease to be able to function as a port.

Although there were comparable changes in the courses of the Tigris and Euphrates, the area below Baghdad was not as densely populated as the plains of the Punjab and the Ganges. Few cities around the Mediterranean and in the land bridge between Anatolia, Syria, Iraq and Iran experienced comparable seismic or hydrological vagaries, although massive earthquakes in Iran and Afghanistan were not uncommon.

'Muslim empires' in the sixteenth and seventeenth centuries (*see* Maps 30 and 42), probably marked Islam's farthest frontier eastwards, apart from a few long-established Muslim communities in Champa and mainland China.

The first Muslims to come to China, as early as the late seventh century, were merchants who settled mainly in the major port cities. By the time of the Sung Dynasty (960–1279) they were playing a major role in China's import and export trade, and their prominence would increase under the Mongol Yuan dynasty (1271–1368), whose rulers regularly employed Muslims in the higher echelons of the administration.

Coastal towns such as Mogadishu, Barawa, Mombasa, Zanzibar, Kilwa and Sofala on the East African coast, Jeddah, Aden and Suhar on the Arabian Peninsula, Basra and Siraf on the Persian Gulf, and Daybul, Cambay, Calicut, Quilon and Kanchipuram on the western and eastern Indian coasts, and Kedah (and later Malacca) on the Malay Peninsula, and Palembang, Sunda Kalapa, Tuban, and Makassar in Indonesia, functioned as the principal 'emporia' for Indian Ocean trade, with their inland trading equivalents, Aleppo, Damascus, Baghdad, Hamadan, Isfahan, Shiraz, Kirman, Herat, Bukhara, Samarkand, Lahore and Delhi along or linked to the caravan routes to and from China.

Map 21

The Islamic World and the Mongol Invasions c.1200–c.1300

THE MONGOL EMPIRE was the last and most extensive of a series of political formations founded by nomadic peoples originating from the steppe lands of northeast Asia. At the height of their powers, the Mongols ruled over an area stretching from Korea to Hungary, but they were never able to maintain centralised control over this vast realm for more than a few decades. The main object of their ambitions was the conquest of the whole of Mongolia and China, but their campaigns to the west had a devastating and lasting effect on the Islamic world. Apart from the huge numbers killed in the course of the conquests, these invasions marked the first major, if eventually temporary, losses of Muslim territories in the east since the beginnings of Islam. In contrast, the Christian *reconquista* in the West had advanced as far south as the Nasrid Sultanate of Granada by the mid-thirteenth century (*see* Map 27). The early Mongol khans were either shamanists or Buddhists, and it was not until the late thirteenth and early fourteenth centuries that the rulers of the western and central Mongol lands and their successors were converted to Islam (*see* Maps 22 and 24).

The founder of the Mongol Empire, Chingiz Khan, was born about 1167 into the minor tribal nobility of what is now eastern Mongolia. His early life is obscure, but Temüjin (= blacksmith) as he was originally named, gradually managed to gain control over the other tribes in the area, principally the Naymans, Merkits and Keraits, and having acquired the title Chingiz Khan (= Universal Lord of Lords), he was acclaimed as their supreme leader in a ceremony in 1206. This was, apparently, the first time that such a confederation had been created and, including the Uighurs who joined in 1209, Chingiz Khan now formed and led a huge army on horseback, against the Hsi-Hsia and the Jin in northern China.

In 1218 the Mongol army advanced westwards into the eastern part of the Islamic world, devastating the territories of 'Ala' al-Din Muhammad Khwarazm Shah, between the Caspian and the Aral Sea, and in Khurasan and Transoxania. The immediate pretext for this invasion was that 'Ala' al-Din greatly insulted an embassy of Chingiz Khan, not least by executing one of his envoys. In the space of two years (1219–21) numerous cities, including Utrar, Bukhara, Samarkand, Marv, Nishapur and Ghazna, were overrun and largely destroyed. Despite a victory at Parwan near Kabul, Khwarazm Shah power collapsed in the face of the relentless Mongol westward onslaught. Although in 1222 Chingiz Khan returned directly to Mongolia with part of his army, another detachment devastated northern Iran, the Caucasus and the south Russian steppe before heading home. Chingiz Khan himself then set off for China on an expedition to subdue the Hsi-Hsia and died after defeating them in 1227.

Chingiz Khan had already nominated his third son, Ögedei, as his successor as Great Khan, but, following tribal custom, the territories he had conquered were divided as appanages (known by the term *ulus*) among his other sons and grandsons.

These were the lands of the Great Khan, including Mongolia and northern China; the western lands (later to be divided between the Ilkhanate and the Khanate of the Golden Horde); and the Chaghatay Khanate in Central Asia (*see* Map 24). Under Ögedei (1229–41) the Empire continued to expand into China and northern Iran and also into southern Russia and eastern Europe. In 1235, Ögedei began building what would become the Mongol capital at Karakorum.

In the same year, Ögedei initiated a major expedition westwards under the command of his nephew, Batu. Advancing through the territories of the Qïpchaq Turks north of the Caspian and the Black Sea in 1237, this expedition overran the Principalities of Russia, sacking Kiev in 1240, and then turned towards eastern Europe, occupying Hungary in 1241. To contemporaries it seemed that the Mongol armies were preparing for the conquest of Europe, and indeed the two halves of the army defeated two European armies, one at Liegnitz in Silesia and the other at

Mohi in Hungary, within two days of each other in April 1241, and eventually reached as far west as Wiener Neustadt, just south of Vienna. At this point, early in 1242, the armies learned of the death of Ögedei in Karakorum; Batu withdrew to the area north of the Caucasus, and no organised force of Mongols ever returned to central Europe. Batu stayed in the Qïpchaq area and founded what later became known as the Khanate of the Golden Horde, with its headquarters at Saray on the Volga, which would maintain 'effective control over Russia for almost a century and a half'; indeed, formal Russian allegiance to the Khanate would only come to an end in 1480 (*see* Maps 24 and 32).

Two years after Ögedei's death, a Mongol army had defeated the Seljuks of Rum near Kösedagh (1243); for the time being the Seljuks retained their independence, but they were forced to pay a substantial annual tribute. The Mongols had also invaded and occupied much of the Kingdom of Georgia, with its capital Tiflis falling in 1238, and its tributary status confirmed by 1243.

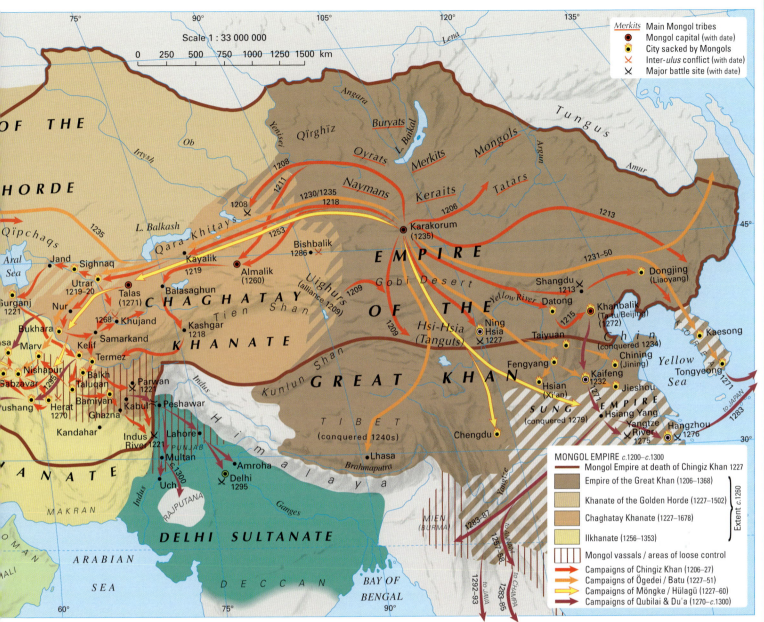

Under Möngke (1251–59), Ögedei's successor as Great Khan, two great expeditions were launched, one towards Sung China and the other towards the west. Möngke's brother Hülagü led the second of these, whose main objectives were to destroy the Isma'ili fortress at Alamut in the mountains of northern Iran, and to obtain the submission of the 'Abbasid caliph of Baghdad (see Map 16).

In 1256 Hülagü arrived at Alamut and secured the submission of the citadel and of other Isma'ili castles in the area. In 1258 his massive armies converged on Baghdad, stormed the city, and put the caliph to death, so ending nearly five centuries of 'Abbasid rule and of Baghdad's domination, however symbolic, of the central lands of the Islamic world. Hülagü attempted to push farther westwards, and indeed briefly occupied both Aleppo and Damascus, but before he could press his advantage further he learned of his brother Möngke's death in Karakorum and withdrew most of his troops to Iran. The remainder of the army was defeated at 'Ayn Jalut in southern

Palestine in 1260. The Mongols never succeeded in occupying Greater Syria, which subsequently became absorbed into the empire of the victors of 'Ayn Jalut, the Mamluks, who had succeeded the Ayyubids as rulers of Egypt in 1250.

Hülagü remained in Iran and founded a new state, the Ilkhanate, with its first capital at Maragha. The rivalry between the descendants of Batu (the khans of the Golden Horde) and the descendants of Hülagü (the Ilkhans) precipitated a series of wars between them in which the rulers of the Golden Horde allied with the Mamluks, especially under Sultan Baybars I (see Map 22). At the same time as this hostility developed between the two western Mongol domains, a rift also appeared between the Chaghatay Khanate and the new Great Khan, Qubilai (1260–94), so that the death of Möngke signalled the end of the united Mongol Empire.

With no strong religious beliefs of their own, the early Mongols were generally tolerant of the beliefs of others. Any initial hostility that they displayed towards Muslim peoples or groups was

almost entirely political, such as their reactions to the treachery of 'Ala' al-Din Khwarazm Shah, or to the challenge which they mistakenly believed the Isma'ilis of Alamut still posed to them.

The only major exception to this was the hostility of Hülagü and his Ilkhanid successors in Iran until 1295 towards Sunni Islam, although this was also 'political', based on opposition to the Sunni 'Abbasids and the Sunni Mamluks. One important result of this was a period of several decades of official tolerance of both Shi'ism and Nestorian Christianity. The increasing influence of Nestorianism in particular gave rise to speculation in some circles in western Europe that a great Christian empire might shortly come into existence in the East; hence the despatch of papal envoys to Karakorum in 1245 and 1253. Such hopes were dashed less than forty years after the fall of Baghdad, when Hülagü's great-grandson, the Ilkhan Ghazan (1295–1304), converted to Sunni Islam, thus bringing much of the western Mongol domain permanently under Muslim rule.

Map 22

The Bahrı Mamluks and the Ilkhanıds c.1250–1382

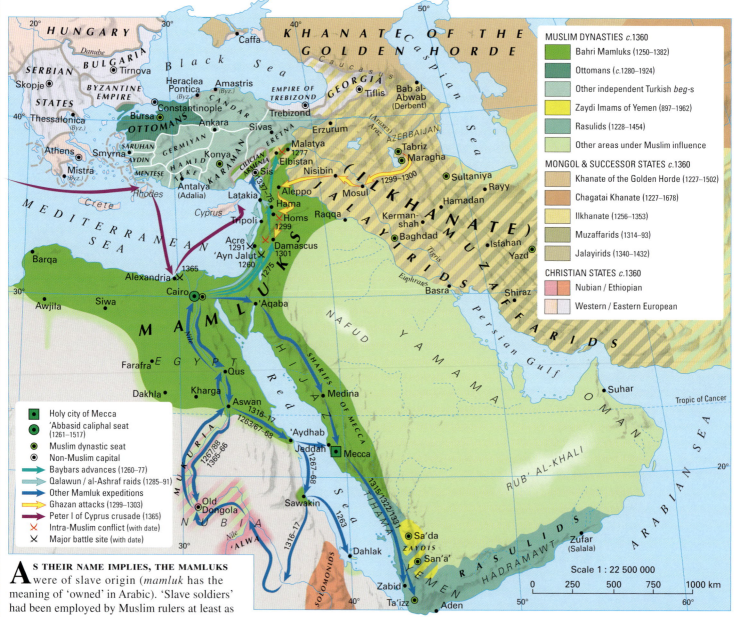

MUSLIM DYNASTIES c.1360
- Bahri Mamluks (1250–1382)
- Ottomans (c.1280–1924)
- Other independent Turkish beg-s
- Zaydi Imams of Yemen (897–1962)
- Rasulids (1228–1454)
- Other areas under Muslim influence

MONGOL & SUCCESSOR STATES c.1360
- Khanate of the Golden Horde (1227–1502)
- Chagatai Khanate (1227–1678)
- Ilkhanate (1256–1353)
- Muzaffarids (1314–93)
- Jalayirids (1340–1432)

CHRISTIAN STATES c.1360
- Nubian / Ethiopian
- Western / Eastern European

- Holy city of Mecca
- 'Abbasid caliphal seat (1261–1517)
- Muslim dynastic seat
- Non-Muslim capital
- Baybars advances (1260–77)
- Qalawun / al-Ashraf raids (1285–91)
- Other Mamluk expeditions
- Ghazan attacks (1299–1303)
- Peter I of Cyprus crusade (1365)
- Intra-Muslim conflict (with date)
- Major battle site (with date)

Scale 1 : 22 500 000

0   250   500   750   1000 km

AS THEIR NAME IMPLIES, THE MAMLUKS were of slave origin (*mamluk* has the meaning of 'owned' in Arabic). 'Slave soldiers' had been employed by Muslim rulers at least as early as the ninth century (*see* Maps 11 and 12). The slaves, mostly 'Turks' captured on raids or purchased outside the *Dar al-Islam*, often rose to positions of great power in the army or the administration, and thus enjoyed a status far superior to that conventionally associated with slavery. In addition, they were normally paid. Many of the Mamluks of the last Ayyubid ruler, al-Salih Ayyub, were Qïpchaq Turks from the steppes north of the Black Sea and the Caspian; his elite force, the Bahriya, was stationed on an island in the Nile (*Bahr al-Nil*).

al-Salih died in 1249 as the crusade led by Louis IX of France was landing at Damietta (*see* Map 18). He was succeeded briefly by his son, then by his wife, and then by what became the Bahri Mamluk dynasty, whose real founder was al-Zahir Baybars I (1260–77). Baybars swiftly took control of the former Ayyubid domains in Syria and the Hijaz, as well as advancing south to Nubia and Sawakin. In order to legitimate his rule, he installed a claimant to the 'Abbasid succession as caliph in Cairo in 1261; this 'second 'Abbasid Caliphate' lasted until 1517.

Although the Mamluks' defeat of the Ilkhans at 'Ayn Jalut in 1260 (*see* Map 21) effectively halted the Mongols' westward advance, it initiated a long period of hostility between them, mostly over Syria, which lasted until peace was concluded in 1323 between the Ilkhan Abu Sa'id (1316–35) and the Mamluk al-Nasir Muhammad ibn Qalawun (1293–94; 1299–1309; 1310–41). Meanwhile the recapture of Palestine was completed by Baybars' successor al-Mansur Qalawun (1279–90) and the latter's son al-Ashraf Khalil (1290–93). The fall of Acre to the Mamluks in May 1291 marked the end of two centuries of crusader presence in the East; Peter I of Cyprus' sack of Alexandria in 1365 was a short-lived revival of Western fortunes. In 1375, the kingdom of Cilician Armenia, formerly an ally of the Mongols, was conquered by the Mamluks. Ironically the Mamluks benefitted from good relations with the Byzantines and the Golden Horde, and there was a lively trade between them (*see* Map 19).

On the other side of the Fertile Crescent, Hülagü (1256–65), the founder of the Ilkhanid dynasty, had sacked Baghdad in 1258 and killed the last of the long line of 'Abbasid caliphs there (*see* Map 21). Hülagü's grandson Ghazan (1295–1304) converted to Sunni Islam, and all his successors followed his example. Processes of acculturation increasingly led the Ilkhanids, whose domains extended over eastern Anatolia, Azerbaijan, Iran and Iraq, to absorb important elements of the civilisation which they ruled. In an almost seamless manner, the dynasty appropriated the 'Persian' administrative system that had prevailed in the region at least since Seljuk times, and contributed generously to the beautification of its capitals at Maragha, Tabriz and Sultaniya. By the 1340s the Ilkhanids had been weakened by a combination of outbreaks of the bubonic plague that would devastate the region until the early sixteenth century, and by constant family feuding. They were replaced first by several local dynasties, including the Muzaffarids in southern and western Iran, the Jalayirids (also nomadic Mongol converts to Islam) in Iraq, Kurdistan and Azerbaijan, and then later by Timur and his successors (*see* Map 24).

Map 23

The Burji Mamluks and the Ottomans 1382–1517

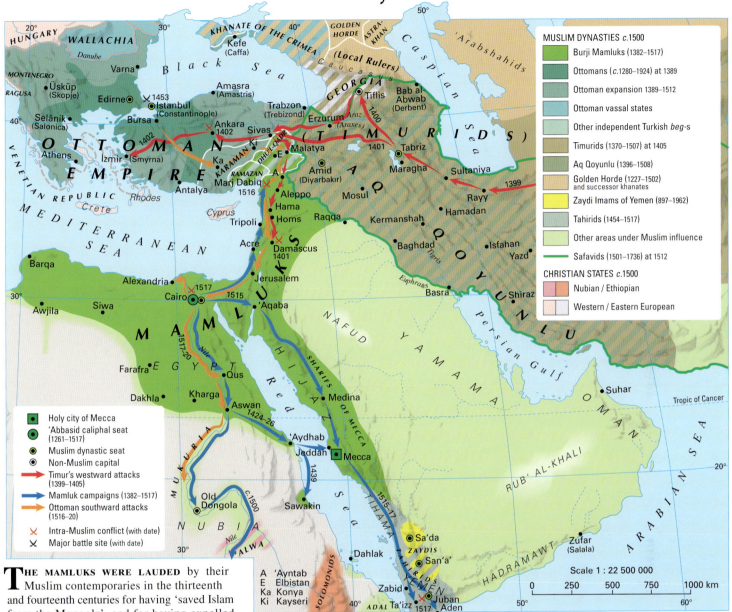

MUSLIM DYNASTIES c.1500
- Burji Mamluks (1382–1517)
- Ottomans (c.1280–1924) at 1389
- Ottoman expansion 1389–1512
- Ottoman vassal states
- Other independent Turkish *beg*-s
- Timurids (1370–1507) at 1405
- Aq Qoyunlu (1396–1508)
- Golden Horde (1227–1502) and successor khanates
- Zaydi Imams of Yemen (897–1962)
- Tahirids (1454–1517)
- Other areas under Muslim influence
- Safavids (1501–1736) at 1512

CHRISTIAN STATES c.1500
- Nubian / Ethiopian
- Western / Eastern European

- ▣ Holy city of Mecca
- ◉ 'Abbasid caliphal seat (1261–1517)
- ◉ Muslim dynastic seat
- ◉ Non-Muslim capital
- → Timur's westward attacks (1399–1405)
- → Mamluk campaigns (1382–1517)
- → Ottoman southward attacks (1516–20)
- ✕ Intra-Muslim conflict (with date)
- ✕ Major battle site (with date)

Scale 1 : 22 500 000
0   250   500   750   1000 km

A 'Ayntab
E Elbistan
Ka Konya
Ki Kayseri

THE MAMLUKS WERE LAUDED by their
Muslim contemporaries in the thirteenth
and fourteenth centuries for having 'saved Islam
from the Mongols', and for having expelled
the crusaders from Muslim territory. They also
gained great prestige among Muslims from their
control of the three holy cities of Mecca, Medina
and Jerusalem. However, in the forty years after
the death of al-Nasir Muhammad ibn Qalawun in
1341, twelve of his sons and grandsons, almost
all dominated by their powerful *amirs*, succeeded
him until the line was replaced in 1382 by the
Burjis, so named as many of them had been
stationed at the citadel (*al-Burj*) of Cairo. In the
1340s, the Black Death, which also swept over
Europe and the domains of the Golden Horde
and the Ilkhanids, is estimated to have carried off
a third of the population of Egypt and Syria. It
was followed by outbreaks of pneumonic plague
perhaps once every three years between the 1340s
and the Ottoman conquest in 1517; these catas-
trophes caused major falls in agricultural revenue,
and thus in the incomes of the Mamluk *amirs*.

The changeover between the Bahri and Burji
Mamluks, from Qïpchaqs (from the Crimea and the
Ukrainian steppes) to Circassians (from the Caucasus),
had already begun before the accession of the

Circassian Barquq (1382–89; 1390–99), but that
date is also significant in marking the end of the
rule of the house of Qalawun, which had lasted
for more than a century. Several theories have
been advanced as to how the Mamluk sultanate,
'a militarized Turkish state implanted on Egyptian
soil', based on a non-hereditary aristocracy and
with episodes of spectacular violence surround-
ing almost every succession, was able to survive
for more than two and a half centuries. In part,
this was because it operated a highly centralized
administration (based on assignments of tax on
lands or commodities by the sultan to individual
office-holders) and also because it faced few major
external threats, at least between the early fourteenth and late fifteenth centuries. (Although highly
destructive, the attack mounted by Timur at the beginning of the fifteenth century, when both Aleppo
and Damascus were sacked, did not do permanent
damage to the dynasty; *see* Map 24.) In the late
fifteenth and early sixteenth centuries the sultanate
was held by members of Mamluk households: thus
Qa'itbay (1468–96) was succeeded briefly by his

son and then by five of his own Mamluks.

Meanwhile, the Mamluks' nemesis was gathering
strength. The Ottomans had conquered much of
southeastern Europe in the fourteenth century, and
in spite of the battering they endured from Timur in
the early fifteenth century, they gradually resumed
the conquest of Anatolia (*see* Map 25). Following
the capture of Constantinople in 1453, the Byzantine enclave of Trebizond was absorbed in 1461,
and by 1483, Karaman, the Ottomans' last serious
local rival, had been annexed. Only Dhu'l-Qadr
and Ramazan remained as weak buffer-states on
what had become the frontier between the Ottomans
and the Mamluks. Fighting broke out between them
in 1485, and continued intermittently for the next
thirty years. In 1516, Selim I (1512–20) decided
to quash the Mamluk threat. The two armies met
at Marj Dabiq near Aleppo, where Ottoman artillery
proved decisive. By early 1517, Selim had pushed
on to Cairo and defeated the remaining Mamluk
forces. All the Mamluk territories were speedily
incorporated into the Ottoman Empire, which now
extended from the upper Nile to the lower Danube.

Map 24

Mongols and Turkmens in Iran, Russia and Central Asia c.1300–c.1500

MONGOL KHANATES
- Golden Horde (1227–1502) and successor khanates c.1500
- → Campaigns of Toqtamïsh (1377–95)
- Chaghatay Khanate (1227–1678) post-Timur remnant c.1500
- — Ilkhanate (1256–1353) maximum extent c.1300
- (KARTS) Ilkhanate successors c.1300– c.1400

CHRISTIAN STATES
- Western European c.1500
- Eastern European c.1500

TIMURID EMPIRE
- Timurids (1370–1507) max. extent on death of Timur 1405 and appanages c.1500
- Campaigns of Timur
- → 1370–89
- → 1390–99
- → 1400–05
- ☉ City sacked by Timur

TURKMEN STATES
- — Qara Qoyunlu (1351–1469) maximum extent 1435
- — Aq Qoyunlu (1396–1508) extent 1435
- Aq Qoyunlu extent 1478 ('empire' of Uzun Hasan)
- Other Turkmen groups

OTHER MUSLIM STATES
- Delhi Sultanate (1206–1555) and successor states c.1500
- Mamluks (1250–1517) extent c.1500
- Ottomans (c.1280–1924) extent c.1500
- Other independent areas under Muslim influence
- ◉ 'Abbasid caliphal seat (1261–1517)
- ◉ Muslim dynastic seat
- ◉ Non-Muslim capital
- ✕ Intra-Muslim conflict (with date)
- ✕ Major battle site (with date)

AFTER THE DEATH OF MÖNGKE IN 1259, the vast empire of Chingiz Khan began to fall apart; the territories in the east came under control of the Yüan dynasty and the three western khanates were generally at odds with each other. The Ilkhanate converted permanently to Islam under Ghazan in 1295, and the Golden Horde under Özbek (1313–41). The conversion of the Chaghatays is less clear-cut; the western part, Transoxania and Farghana, was initially taken over by Timur (1370–1405), who made his capital at Samarkand. The Islamisation of the eastern part was uneven; individual rulers converted, but the process was not continuous.

In Russia the exactions of the Golden Horde profoundly affected the economy and accentuated the country's isolation. Moscow was sacked in 1293 and 1298. However, the fourteenth century saw the gradual rise of Muscovy; in 1380, Grand Prince Dmitrii defeated Khan Toqtamïsh (1377–95) at Kulikovo, although the Horde sacked Moscow two years later and devastated the state in 1408 for not paying tribute. Further south, the Ottoman capture of Constantinople in 1453 by Mehmed II (1444–46; 1451–81) added

to the isolation of the Russian Orthodox Church. In 1480 Ivan III renounced his allegiance to the Horde, which had begun to fragment into smaller khanates: Astrakhan, Crimea, Kazan and Qasimov (see Map 32).

Meanwhile, south of the Caucasus, a weakened Ilkhanate was replaced by several local dynasties, which in turn were eclipsed by Timur in the 1380s as part of a well-planned military campaign. Later in 1395 Timur vanquished his great rival Toqtamïsh at Terek River; in 1398 he devastated Delhi; in 1400 he besieged Aleppo, and in 1401 ordered the sack of both Damascus and Baghdad. In 1402 he defeated and captured Sultan Bayazid I (1389–1402) near Ankara; Bayazid subsequently died in captivity, and the Ottoman state took decades to recover. At its height Timur's empire stretched from the Euphrates in the west to the Indus in the east and to the Syr Darya in the north. However, largely because of the Turkic tradition of parcelling out territories among sons and grandsons, it fell apart on the death of his son Shah Rukh in 1447 (see Map 32).

In the vacuum that followed, two Turkmen dynasties took over the western part of Timur's former

empire. Like the Ottomans, and the Safavids (who would become the rulers of Iran in 1501; see Map 31), the Qara Qoyunlu (1380–1468) and the Aq Qoyunlu (1389–1508) were nomadic tribes which had been pushed westwards by the Mongols. The Qara Qoyunlu ruled most of northern Iraq from Tabriz from about 1410 until the late 1460s, when their territories were taken over by the Aq Qoyunlu, who had been Timur's vassals and became his successors in the west. Their leader Qara 'Uthman (1403–35) had played an important part in Timur's defeat of Bayazid I in 1402. Under the dynasty's most notable ruler, Uzun Hasan (1457–78), its domains expanded into an 'empire' which covered much of Azerbaijan, Iraq and Iran.

After his victory over the Mamluks, which gave him possession of the Hijaz, Selim I and his successors described themselves as 'the Servant[s] of the Two Noble Sanctuaries' (Mecca and Medina), a title for which Uzun Hasan had been angling towards the end of his reign. The Ottomans also proved to be Uzun Hasan's undoing, defeating his troops at Tercan near Erzincan in August 1473.

Map 25

Ottoman Expansion in Anatolia, the Balkans and Black Sea Lands c.1300–c.1520

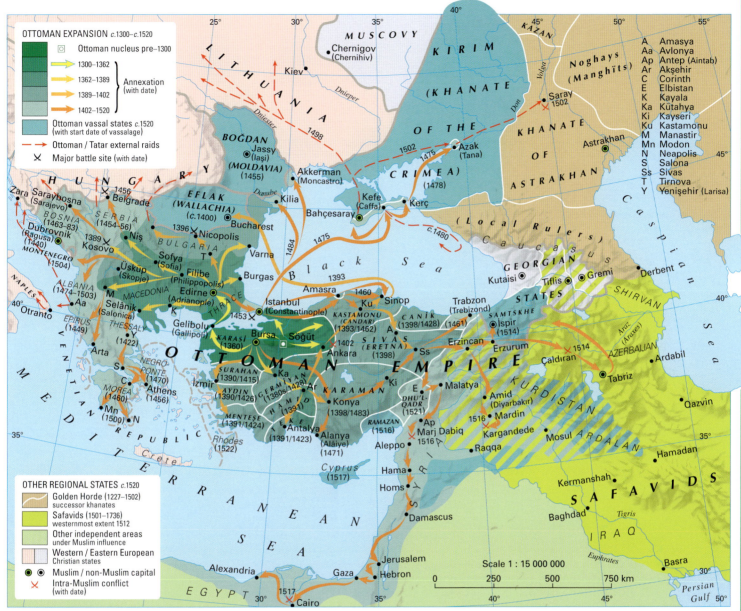

OTTOMAN EXPANSION c.1300–c.1520

- ⊡ Ottoman nucleus pre–1300
- → 1300–1362 ⎫
- → 1362–1389 ⎬ Annexation (with date)
- → 1389–1402 ⎪
- → 1402–1520 ⎭
- Ottoman vassal states c.1520 (with start date of vassalage)
- ⤏ Ottoman / Tatar external raids
- ✕ Major battle site (with date)

OTHER REGIONAL STATES c.1520

- Golden Horde (1227–1502) successor khanates
- Safavids (1501–1736) westernmost extent 1512
- Other independent areas under Muslim influence
- Western / Eastern European Christian states
- ◉ ◉ Muslim / non-Muslim capital
- ✕ Intra-Muslim conflict (with date)

A Amasya
Aa Avlonya
Ap Antep (Aintab)
Ar Akşehir
C Corinth
E Elbistan
K Kayala
Ka Kütahya
Ki Kayseri
Ku Kastamonu
M Manastir
Mn Modon
N Neapolis
S Salona
Ss Sivas
T Tirnova
Y Yenişehir (Larisa)

Scale 1 : 15 000 000

0   250   500   750 km

THE OTTOMAN EMPIRE lasted for over six hundred years, from the late thirteenth century to the early 1920s. The Ottomans were another Turkic people pushed westwards by the Mongols; after their consolidation around Bursa in the early fourteenth century they rolled back Byzantine authority through their conquest of the Balkans. Southern Bulgaria, Macedonia, and Thrace were annexed by the 1380s, and after major victories over the Serbs at Kosovo (1389) and the Hungarians at Nicopolis (1396), northern Bulgaria, Thessaly, Epirus, Serbia, Athens, the Morea, southern Bosnia and Albania became part of their domains. The Ottomans absorbed the territories of their Turkic rivals in Anatolia between 1360 and 1521 (in spite of a temporary setback following Timur's attack in 1402; *see* Map 24), while Wallachia, Moldavia and the Khanate of the Crimea became vassal states in the fifteenth century (*see* Map 31).

Many factors contributed to the longevity of the Ottoman Empire. One of these was that almost from the beginning, its rulers practised a policy of systematic institution-building. The earliest Ottoman sultans struck coins in their own names, established chanceries where clerks issued documents, and created courts in their successive capitals, Bursa (1326–60s), Edirne (1360s–1453) and then Istanbul (Constantinople). Murad I (1362–89) exacted a tax of one fifth on slaves and booty captured in raids into Europe, and used the proceeds to create a professional infantry, the Janissaries (*yeni çeri*, new troops). Also in the fourteenth century, the Ottomans instituted the *devşirme*, 'collection', a levy of Christian boys from Anatolia and the Balkans (and of Muslim boys from Bosnia), which provided recruits for both the army and the bureaucracy until the end of the sixteenth century.

Another key element contributing to the long life of the dynasty was that, unlike almost all its Turkic predecessors, it did not countenance the 'appanage' notion of sovereignty, under which the 'imperial territories' were co-ruled by several members of the same family. By the early fifteenth century it seems to have been established that the sum of Ottoman territory was indivisible, and this principle was fully upheld for the remainder of the Empire's existence.

A number of other features of the Ottoman state should be mentioned. The first was a highly centralised system of taxation, based on periodic censuses, which were taken very meticulously. Eventually, the system found it difficult to accommodate the price inflation of the late sixteenth and early seventeenth centuries, and it could also not cope with the state's increasing demands for trained paid soldiery to fight off invasions, but at least during the Ottoman 'golden age' (1451–1600) it worked relatively well. Another important institution was the provincial cavalry, whose officers governed the provinces in return for being assigned *timar*-s, or 'fiefdoms', which included the right to collect revenue and administer the rural areas.

After consolidating their conquests in Europe and Anatolia, the Ottomans turned their attention eastward. Selim I (1512–20) established a semi-permanent frontier with Iran after defeating the Safavids at Çaldıran in 1514. Two years later he led a successful expedition to Syria and Egypt, after which all the Mamluk territories were fully incorporated into the Ottoman state (*see* Map 31).

Map 26

North Africa and Spain under the Almohads c.1130–c.1250

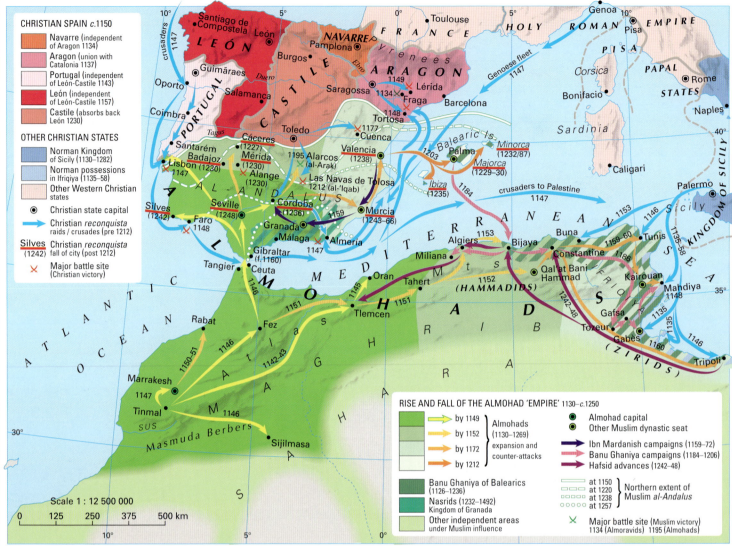

CHRISTIAN SPAIN c.1150

- Navarre (independent of Aragon 1134)
- Aragon (union with Catalonia 1137)
- Portugal (independent of León-Castile 1143)
- León (independent of León-Castile 1157)
- Castile (absorbs back León 1230)

OTHER CHRISTIAN STATES

- Norman Kingdom of Sicily (1130–1282)
- Norman possessions in Ifriqiya (1135–58)
- Other Western Christian states
- ◉ Christian state capital
- → Christian *reconquista* raids / crusades (pre 1212)
- <u>Silves</u> (1242) Christian *reconquista* fall of city (post 1212)
- ✕ Major battle site (Christian victory)

RISE AND FALL OF THE ALMOHAD 'EMPIRE' 1130–c.1250

- by 1149 ⎫
- by 1152 ⎪ Almohads (1130–1269)
- by 1172 ⎬ expansion and counter-attacks
- by 1212 ⎭
- Banu Ghaniya of Balearics (1126–1236)
- Nasrids (1232–1492) Kingdom of Granada
- Other independent areas under Muslim influence
- ◉ Almohad capital
- ◉ Other Muslim dynastic seat
- ➤ Ibn Mardanish campaigns (1159–72)
- ➤ Banu Ghaniya campaigns (1184–1206)
- ➤ Hafsid advances (1242–48)
- at 1150 ⎫
- at 1220 ⎪ Northern extent of
- at 1238 ⎬ Muslim *al-Andalus*
- at 1257 ⎭
- ✕ Major battle site (Muslim victory) 1134 (Almoravids) 1195 (Almohads)

Scale 1 : 12 500 000
0 125 250 375 500 km

IN THE SIXTY-TWO YEARS between the victory of Yusuf ibn Tashufin over Alfonso VI at Zallaqa in 1086 and the fall of Seville to Ferdinand III in 1248, all but the southeastern corner of *al-Andalus* fell into Christian hands. This was partly because of the growing strength, confidence and unity of the forces of the *reconquista* (and especially with the rise of Aragon under Alfonso I 'El Batallador', 1104–34) but even more so because of disunity, lack of organisation and disaffection among the Muslims.

For almost two hundred years, first under the Almoravids (c.1050–1147; *see* Map 14) and then under their successors the Almohads (1130–1269), it is difficult to disentangle the history of *al-Andalus* from that of the Maghrib. Both dynasties were based in Marrakesh, and generally controlled *al-Andalus* from there. From the point of view of the continuing vitality of Islam in Spain, this arrangement had obvious disadvantages, in the sense that the rulers were often either preoccupied with potential opposition in Morocco or obliged to delegate power to others to rule Spain on their behalf, or, if they did reside briefly in Spain, might have to return to Marrakesh to deal with problems there.

Initially, the Almoravid 'Ali ibn Yusuf ibn Tashufin (1107–42) had continued his father's tradition of confining the bestowal of high office

to his close relatives from North Africa, but he became increasingly assimilated to Andalusian culture, appointing Andalusians to his court and chancery and recruiting Christians to his militia (*hasham*). This seems to have been a major factor in the rise of a protest movement among the Masmuda Berbers of the Atlas Mountains south of Marrakesh, the *al-Muwahhidun*, or Almohads, 'those who proclaim the unity of God', led by Ibn Tumart.

Ibn Tumart (c.1080–1130), a Moroccan from the Sus, had studied in the Arab east, possibly with the great theological reformer al-Ghazali. He returned to Marrakesh around 1120, preaching an austere form of Islam based only on the Qur'an and *hadith* (rejecting the authority of the *'ulama'*), and tried to win over 'Ali ibn Yusuf ibn Tashufin to his cause. When this failed, he proclaimed himself *Mahdi* and took refuge at Tinmal with a Masmuda Berber tribe whom he led in a series of attacks on the Almoravids until his death in 1130. He was succeeded as 'caliph' by his principal lieutenant, 'Abd al-Mu'min (1130–63), who took Marrakesh from the Almoravids in 1147, made members of his own family governors of Córdoba, Granada and Seville, and then proceeded to occupy much of North Africa in the 1150s.

At this point the Almohads found themselves

confronted with two serious revolts. The first was led by Ibn Mardanish, the ruler of Valencia and Murcia, who held out against them until his death in 1172. Subsequently, the campaigns of the pro-Almoravid Banu Ghaniya hastened the decline of Almohad power in the eastern Maghrib. Also, during this period Lisbon fell to the Christians, and the Normans gained a temporary foothold in Ifriqiya. In spite of this, the Almohads succeeded in uniting the Muslim west into a single 'empire' between the 1170s and the late 1240s, with its capitals at Marrakesh and Seville. Yusuf ibn 'Abd al-Mu'min (1163–84) and his son Ya'qub (1184–99) both resided at Seville, where they patronised a brilliant court and built many of the city's most famous monuments.

Like their Almoravid predecessors, the Almohads eventually fell victim to a combination of internecine rivalries, doctrinal disagreements and the increasing determination of the Christians. Ya'qub's victory at Alarcos in 1195 was the last of its kind, and the Muslim defeat at Las Navas de Tolosa in 1212 occasioned a series of local revolts against the Almohads. In North Africa, their territories were subsequently split between three other Berber dynasties, the Marinids, the Ziyanids and the Hafsids. After the fall of Seville in 1248, the emirate of Granada was all that was left of Muslim Spain.

Map 27

Muslim Rule in North Africa and Spain at the End of the Reconquista c.1250–c.1550

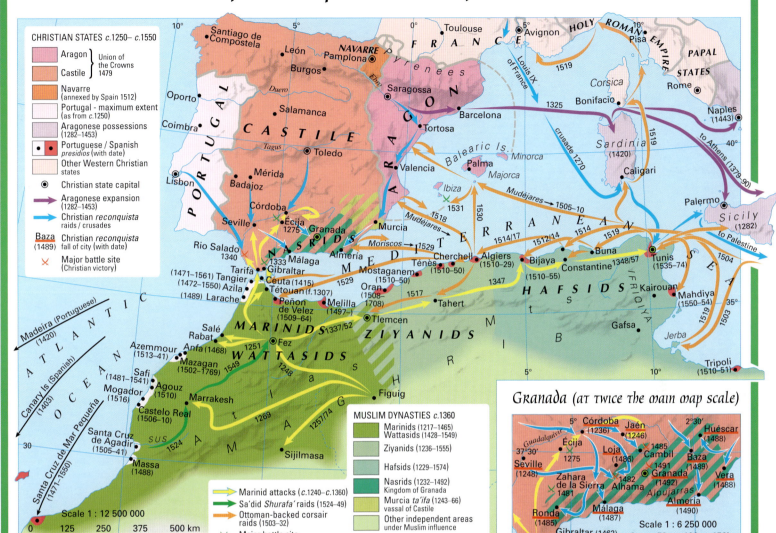

CHRISTIAN STATES c.1250– c.1550

- Aragon } Union of
- Castile } the Crowns 1479
- Navarre (annexed by Spain 1512)
- Portugal - maximum extent (as from c.1250)
- Aragonese possessions (1282–1453)
- Portuguese / Spanish *presidios* (with date)
- Other Western Christian states
- ⊙ Christian state capital
- → Aragonese expansion (1282–1453)
- → Christian *reconquista* raids / crusades
- Baza (1489) Christian *reconquista* fall of city (with date)
- ✕ Major battle site (Christian victory)

MUSLIM DYNASTIES c.1360

- Marinids (1217–1465)
- Wattasids (1428–1549)
- Ziyanids (1236–1555)
- Hafsids (1229–1574)
- Nasrids (1232–1492) Kingdom of Granada
- Murcia *ta'ifa* (1243–66) vassal of Castile
- Other independent areas under Muslim influence
- ⇒ Marinid attacks (c.1240–c.1360)
- ⇒ Sa'did *Shurafa'* raids (1524–49)
- ⇒ Ottoman-backed corsair raids (1503–32)
- ✕ Major battle site (Muslim victory)
- ⊙ Muslim dynastic seat

Scale 1 : 12 500 000
0 125 250 375 500 km

Granada (at twice the main map scale)

Scale 1 : 6 250 000
0 50 100 150 km

I**N 1232, MUHAMMAD AL-AHMAR**, a soldier of humble origins from the countryside near Jaén, took over Granada, the southernmost part of a rapidly shrinking Muslim *al-Andalus*. With the backing of his clan, the Banu Nasr, al-Ahmar founded a dynasty, the Nasrids, which was to last, through many compromises and many vicissitudes, until 1492. Like the revolt of Ibn Mardanish (*see Map 26*), al-Ahmar's original rebellion against the Almohads has sometimes been interpreted as an 'Andalusian' movement against 'alien', that is North African Berber, rule. Some of al-Ahmar's actions as ruler of Granada (1232–73) are not easy to interpret, particularly his alliance with Ferdinand III of Castile (1217–52), to whom he sent troops to assist in the siege of Seville in 1248. In general, al-Ahmar seems to have had a fairly shrewd sense of the limitations of his position.

Surrounded by high mountain ranges, Granada's boundaries remained fairly constant until the 1480s. The Nasrid kingdom was quite densely populated, and its capital city was the centre of a rich agricultural area. Granada's natural defences generally enabled the early Nasrids to keep out both their Castilian overlords and the Marinids, the Almohads' principal successors in the Maghrib.

Meanwhile in the Maghrib, the Marinids, a Zanata Berber tribe based near Figuig in the northern Sahara, progressively made assaults on the Almohad state, culminating in the conquest of Marrakesh in 1269, and began to build their own new capital at Fez in 1276. Several Marinid rulers fought in Spain against the *reconquista*, and the dynasty gradually extended its influence eastwards at the expense of the Ziyanids and Hafsids until checked by a series of attacks by Castile and Portugal and by the rise of the Wattasids, a collateral branch of the Marinids, in the 1420s.

The great days of the Nasrids were the reigns of Yusuf I (1333–54) and Muhammad V (1362–91), during which the Alhambra was built and Castile expelled the Marinids from *al-Andalus*. After this, the Nasrids' complex and often obscure history seems to slide toward the seemingly inevitable ouster of Muhammad XII (1482–83:1487–92) in 1492 by the forces of Ferdinand and Isabella, the end of nearly 800 years of Muslim rule in the Iberian Peninsula.

Since the middle of the thirteenth century, the great majority of the Muslims of *al-Andalus* had acquired the status of *Mudéjares,* Muslims living under Christian rule. For the last two and a half centuries of Muslim Spain they were generally able to maintain and practise their faith, but all this changed after the anti-Castilian revolts (1499–1502) in the Alpujarras and other parts of Granada. First, the Muslims of Granada, then, later in the 1520s, those in Castile and Aragon, were obliged either to convert to Christianity, to refuse baptism and to become enslaved, or – a desirable but difficult alternative, since destinations were very restricted – to leave the country altogether. Eventually, the Spanish monarchy decided to expel them, and between 1609 and 1614, some 300,000 *Moriscos*, Muslim converts to Christianity, were obliged to leave the Peninsula, mainly for Morocco or Greece.

In the fifteenth and early sixteenth centuries, encouraged by the successes of the *reconquista*, Spain and Portugal established *presidios*, fortified ports, on the Atlantic and Mediterranean coasts of North Africa, a development that the weak Muslim states of the region were unable to oppose. Various explanations have been suggested: that the *presidios* would provide the basis for a fresh crusade, and/or that they would enable Spain and Portugal to take control of the trans-Saharan gold trade. In time, the wider colonial undertakings of the Iberian states gradually reduced the importance of the *presidios*. Most of those on the Mediterranean were lost to the Ottomans, while those on the Atlantic were eventually absorbed into the Moroccan state, which would undergo a remarkable revival under the rule of the Sa'did dynasty between 1510 and 1659 (*see Map 33*).

Map 28
India under the Delhi Sultanate 1206–c.1400

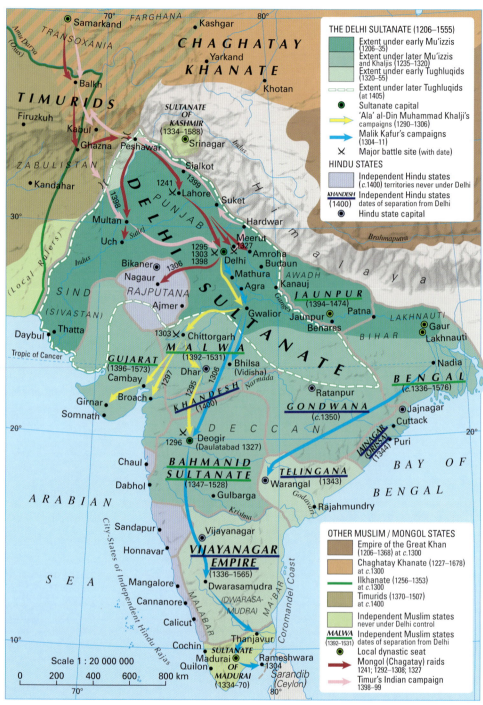

While some of these victories were permanent, many local Hindu rulers managed to maintain their positions, or were able to regain them over time. In addition, although the foundation of the Delhi Sultanate in 1206 marked the beginning of a distinctively new direction for Islamic rule in India, its first century was not especially stable: ten sultans ruled between the death of Iltutmish in 1236 and 1296 (including, remarkably, his daughter Raziya [1236–40]), most of them for periods of less than three years. Almost all of them were faced with constant and often lethal challenges to their authority from other members of the elite.

In 1290, the Mu'izzi dynasty was followed by the Khaljis, who originated in Zabulistan (south-eastern Afghanistan), and were thus not properly 'Turks'. Among the achievements of 'Ala' al-Din Muhammad (1296–1316) was to extend the Delhi Sultanate into the northern Deccan (in 1296), and into the rich province of Gujarat (in 1299–1300). Under the command of his na'ib, or deputy, Malik Kafur, 'Ala' al-Din's armies penetrated to Madurai, near the 'Coromandel Coast' in the far south of India. Although these conquests were temporary, in the sense that local power brokers soon began to challenge the authority of Delhi, both 'Ala' al-Din and the founder of the successor dynasty, Muhammad b. Tughluq, encouraged the Islamisation of the Deccan, although much of the region would remain in the hands of tributary Hindu rajas. Between 1292 and 1316, 'Ala' al-Din managed to ward off at least eight attacks from the Mongols (who had occupied Lahore temporarily at the end of 1241, and Uch and Multan in 1257–58), including a siege of Delhi in 1295.

The Khalji dynasty lasted only thirty years and was replaced by the Turco-Indian Tughluqids (1320–c.1414), who probably originated in Khurasan. Muhammad b. Tughluq (1325–51) began by controlling more territory than any of his predecessors, but, partly because of a disastrous drought between 1335 and 1342, and partly as a result of constant rebellions against his attempts to centralise the administration of the further flung provinces, he died having lost both Bengal and much of South India. His cousin Firuz Shah (1351–88) restored the authority of the Delhi Sultanate in Sind, but could not prevent the continuing independence of the Hindu empire of Vijayanagar and the Muslim states of the Deccan (the Bahmanids) and Madurai. Both before and after Firuz's death, the Sultanate endured a series of civil wars with numerous rival claimants to the succession. The resulting chaos proved enormously tempting to Timur, who sacked and occupied Delhi in 1398 with a vast army in what was to be the last major nomadic incursion across the Indus (see Map 24). This was to be instrumental in hastening the collapse of the Delhi Sultanate, and in paving the way for the rise of a number of independent Muslim states: Jaunpur, Gujarat, Malwa, and later Berar, Bidar, Bijapur, Ahmadnagar and Golconda, the five successors of the Bahmanid Sultanate in the Deccan.

IN 1215–16 THE GHURID RULERS lost control of Ghazna to the Khwarazm Shahs, and shifted their attention to India (see Map 16). Beginning with the campaigns of Mu'izz al-Din Ghuri (1173–1206) and his general Aybak, much of northern and central India came under Muslim, more specifically Turkish-Afghan, control. Thus at some point in the early thirteenth century, Delhi became the 'capital of Muslim India'. According to both Sanskrit and Muslim sources, the success of the early Muslim invaders and of the conquests carried out by their descendants was the result of a combination of the sheer size of their armies and their extensive use of archers and armoured cavalry, mounted on Nisean horses imported from Central Asia and Iran.

Early in the thirteenth century, Ikhtiyar al-Din Muhammad Khalji, a general in Aybak's service, conquered Bihar and western Bengal, where he ruled until his death in 1206. Iltutmish, a general in Aybak's service, ruled as sultan in Delhi between 1211 and 1236, added Sind to the Sultanate, and in 1229 received recognition from the caliph al-Mustansir (1226–42) as *Nasir Amir al-Mu'minin*, Assistant/Helper of the Commander of the Faithful, a title which he and many of his successors maintained until (and after) the fall of the 'Abbasids in 1258. The court of Iltutmish became a haven for Muslim notables and scholars fleeing the Mongol invasions. During and after his time Delhi became, and long remained, the pre-eminent Muslim city of the east.

Map 29

India under the Sayyids, Lodis and early Mughals c.1400–1605

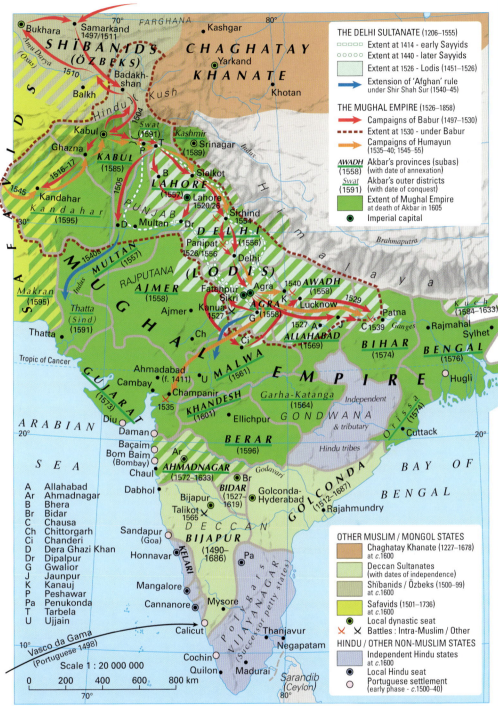

AFTER TIMUR'S SACK OF DELHI IN 1398, the power of the Delhi Sultanate virtually collapsed. For some forty years, the Sayyids (1414–51), who claimed both descent from the Prophet Muhammad and appointment to their position from Shah Rukh (1405–47; the son of Timur, and ruler of Transoxania, Khurasan and Iran), reigned over a greatly reduced domain which included Delhi and its immediate surroundings, Multan (where the dynasty originated), and parts of the Punjab.

In an attempt to recoup some of the Sultanate's losses, the first Sayyid ruler recruited a sizeable army, mostly of warlords of Afghan origin and their military dependents. One of the Afghan commanders, Bahlul Lodi, restored the authority of Delhi over the Punjab, and eventually took over the Sultanate in 1451. In the course of a long reign (1451–89) he forced the submission of the sultanate of Jaunpur, and re-established control over much of central India. He also invited other Afghan warriors to join him in India, and divided his conquests between his many sons and numerous other male relatives. His third son, Sikandar (1489–1521) preferred a more centralised administration, moving the capital to Agra, and cultivating local notables, even promoting Rajput Hindus to important civil and military offices. The last Lodi ruler, Ibrahim b. Sikander (1517–26) was even more determined to 'Indianise' his administration. In consequence, the (Afghan) governor of the Punjab, Dawlat Khan, approached Babur, a descendant of both Chingiz Khan and Timur, who had been claiming Delhi on behalf of his Timurid forbears at least since his first military foray into India in 1519, offering him an alliance to unseat Ibrahim. In 1526, Babur's forces, using Central Asian cavalry tactics to encircle the Afghans, decisively defeated the Lodi army at Panipat, some fifty miles from Delhi. Two weeks later he entered Agra, which became his capital.

In spite of Babur's considerable military and administrative skills, the state which he founded long remained precarious. 'Afghan warlords' continued to hold several important military strongholds in the Ganges valley, and by the time of his death at 57 in 1530, Timurid/Mughal rule was still more of a military occupation than an empire. This was to last for some time, to the extent that an 'Afghan dynasty' founded by Shir Shah Sur (1540–45) not only defeated Babur's son Humayun (1530–40, then 1555–56) in battle in 1539 and 1540, but managed to keep him out of India for much of the next fifteen years. During this time he sought refuge at the court of the Safavid Shah Tahmasp I (1524–76), whose loan of troops was crucial to Humayun's eventual restoration. Beginning with his successful siege of Kandahar in 1545, the process took a further ten years. Humayun died after a fall in the fortress of Delhi in 1556, and was succeeded by his twelve-year old son, Akbar (1556–1605), under whom Mughal rule was 'permanently' established.

By 1558 Akbar had reconquered most of the Punjab, Rajputana and the Ganges valley as far east as Jaunpur; by 1561 he had become his own commander-in-chief and had added Malwa to his domains. In 1571, he transferred the capital to the newly built city of Fatehpur Sikri near Agra. Akbar had constructed the city around a great mosque which contained the tomb of the Sufi saint Salim Chishti (d.1571), to whom he and his successors were deeply devoted. By 1573, he had conquered Gujarat, and later annexed Bengal, Bihar and Orissa; in 1585, largely to counter threats from the fearsome Shïbanid/Özbek ruler 'Abdullah II (1583–98; see Map 32) he moved his capital to Lahore, from which he annexed Kashmir and Sind. In 1565, the five Muslim sultanates of the Deccan had defeated the Vijayanagar Empire at a crucial battle at Talikota which caused the collapse of the last great Hindu kingdom of South India.

Akbar was always interested in religious debate, initially on Islamic theology, but he later widened the discussions to include Hindu holy men, Christian priests, and Mahdist (and thus in Indian terms heterodox) *'ulama'*. He also propagated *Din-i Ilahi,* a form of theism which attempted to express the common elements of Islam and Hinduism. In addition he recruited a number of (unconverted) Rajputs to senior positions in his administration.

In 1598 Akbar moved his capital back to Agra. From there, he conquered and annexed Khandesh and Berar and began the conquest of Ahmadnagar by occupying its capital. His last years were clouded by the rebellion of his son Salim, but the two were reconciled on Akbar's deathbed, when he nominated Salim as his heir.

Map 30

The Spread of Islam in Southeast Asia c.1275–c.1600

THE SPREAD OF ISLAM IN SOUTHEAST ASIA should be understood in terms of a series of long-term incremental developments, which began slowly with the arrival of Muslim merchants in the region in the eighth century, perhaps even earlier. Arab and Chinese accounts attest to the presence of Muslim merchants in southern China in the ninth century (*see* Map 20). From the tenth through twelfth centuries, Muslim merchants were active in the south Sumatran entrepôt of Palembang, the capital of Srivijaya (*Zabaj*), and in the west Sumatran port of Barus (*Fansur*). Larger scale conversion to Islam, however, was 'a process rather than an event,' which took on greater momentum between the late thirteenth and fifteenth centuries, generally spreading from the coastal areas to the interior of the islands, and generally, although not always, in a top-down process in which rulers were converted and then introduced more or less orthodox versions of Islam to their peoples.

The identities of the first Muslim merchants are not entirely clear: some modern historiography in Malaysia and Indonesia stresses the role of Hadrami Arabs, but earlier evidence from Aceh and elsewhere in Sumatra suggests the important roles played by Indian Muslims from Gujarat, Malabar and Tamil Nadu. In any case, the process of Islamisation was quite long and drawn out. By the sixteenth and seventeenth centuries, many members of the *'ulama'* in the region were linked to various Sufi orders. The *barakat* or spiritual power of Sufi 'holy men' and rulers, whose tombs were and are still visited by the faithful, seems to have played an important role in easing the transition from previous belief systems. In Java, where Muslim migrants from China were also present, Islam expanded from communities on the north coast to the interior where it established itself in relation to a complex Hindu-Buddhist court culture. Despite the generally low esteem in which trade and merchants were traditionally held, Islam gradually became 'identified with wealth, success and power' since many Muslim merchants became wealthy and enjoyed a prosperous lifestyle. When the Hindu-Buddhist polities did convert, their elaborate court ceremonies were often retained.

By the end of the thirteenth century Marco Polo recorded the existence of two small Muslim polities in Aceh in northern Sumatra, in Perlak and Samudra-Pasai. The Moroccan traveller Ibn Batuta, who visited the island in the 1340s, noted that the ruler and people of Samudra followed the Shafi'i *madhhab* (school of [Islamic] religious law) and engaged in *jihad* against their non-Muslim neighbours. By the late fourteenth century, Islam had begun to spread to the east coast of the Malay peninsula, and Brunei, and later to Sulu and Mindanao, where sultanates established in the fifteenth and sixteenth centuries resisted subjugation during the Spanish conquest of the Philippines in the 1570s. A greater degree of political institutionalisation began with the establishment of the sultanate of Aceh in the late fifteenth century, which came to dominate trade with India and China and seriously rivalled the Portuguese at Malacca (*see* Map 42).

In the early fifteenth century, the rulers of Malacca converted to Islam. The city became the centre of

ISLAM IN SOUTHEAST ASIA c.900–c.1600

- ⭐ Earliest evidence of Muslim presence (c.900–c.1300)
- [1211]
- → Early routes of Muslim traders / refugees (c.1250–c.1500)
- ☾ Early Muslim polities / communities (with date)
- Islamised by c.1400
- Islamised by c.1500
- Islamised by c.1600
- **DEMAK** (c.1500–88) First major Muslim trading sultanates (with dates of regime power)
- *Pajang* (1550–88) Other minor / successor sultanates (with dates of regime power)
- ⊸ ⊸ Spheres of trade / influence (Malacca / Demak)
- → Chinese naval expeditions (c.1400–c.1500)
- ⇒ Demak / Banten expansion (c.1500–88)
- ⇒ Mataram early conquests (1575–1625)
- ⇒ Other sultanate expansion / raids (c.1550–c.1620)
- 🟢 Major Islamic centres / holy sites of *wali sanga* in Java
- ⊙ Muslim sultanate capital
- ✕ ✕ Major conflicts : Intra-Muslim / Other

an important trading empire, with vassals in Malaya and Sumatra and connections with Java and China. Its rulers imposed tolls on ships sailing through the Straits of Malacca, and were also involved in the conversion of Brunei. Malacca's powers were eventually eclipsed when the Portuguese captured the city in 1511, and Muslim trade dispersed to other centres in the archipelago. According to the Portuguese chronicler Tomé Pires, describing Malacca between 1512 and 1515, all the rulers of northern and eastern Sumatra were Muslims.

Much of the wealth of the area came from the spices obtained from the Moluccas or Spice Islands, especially Ternate and Tidore, whose rulers converted to Islam in the late fifteenth century. At that time the islands were exporting fifty-two tonnes of cloves and twenty-six tonnes of nutmeg annually. The Portuguese and the Ottomans became major contenders for control of this trade during the late fifteenth and sixteenth centuries; as it happened, Ottoman interest in the region coincided with the rise of the Muslim polities, and some of the emerging Muslim sultanates received Ottoman military assistance in their struggles

against the Portuguese in return for the recognition of Ottoman 'caliphal legitimacy'.

The leading power in Java at this time was the Hindu-Buddhist kingdom of Majapahit (1293–1527). In the mid-fourteenth century Ibn Battuta described Java as 'the country of the infidels (*kuffar*)', and the process of Islamisation would begin some decades after his visit. Recent research (based mostly on inscriptions on Muslim gravestones) suggests the influential role in this process played by 'refugees' from the long-established Muslim community at Quanzhou/Zaiton in the province of Fujian in southern China. This region came under attack during the chaos and lawlessness of the 1360s that heralded the end of the Yuan dynasty and the rise of the Ming. Some Muslims found their way to the court of Majapahit, while other arrived in Surabaya, Gresik and Cirebon from Quanzhou and Champa (in the centre and the south of modern Vietnam) in the late fourteenth and early fifteenth

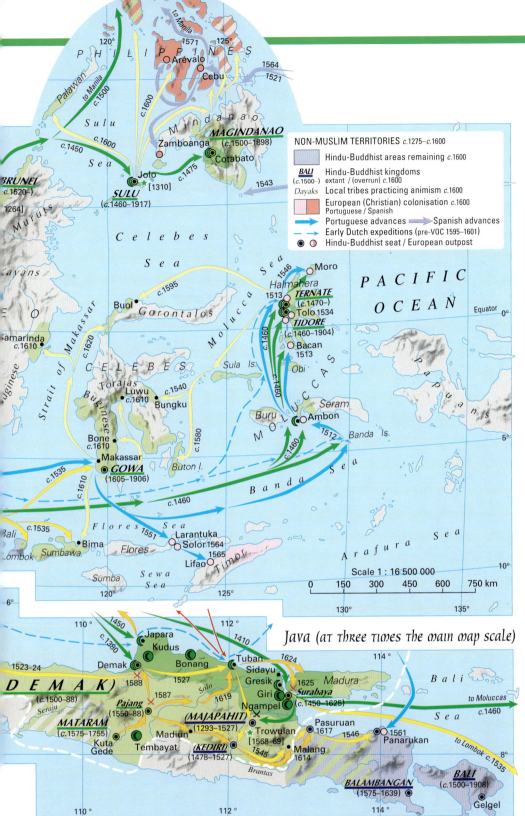

political and religious transition of the Hindu-Buddhist state to an Islamic polity.

In the west of the island, the influence of Demak was crucial in the consolidation of Islam in Cirebon in the 1520s. At the same time an army from Demak led by Sunan Gunungjati (or Fatah-Ilah) eventually created the sultanate of Banten in Pajajaran in western Java, which lasted until 1918. In the course of this expedition he took the port of Sunda Kalapa, which he renamed Jayakarta. His descendants eventually became independent of Demak, and a grandson or great-grandson, Molana Yusup (c.1570–80), conquered the rest of Pajajaran, the last major Hindu-Buddhist state in western Java to accept Islam. Other major Islamic centres founded in Java in the sixteenth century include Kudus, associated with Sunan Kudus, a doughty campaigner against Majapahit, and Giri, associated with Sunan Giri. These two men, together with Gunungjati, are numbered among the revered *wali sanga*, the 'nine saints' associated with the conversion of Java to Islam. Sunan Giri and his successors are said to have been instrumental in bringing Islam to Lombok and Makassar in the sixteenth century, while in turn the Islamisation of Bima and Sumbawa was largely undertaken from Makassar in the early seventeenth century. Other accounts attribute the Islamisation of southern Celebes to missionaries from Minangkabau.

The fall of Majapahit/Kediri in 1527 did not lead to its immediate replacement by a Muslim state, and much of the power of Demak was dissipated when Trenggana was killed in the course of a *jihad* against the Hindu state of Pasuruan in 1546. In general, there seems to have been a long period of intra-Muslim fighting and rivalry before the emergence of the 'Empire of Mataram' in the 1570s (*see* Map 42), under the leadership of Senapati (c.1575–c.1601), who, like Raden Fatah some sixty years earlier, was a putative descendant of the royal family of Majapahit.

Senapati's life and career cannot be precisely reconstructed from the Javanese chronicles, and it is possible that the first 'real' Muslim ruler of Mataram was either Senapati's son Krapyak (c.1601–13) or his grandson Sultan Agung (1613–46). Krapyak initiated a series of military campaigns against the sultanate of Surabaya, Mataram's main Muslim rival, and he was also the first Javanese ruler to make contact with the Dutch East India Company, the VOC, which had been chartered in 1602. The VOC, which would force the Portuguese out in the 1640s, would play a major role in the economics and politics of Southeast Asia for more than three centuries, and the detailed correspondence of its employees facilitates the construction of an accurate chronology of the subsequent history of the region.

Eventually, after a long siege ending in 1625, Agung, the 'Great Sultan' of Mataram, conquered Surabaya, which also controlled Gresik (near the renowned Islamic site of Giri) and Sidayu, Madura, and possibly east central Java as far south as the Brantas valley. For a brief period after this, Mataram came to control most of Java, with the exception of the sultanate of Banten, and the newly founded Dutch settlement of Batavia (*see* Map 42).

centuries, assisting in the gradual conversion of eastern and central Java. In the early fifteenth century, many of the senior commanders of the huge naval expeditions sent out by the Yongle Emperor from southeastern China (to Malacca and northern Sumatra, amongst other places) were Muslims, and this undoubtedly facilitated the spread of Islam in this region. Most prominent among these was the Admiral Zheng He (1371–1433), who made many visits to Southeast Asia and India.

Chinese sources also suggest the significant role played by Muslims who had fled from China in the conversion of northern Java. The origins of the sultanate of Demak (c.1500–88) are obscure although the town itself was probably founded in the last quarter of the fourteenth century, also by

'Muslim refugees' from China. Demak's prosperity as a major exporter of rice from central Java dates from the late fifteenth century and especially to the activities of a wealthy Muslim ship owner named Ko Po (or Cek Ko-po), one of whose relatives, Sultan Trenggana (1505–46) was the principal figure behind Demak's brief domination of Java. Trenggana was also involved in the conversion to Islam of Banjarmasin in south Borneo in the 1520s, and was a major military commander. In some chronicles, the conqueror of Majapahit (and of a successor or parallel Hindu-Buddhist state at Kediri) around 1527 is identified as Raden Patah, a heroic figure in Javanese history who was at once sultan of Demak and a descendant of the royal family of Majapahit, thus legitimising the

Map 31

The Rise of the Safavids and the Expansion of the Ottoman Empire c.1500–c.1700

THE SEIZURE OF POWER BY THE SAFAVIDS in 1501 marked the beginning of a new era in the socio-political history of Iran. Isma'il (1501–24), the founder of the dynasty, was the grandson of the Aq Qoyunlu leader Uzun Hasan (*see* Map 24). On his father's death in 1488, he had become the grand master of a Sufi order in Ardabil that had once been Sunni, but he and his father had gradually leaned towards Shi'ism. His Shi'ism attracted support both from the heterodox Turkmen population of eastern Anatolia, Kurdistan and Azerbaijan, who became his foot soldiers, called the *qızılbaş*, 'red-heads', after their distinctive turbans, and from the Iranian bureaucracy and *sayyid* class, for whom Persian was the language of administration and literature. Isma'il's own identification with Shi'ism is clear but the wider spread of Shi'ism across Iran took place after his reign, and the process was likely incomplete until well into the seventeenth century. The main centres of Shi'ism remained in Lebanon, the northeastern coast of the Arabian Peninsula, and Iraq, which was only very sporadically under Safavid control and which would become permanently part of the Ottoman Empire after 1639.

The Ottoman state also enjoyed a period of consolidation and expansion during the long reign of Sultan Süleyman II (1520–66), popularly known in the West as 'the Magnificent', and in the East as 'the Lawgiver' (*Kanuni* in Turkish) for his complete reconstruction of the Ottoman legal system. His father Selim I had declared Isma'il a heretic, and partly to pre-empt the formation of a Safavid/Mamluk alliance, joined battle with him at Çaldıran in 1514. The Safavids lacked handguns and artillery, and were defeated relatively easily, but although the Ottomans captured Tabriz they did not maintain their advantage and soon abandoned it. During the reign of Isma'il's son Tahmasp (1524–76) the Ottomans invaded Iran several times, occupying Tabriz and Baghdad (which gave the Ottomans access to the Gulf) in 1534. In 1555 hostilities came to an end for a while with the Treaty of Amasya, which defined the frontiers between Iran and the Ottoman Empire, and divided Georgia between the two. Tahmasp also gave shelter to the Mughal ruler Humayun during his exile from India at the hands of his 'Afghan' rivals (*see* Map 29). In the 1540s, following his father's claim to have been the 'defender of Sunni Islam' (against the 'heretical' Iranian Shi'is), Süleyman encouraged the notion that members of the Ottoman ruling house were the 'successors' (*khulafa'*, caliphs) of the Prophet Muhammad, although this emphasis on the sultan's religious functions gradually dropped out of sight.

During the sixteenth century the Ottoman Empire reached its territorial apogee in Africa, Asia and Europe. Selim I's conquest of Egypt in 1517 also gave him control of the Hijaz, and thus of the Holy Places of Islam. By this time the Ottomans had taken over from the Venetians as the dominant naval power in the eastern Mediterranean, and became the main challengers to the Portuguese in the Red Sea, gaining a foothold in Yemen in 1538 and occupying the inland cities of Ta'izz and San'a'

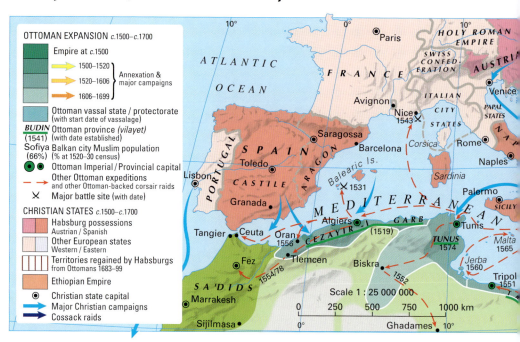

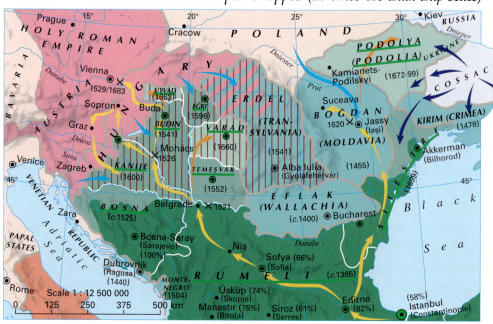

Dubrovnik – Danube Lands – Dnieper Steppes (at twice the main map scale)

in 1547 and 1552. In North Africa, the Barbarossa brothers, corsairs from Lesbos who would become high Ottoman officials, took Algiers in 1516, while expeditions in the 1550s and 1560s added Tripoli, Oran, Jerba and Malta (*see* Maps 27 and 33).

In the 1520s, Ottoman armies captured Belgrade, Rhodes and Buda, routing the Hungarian army at Mohács in 1526. The rulers of Hungary became Ottoman vassals, although their domain was greatly reduced as the rich Danube lands of Budin, Eğri, Kanije and Temeşvar became part of the Empire, and Transylvania (Erdel) accepted tributary status. In 1537 Süleyman made an alliance with Francis I of France against the Habsburg Charles V, signalling the arrival of the Ottomans as a major power broker on the European stage.

The Balkans formed the main economic 'backbone' of the Empire as the principal supplier of food

and raw materials to the capital via the Danube. Further west, the city state of Dubrovnik was the crucial entrepôt between the Empire, the Balkans and Venice, even when the Ottomans and Venetians were at war. It also acted as the Empire's main access to the rest of Europe and to Western military and commercial technology. On the northern shores of the Black Sea, Moldavia and the Crimea produced (and exported) large quantities of grain, meat and fish, which would become extremely crucial when bands of outlaws (*celali*-s) caused havoc with agriculture in eastern Anatolia between 1596 and 1610. An Ottoman census taken in the European provinces in the 1520s shows that 18.8 per cent of households were Muslim, mostly living in a wide arc from what is now Bosnia to Thrace, with large majorities of Muslims in such cities as Sarajevo, Manastır, Yenişehir, Üsküp and Edirne.

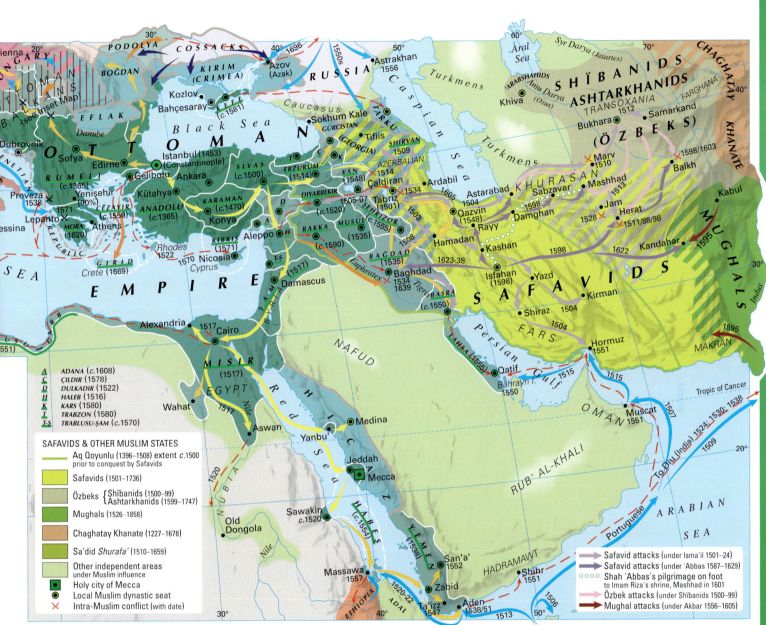

SAFAVIDS & OTHER MUSLIM STATES

— Aq Qoyunlu (1396–1508) extent *c.*1500 prior to conquest by Safavids

Safavids (1501–1736)

Özbeks { Shïbanids (1500–99) / Ashtarkhanids (1599–1747)

Mughals (1526–1858)

Chaghatay Khanate (1227–1678)

Sa'did *Shurafa'* (1510–1659)

Other independent areas under Muslim influence

⬢ Holy city of Mecca

◉ Local Muslim dynastic seat

✕ Intra-Muslim conflict (with date)

➤ Safavid attacks (under Isma'il 1501–24)

➤ Safavid attacks (under 'Abbas 1587–1629)

⚬⚬⚬ Shah 'Abbas's pilgrimage on foot to Imam Riza's shrine, Mashhad in 1601

➤ Özbek attacks (under Shïbanids 1500–99)

➤ Mughal attacks (under Akbar 1556–1605)

ADANA (c.1608)
ÇİLDİR (1578)
DULKADIR (1522)
HALEB (1516)
KARS (1580)
TRABZON (1580)
TRABLUSU-ŞAM (c.1570)

Cyprus was captured from the Venetians in 1570, but in the following year the Ottoman fleet was destroyed off Lepanto by a new Holy League of the Habsburgs, the Venetians and the papacy. In the 1580s and 1590s the Ottoman conquest of western Iran brought the Empire to its maximum geographical extent, but continuous warfare had severely strained its social and economic fabric. In 1606, the Habsburgs and the Ottomans signed the Peace of Zsitva Torok, which ended hostilities between the two until the 1660s, and left the Ottomans free to concentrate on their eastern frontier. Meanwhile, at Jassy in 1620 an Ottoman force defeated the combined armies of Poland and Moldavia, which had done nothing to stop years of Cossack raids into Ottoman territory.

The peak of Safavid power was achieved during the reign of Shah 'Abbas I (1587–1629), whose most enduring legacy is the extraordinary complex of magnificent buildings, avenues and squares in his new capital, Isfahan. 'Abbas consolidated his rule with a series of determined campaigns to reverse earlier territorial losses to the Ottomans and the Özbeks. Like previous Safavid rulers, he

not only had to fight his Sunni enemies on two fronts, in the west and the northeast, but was also faced with a revolt by the *qızılbaş*. However, his forces recaptured Herat, Mashhad, Astarabad and briefly Balkh from the Özbeks in 1598, and Tabriz, Azerbaijan and the Caucasus from the Ottomans by 1606 and Baghdad in 1623. Conflict with the Ottomans continued intermittently until 1639, when the Treaty of Zuhab, concluded by 'Abbas' son Safi (1629–42) reaffirmed the provisions of the Treaty of Amasya, restored western Iran to the Safavids, and returned Baghdad and the rest of Iraq to the Ottomans, thus initiating a long period of peace.

'Abbas actively encouraged trade and commerce, especially in silk, and instituted regular trading links with a number of European countries, especially through the East India Company and its Dutch counterpart, the VOC. He asserted his religious credentials by numerous pilgrimages to Mashhad, to his family's shrine in Ardabil and to the Iraqi holy cities, and by building up the religious infrastructure of his capital Isfahan. He also stabilised the Iranian state to the extent that it was able to survive a century of less able rulers. At times Safavid rule

extended eastwards deep into Afghan territory, which remained staunchly Sunni. An Afghan invasion took place in 1722, which the Safavids were unable to resist. Eventually Nadir Shah, a Turkmen leader from Khurasan, took effective charge of the country, forcing the Afghans out of eastern Iran and Ottoman forces out of the northwest (*see* Map 32).

The seventeenth century marked a crisis for the Ottoman dynasty; nine sultans of varying abilities, some mad, some minors, reigned between 1600 and 1700 (one twice) during a time of economic crisis, constant wars with the Safavids, and continuing Cossack raids. In 1669, after a siege of twenty-two years, Crete was captured from the Venetians. Podolia and southern Ukraine were acquired briefly from Poland in 1672, which brought the Empire into direct contact with the expanding Russian state for the first time (*see* Map 38). In 1683 an attempt to besiege Vienna was thwarted by a coalition of European powers; a sixteen-year war followed, ending in the Treaty of Carlowitz (1699), under which the Ottomans lost Hungary to the Austrians, and Athens and the Peloponnese to Venice. Henceforth the Empire was always on the defensive.

Map 32

Islamic Russia, Central Asia and Iran c.1450–c.1750

see Map 24 At THE END OF THE FOURTEENTH CENTURY, the Golden Horde was devastated by a series of campaigns led by Timur, during which Urgench, the chief city of Khwarazm, was destroyed and the Horde's leader Toqtamïsh subsequently defeated in the Caucasus (see Map 24). After this, the Horde, which had effectively controlled the Russian state since the 1240s, began to disintegrate politically. At this time, nomads from the eastern half of the Horde began to be known as 'Özbeks', possibly after the first of their rulers to convert to Islam, Khan Özbek (1313–41); by the end of the fifteenth century some of these nomads moved from Siberia to Transoxania, giving their name eventually to the present-day inhabitants of Uzbekistan. Their leader, Abu'l-Khayr (1438–68), was the founder of the Abu'l-Khayrids or Shïbanids, who would dominate Central Asia and become the hostile neighbours of the Safavids for much of the sixteenth century. In the late 1450s some of the tribes abandoned Abu'l-Khayr and migrated to the area southwest of Lake Balkhash; these are the progenitors of the modern Kazakhs. By c.1520 these nomads had occupied the vast Dasht-i Qïpchaq steppe that extends over most of what is now Kazakhstan.

In the course of the fifteenth century the western part of the Horde began to break up into smaller entities, beginning with the Khanate of Kazan, which was eventually absorbed into Russia in 1552. Similarly, the Khanate of the Crimea, which included much of southern Ukraine and the lower Don basin, became a separate entity, and was at different times either a partner or a vassal of the Ottoman state until its annexation to Russia in 1783 (see Maps 24, 25, 31 and 38). In 1452, Qasim Khan, a son of the khan of the Golden Horde, became a vassal of Basil II [the Blind] (1425–62) and obtained an independent state southeast of Moscow, the Qasimov Khanate, for himself and his descendants, which lasted until 1681. Some years later, the khans of Astrakhan also established an independent state, which lasted until its incorporation into Russia in 1556. The emergence of a vigorous 'Muscovite Russia' under Ivan III (1462–1505) and Basil III (1505–33) established the foundations for Moscow's independence, a process that was more or less completed by 1480. The direct heirs to the old Golden Horde, by then ruling a polity known as the 'Great Horde', fell victim to a short-lived alliance between Moscow and the Khans of the Crimea, which led to their defeat at Saray in 1502.

Under Ivan IV [the Terrible] (1533–84) and his successor Fyodor (1584–98) there were further advances into 'Muslim territory' down the Volga and east of the Urals. In addition to the absorption of Kazan and Astrakhan in the 1550s, the Khanate of Sibir was incorporated into the Russian state between 1582 and 1598. These conquests regularly involved the forced conversion of Muslims to Christianity and the importation of Russian peasants from further west, and often encountered strong resistance. Saraychiq, the capital of the Noghay or Manghït Horde, north of the Caspian, was burned down by Cossack raiders in 1581, and in 1591 a son of Kuchum, the last khan of Sibir, converted to Christianity and the family became absorbed

into the Russian nobility. Most subsequent Russian expansion until the mid-nineteenth century took place to the north and east of Islamic Central Asia, and significantly, Peter the Great (1682–1725) began the construction of extensive fortifications to protect Russian settlements on the steppe frontier from increasing Kazakh and Junghar raids (see below).

Meanwhile, in western Iran, the Qara Qoyunlu and the Aq Qoyunlu took over much of the western territories of the former Timurid Empire (see Map 24), which later became part of the Safavid and Ottoman empires (see Map 31). Timur's son Shah Rukh (c.1409–47) continued to rule over the eastern part of his father's empire in Transoxania and Khurasan, although his successors were ultimately unable to withstand the military might of the Shïbanids in the sixteenth century. Further east, the Chaghatay khans of Mughulistan continued the Islamisation of the northern Tarim

Basin in the late fifteenth and sixteenth centuries.

Beginning in 1500, Muhammad Shïbani (1500–10), the grandson of the founder of the dynasty, led an army of nomadic Özbeks, together with detachments of disaffected local forces, on raids that led to the conquest of Transoxania, and briefly of Khurasan, effectively putting paid to the Timurids. In addition, the southward migration of large numbers of Özbeks left the northern part of the Dasht-i Qïpchaq steppe to the Kazakhs, whose rulers claimed descent from Jochi's son Toqay Timur. Continuing hostilities between north and south resulted in the gradual emergence of the Kazakhs as a separate ethnic group (see above).

As a further consequence of their acquisition of Transoxania, the Sunni Özbeks became the immediate neighbours of the Shi'i Safavids, and much conflict ensued; in fact, Muhammad Shïbani was killed near Marv in 1510 by Isma'il Safavi's army,

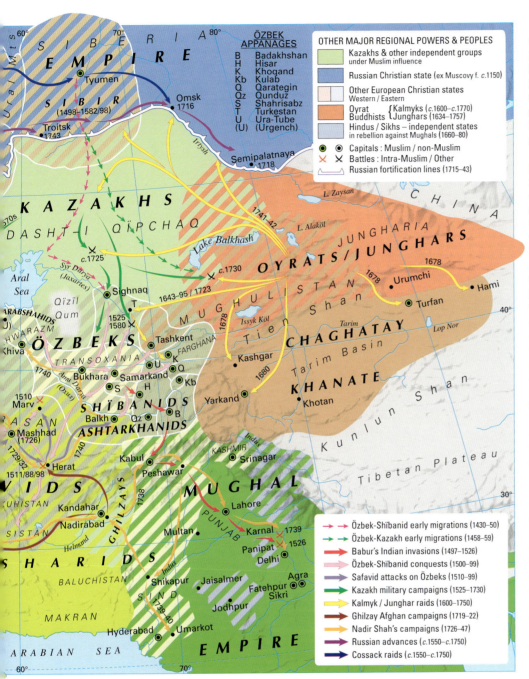

ÖZBEK APPANAGES
B Badakhshan
H Hisar
K Khoqand
Kb Kulab
Q Qaraategin
Qz Qunduz
S Shahrisabz
T Turkestan
U Ura-Tube
(U) (Urgench)

OTHER MAJOR REGIONAL POWERS & PEOPLES
- Kazakhs & other independent groups under Muslim influence
- Russian Christian state (ex Muscovy f. c.1150)
- Other European Christian states — Western / Eastern
- Oyrat Buddhists { Kalmyks (c.1600–c.1770) / Junghars (1634–1757)
- Hindus / Sikhs – independent states in rebellion against Mughals (1660–80)
- Capitals : Muslim / non-Muslim
- Battles : Intra-Muslim / Other
- Russian fortification lines (1715–43)

- → Özbek-Shïbanid early migrations (1430–50)
- → Özbek-Kazakh early migrations (1458–59)
- → Babur's Indian invasions (1497–1526)
- → Özbek-Shïbanid conquests (1500–99)
- → Safavid attacks on Özbeks (1510–99)
- → Kazakh military campaigns (1525–1730)
- → Kalmyk / Junghar raids (1600–1750)
- → Ghilzay Afghan campaigns (1719–22)
- → Nadir Shah's campaigns (1726–47)
- → Russian advances (c.1550–c.1750)
- → Cossack raids (c.1550–c.1750)

During the seventeenth century, the Dasht-i Qïpchaq also saw a major expansion of the Oyrats, Buddhist Mongols from Jungharia (the region of high plateau north of the Tien Shan), who were to have a significant impact on Islamic Central Asia. Coinciding with the Russian advance into Siberia at the end of the sixteenth century, groups of Oyrats had begun to migrate westwards in increasing numbers into the northern Dasht-i Qïpchaq. By the 1630s some of these Oyrats, later known as the Kalmyks, settled in the region north of the Caspian formerly occupied by the Noghay/Manghïts, most of whom were forced to flee across the Volga, some as far as the Caucasus. These Kalmyks then began raiding Khwarazm, Mangïshlaq and even the borders of Iran. Meanwhile in 1634 the Oyrats back in Jungharia formed a confederation known as the Junghars, which posed an increasingly serious threat to the Kazakhs over the next hundred years. During a particularly destructive campaign in 1723 the Junghars captured Tashkent and Turkestan, driving masses of Kazakhs into Transoxania, greatly destabilising the region in advance of Nadir Shah's invasions (see below). By 1678 the Junghars had put an end to the Chaghatay Khanate, installing local Naqshbandi Sufi leaders as their governors, until their own destruction by the Qing Empire in 1757. In general, the eighteenth century saw considerable economic decline in Central Asia; European traders came to prefer the Indian Ocean over the Silk Road to China, and the Russians themselves chose the trans-Siberian routes running much further north.

At the beginning of the eighteenth century the Safavid court chroniclers hailed the dynasty as the main promoter of Shi'ism, the defender of Iran from its Sunni neighbours, the Ottomans and the Özbeks, and it was regarded by the elites as the unifier of the different interests of Turks and Persians within Iran. Often accused of intolerance towards non-Muslims, a recent account suggests that the Safavids' treatment of religious minorities 'stands in favourable contrast to that of contemporary Europe.' Trade, most notably in silk, continued to flourish in the seventeenth and early eighteenth centuries, and the state evidently prospered. The smooth successions of Sulayman I (1666–94), and his son Husayn (1694–1722), described by contemporaries as 'the shadow of God' and 'the just sultan', showed the extent to which the dynasty had become institutionalised.

Peace and stability, and the power of the dynasty itself, came to end with an invasion by the staunchly Sunni Ghilzay Afghans who took Isfahan in 1722. The Safavids were subsequently replaced by the Afsharids, whose Turkmen founder, Nadir Shah, had himself appointed regent for Shah Husayn's son Shah Tahmasp II (1722–32). Nadir Shah (1736–47) campaigned against the Ottomans in Azerbaijan and Qarabagh, and penetrated as far as Daghestan. He also invaded India in 1738–40, taking Kandahar from the Afghans and annexing all the northwestern Mughal domains; he conquered Bukhara and Khiva by 1740 and Oman by 1744. Nadir Shah's assassination in 1747, which was followed by the eclipse of his dynasty, coincided with the collapse of the Mughals in India, and with the emergence of the Afghan state under the Durranis (see Maps 35 and 37).

which went on to take Herat (see Map 31). At the same time, Zahir al-Din Babur, a Timurid prince from Farghana, tried to regain power in Samarkand, with the assistance of Isma'il Safavi, whom he acknowledged as his suzerain, even briefly accepting Shi'ism. Babur would eventually leave Central Asia behind, conquering Delhi in 1526, and founding the Mughal Empire (see Map 29).

The Özbeks continued the Central Asian system of appanages, which produced multiple centres of political power. A balance of sorts between them existed until the mid-sixteenth century, and after years of infighting political authority in the region eventually became concentrated in the hands of 'Abdullah ibn Iskandar (1583–98). The 'Arabshahids, also descendants of Shïban, the fifth son of Jochi, ruled over much of Khwarazm and northern Khurasan; early in the seventeenth century they moved their capital to Khiva, which remained

an independent khanate under a later dynasty, the Qonghrats, who survived until 1920 (see Map 37).

In the third quarter of the sixteenth century the Özbek appanages were almost constantly at war with one another. Nevertheless, particularly in the reign of 'Abdullah b. Iskandar, they also directed their energies against the Safavids, conquering Herat in 1588 and taking over Kuhistan and Sistan. The Safavids regained the initiative under Shah 'Abbas (1587–1629), retaking Herat, Mashhad, Astarabad and Marv, in a campaign which temporarily brought the Özbek/Safavid conflict to an end. In 1599 the Shïbanids were replaced in Transoxania and what is now northern Afghanistan by the Janids or Ashtarkhanids, who ruled somewhat loosely from Bukhara and Balkh until 1747. In 1756 the Manghïts, who had become the Ashtarkhanids' ataliq-s, 'advisers', took over Bukhara and ruled there until 1920 (see Map 37).

Map 33

The Development of Muslim States in North and West Africa c.1500–c.1650

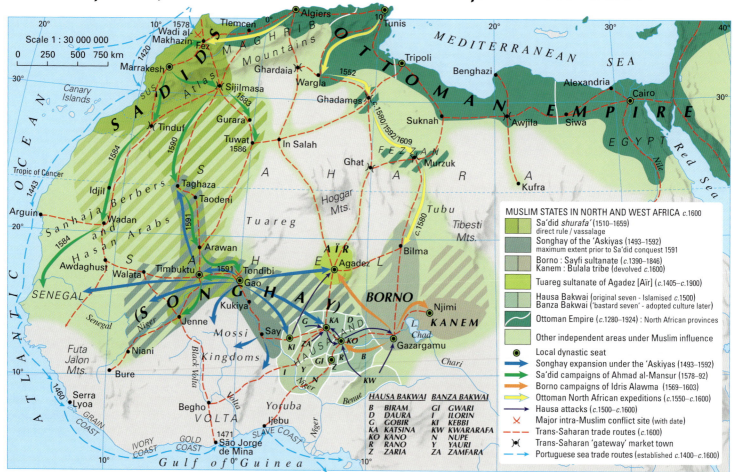

MUSLIM STATES IN NORTH AND WEST AFRICA c.1600

- Sa'did *shurafa* (1510–1659) direct rule / vassalage
- Songhay of the 'Askiyas (1493–1592) maximum extent prior to Sa'did conquest 1591
- Borno : Sayfi sultanate (c.1390–1846) Kanem : Bulala tribe (devolved c.1600)
- Tuareg sultanate of Agadez [Aïr] (c.1405–c.1900)
- Hausa Bakwai (original seven - Islamised c.1500) Banza Bakwai ('bastard seven' - adopted culture later)
- Ottoman Empire (c.1280–1924) : North African provinces
- Other independent areas under Muslim influence
- ◉ Local dynastic seat
- → Songhay expansion under the 'Askiyas (1493–1592)
- → Sa'did campaigns of Ahmad al-Mansur (1578–92)
- → Borno campaigns of Idris Alawma (1569–1603)
- → Ottoman North African expeditions (c.1550–c.1600)
- → Hausa attacks (c.1500–c.1600)
- ✕ Major intra-Muslim conflict site (with date)
- – – Trans-Saharan trade routes (c.1600)
-)●(Trans-Saharan 'gateway' market town
- – – Portuguese sea trade routes (established c.1400–c.1600)

HAUSA BAKWAI		BANZA BAKWAI	
B	BIRAM	GI	GWARI
D	DAURA	I	ILORIN
G	GOBIR	KI	KEBBI
KA	KATSINA	KW	KWARARAFA
KO	KANO	N	NUPE
R	RANO	Y	YAURI
Z	ZARIA	ZA	ZAMFARA

IN NORTH AND WEST AFRICA, the sixteenth and seventeenth centuries marked the establishment of an ambitious Moroccan state, originally under the Sa'dids (1510–1659) and then under the 'Alawi/Filali dynasty, which still rules today. In addition, after the overthrow of the Songhay Empire in 1591, the focal point of Islam in the Sahel shifted to Borno, and new Muslim states emerged in Hausaland. Finally in this period, Ottoman rule extended westwards through Tunisia as far as western Algeria.

The legitimacy of the Sa'dids, *shurafa'* from the Sus, who captured Marrakesh and Fez from the Wattasids in 1524 and 1549 (*see* Map 27), rested on their descent from the Prophet, their *jihad* against the Christians, and the messianic fervour with which they inspired their subjects. In addition, the Muslims of the Maghrib and West Africa had long been powerfully influenced by the Sufi orders. These orders functioned as formal religious organisations, but individual Sufis also gained reputations as 'holy men' (*marabout*-s), whose persons and shrines were the focus of popular devotion throughout the region.

In 1576 the Sa'did Sultan Muhammad II al-Mutwakkil, who had been deposed by his uncle 'Abd al-Malik, asked King Sebastian of Portugal to help restore him to the throne. Sebastian, who had long been planning a crusade against Morocco, responded with enthusiasm, and led a large army across to Morocco in 1578. However, he was defeated at Wadi al-Makhazin in the Battle of the Three Kings, so called because al-Mutwakkil drowned, 'Abd al-Malik died of a heart attack, and Sebastian himself was killed. 'Abd al-Malik was

succeeded by his brother, Ahmad (1578–1603) subsequently known by the honorific *al-Mansur*, 'the Victorious'. The spoils of this battle enabled him to strengthen his army and to undertake major building projects in his capital Marrakesh.

Perhaps Ahmad's greatest achievement was his expedition to the south that led to the defeat of the Songhay Empire at Tondibi in 1591. Songhay power had reached its zenith under the rule of the 'Askiyas (1493–1591), who had extended its territory to Senegal in the west and to Hausaland in the east as well as having acted as major patrons of Islamic learning in Timbuktu. Crucially, the 'Askiyas controlled the trans-Saharan trade in gold and salt, which made the Songhay Empire especially attractive to its northern neighbour. Ahmad's conquest enriched the Moroccan court sufficiently for him to gain the additional soubriquet of *al-Dhahabi*, 'the Golden One', although he was criticised by some of the '*ulama*' for having invaded a friendly Muslim state. In fact, Morocco's control of the Songhay Empire was limited in both time and extent; it only occupied the main cities of the Niger Bend for some forty years before domestic turmoil led to the Sa'dids' demise (*see* Map 40).

However, Songhay power was permanently broken, and this would have a significant effect on the patterns of trans-Saharan trade. As the economic influence of Gao, Jenne and Timbuktu declined, an expanding trade in gold, ivory and slaves from the Volta region and the Sahel to North Africa and Europe was redirected though Aïr, Borno and Hausaland.

Although the sultans of Borno never regained their lands in Kanem (*see* Map 15) the kingdom gradually expanded and strengthened its Islamic core to become a significant Muslim force in the Sahel, with its capital Gazargamu growing into a major regional trading hub and cultural centre. These developments reached their peak under the rule of the redoubtable Idris Alawma (1569–1603) who obtained firearms and musketeers through contact with the Ottomans via the Fezzan, thus giving Borno a military edge over its rivals in Aïr and Hausaland. Here, several small warring city-states, including Agadez, Kano, Katsina, Kebbi and Zaria, emerged on routes used by Muslim traders in an area that had been gradually Islamising since the late fifteenth century.

Ottoman expansion into North Africa had begun with the Barbarossa brothers' decision to seek imperial protection in 1519, thus bringing Algiers and Tunis into the Empire (*see* Maps 27 and 31). The Habsburgs and the Ottomans competed for the possession of various ports in the eastern Maghrib during the 1550s and 1560s. In 1574 the Ottomans recaptured Tunis from Spain; after this Philip II of Spain, who benefitted from the unexpected death of his nephew Sebastian of Portugal in 1578 (*see above*), showed little interest in Algeria and Tunisia. During this period the enduring strength of the Moroccan state generally ensured that Ottoman influence did not extend west of Tlemcen. Tunisia and Tripoli came to be ruled by Ottoman vassals, while Algiers maintained its role as the corsair capital of the western Mediterranean.

Map 34

The Mughal Empire from the Death of Akbar to the Death of Awrangzib 1605–1707

IN INDIA, the sixteenth and seventeenth centuries were the heyday of the Mughal Empire, the greatest of the 'Muslim gunpowder empires of the early modern era'. At its height it ruled nearly five times as many subjects as the Ottomans and extended over most of the subcontinent. Its success owed much to the personalities of its most capable rulers, and, in spite of frequently bloody struggles over the succession, their relatively long reigns: Akbar, 1556–1605; Salim/Jahangir b. Akbar, 1605–27; Shah Jahan b. Jahangir, 1628–57, and finally Awrangzib b. Shah Jahan, 1658–1707. Both Babur, the founder of the dynasty (*see* Map 29) and Jahangir wrote personal memoirs covering much of their lives; in addition there are chronicles of the period written by officials and others employed at the various courts, as well as accounts by European travellers, missionaries and diplomats. The Mughals were also great patrons of the arts, most notably architecture (mosques, palaces, tombs and the *chaharbagh*, or formal irrigated garden), miniature painting and portraiture, and Persian poetry.

Like almost all Mughal rulers, Jahangir faced risings throughout the Empire, particularly in Bengal, the Deccan and 'Afghanistan', as well as opposition from members of his own family, the latter partly because of the extraordinary influence wielded by his wife, Nur Jahan, and her father. Jahangir's son (and successor) Shah Jahan rebelled against him, and the two were not reconciled before Jahangir's death in 1627. Shah Jahan is perhaps best known for his devotion to his wife Mumtaz Mahal, who died in 1631, and the Taj Mahal, the magnificent mausoleum which he had built for her near Agra.

Shah Jahan also built Shahjahanabad, an imposing new capital at Delhi. He and his sons extended Mughal rule to south India, annexing Ahmadnagar and exacting tribute from Bijapur and Golconda. In addition he attempted to assert Mughal power against the Özbeks and the Safavids. In 1646 his son Murad succeeded in occupying Balkh, but Shah Jahan was soon obliged to withdraw the army to Kabul, largely because it was unable to live off the harsh steppe lands; thus the Emperor's attempts to recover the old Timurid heartland in Transoxania remained un-realised. He also sent several expeditions against Kandahar, but it remained in Safavid hands until early in the eighteenth century. In 1657 Shah Jahan fell gravely ill and a ferocious struggle over the succession took place between his four sons. His third son, Awrangzib, seized his father and imprisoned him in the fort at Agra until his death in 1666. Meanwhile, Awrangzib's other brothers were either killed in battle or executed at his behest between 1657 and 1659.

Under Awrangzib, the most austere and most religiously orthodox member of the dynasty, the Mughal Empire reached its furthest extent. The remaining Shi'i sultanates of Bijapur and Golconda (later Hyderabad) were eventually incorporated in 1686–87. Almost all his predecessors, perhaps most famously Akbar, had been notable for their religious tolerance, while some were known for their relatively catholic approach to religion and others for their devotion to Sufism. In contrast,

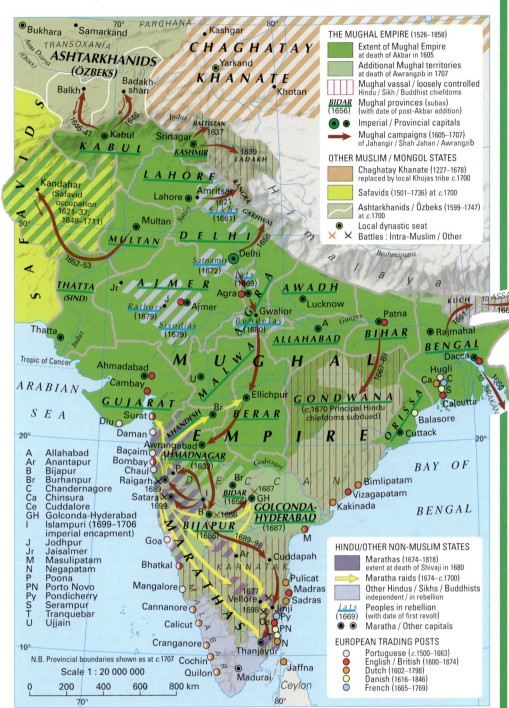

Awrangzib reimposed the *jizya*, destroyed Hindu temples, rewarded conversion to Islam, and generally boosted the status of the Sunni *'ulama'*, especially with the construction of the Firangi Mahal *madrasa* in Lucknow in 1691. He also faced the onset of a new threat from the Marathas, Hindu warriors based in the central and western Deccan, although their political disunity meant that they were a sporadic rather than a coherent challenge as long as Awrangzib lived. Nevertheless he spent much of his time and treasury campaigning against them during the last thirty years of his reign, never returning to Delhi or Agra but making the imperial encampment his capital.

In the sixteenth century the Portuguese had dominated European trade with India, but in the

seventeenth they were gradually supplanted by the English and the Dutch. In 1600 and 1602 the English and Dutch East India Companies were founded with exclusive national rights to trade with India (a similar French company was established in 1665). The companies exported Indian goods to Europe, including pepper, indigo, raw silk, cotton cloth and saltpetre (used to make munitions). The Europeans paid for these products with New World gold and silver. Trading posts or 'factories' were established both at the ports and in some inland cities, and their activities directly stimulated the regional economy. In contrast with China and Japan, the Mughal state placed very few restrictions on the activities of foreign merchants (*see* Map 35).

Map 35

The Decline of the Mughal Empire 1707–c.1820

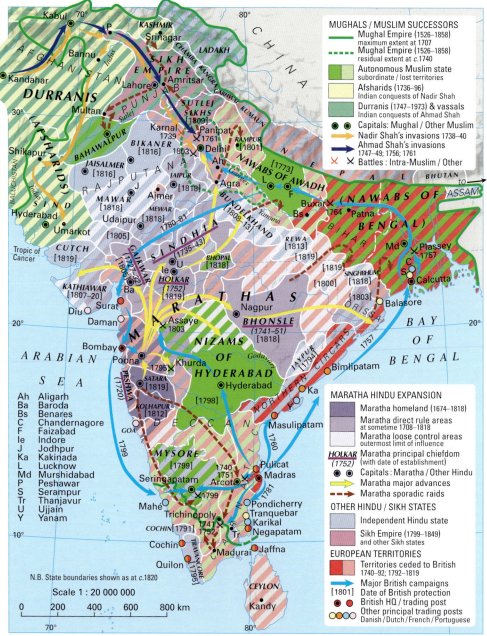

MUGHALS / MUSLIM SUCCESSORS
— Mughal Empire (1526–1858) maximum extent at 1707
- - - Mughal Empire (1526–1858) residual extent at c.1740
Autonomous Muslim state subordinate / lost territories
Afsharids (1736–96) Indian conquests of Nadir Shah
Durranis (1747–1973) & vassals Indian conquests of Ahmad Shah
⦿ ⦿ Capitals: Mughal / Other Muslim
→ Nadir Shah's invasions 1738–40
→ Ahmad Shah's invasions 1747–49; 1756; 1761
✕ ✕ Battles : Intra-Muslim / Other

MARATHA HINDU EXPANSION
Maratha homeland (1674–1818)
Maratha direct rule areas at sometime 1708–1818
Maratha loose control areas outermost limit of influence
HOLKAR (1752) Maratha principal chiefdom (with date of establishment)
⦿ ⦿ Capitals : Maratha / Other Hindu
→ Maratha major advances
→ Maratha sporadic raids

OTHER HINDU / SIKH STATES
Independent Hindu state
Sikh Empire (1799–1849) and other Sikh states

EUROPEAN TERRITORIES
Territories ceded to British 1740–92; 1792–1819
→ Major British campaigns
[1801] Date of British protection
⦿ ⦿ British HQ / trading post
⦿⦿⦿⦿ Other principal trading posts Danish / Dutch / French / Portuguese

Ah Aligarh
Ba Baroda
Bs Benares
C   Chandernagore
F   Faizabad
Ie Indore
J   Jodhpur
Ka Kakinada
L   Lucknow
Md Murshidabad
P   Peshawar
S   Serampur
Tr Thanjavur
U   Ujjain
Y   Yanam

N.B. State boundaries shown as at c.1820

Scale 1 : 20 000 000
0   200   400   600   800 km

IN 1700 THE EMPEROR AWRANGZIB ruled the area from Kabul in the west to Assam in the east, and from Kashmir in the north to Thanjavur in the south. However, immediately after his death in 1707 quarrels between his sons initiated the rapid disintegration of the Mughal Empire. A succesion of weak and ephemeral emperors allowed the wealthy Muslim provinces of Bengal, Awadh and Hyderabad to become autonomous, while such groups as the Marathas, Sikhs and Afghans gained control in the Deccan and the north. As part of this process Nadir Shah invaded India from Iran in 1738 (*see* Map 32), annexed all the imperial provinces north and west of the Indus, sacked Delhi, seized the Mughal treasury and the Peacock Throne, thus effectively reducing the Empire to a mere city state. The rise of the Marathas and the Sikhs coincided with the growing influence of the British East India Company as the main contender not only for commercial influence but also for political control.

Bengal was the first part of the Mughal Empire to break away from central control, under a Brahmin convert, Murshid Quli Khan (1704–25), who had been appointed governor (*nawab*) by Awrangzib. Bihar followed suit after its annexation by Bengal in 1733. Bengal was one of the most prosperous regions of India, and British traders had long enjoyed customs privileges there, which seemed in jeopardy at the accession of Siraj al-Dawla (1756–57). The new ruler attacked the British 'factory' at Calcutta to punish the Company for fortifying its settlement, but in 1757 he was defeated at Plassey by Colonel Robert Clive. In 1765 the Company took over the revenue administration of Bengal, Bihar and Orissa (Bengal Presidency) but did not assume full responsibility for governing this and other presidencies until later in the eighteenth century.

Awadh became autonomous from Delhi under Nawab Sa'adat Khan (1722–39) and saw expansion of its territory and wealth as a result. Sa'adat Khan, his son Safdar Jang (1739–54) and his grandson

Shuja al-Dawla (1754–75) attempted to defend the remains of the Mughal state from Afghan and Maratha attacks. In 1764 Shuja al-Dawla's forces, together with those of the Mughal emperor Shah 'Alam II (1759–1806) and the recently deposed Nawab of Bengal invaded (British-controlled) Bihar but they were narrowly defeated at Buxar. Thereafter Awadh became subject to increasing British fiscal and ultimately political control.

Hyderabad became independent in 1724, and was to remain a 'princely state' under a long line of Nizams (honorific title of its Muslim rulers) until it was absorbed into India in 1948. Although surrounded by British Indian territory it maintained its own government, and continued to acknowledge the theoretical suzerainty of the Mughals. Mysore also remained a princely state until independence. A Hindu state that had been usurped by the Muslim military adventurer Haydar 'Ali in the 1760s, it became the last major threat to British power in South India when Haydar 'Ali's ambitious son, Tippu Sultan, allied with the French. In 1799 Tippu Sultan was defeated by the British and was later killed at his capital, Seringapatam.

Meanwhile in the north Ahmad Shah Abdali [Durrani] (1747–73) was acclaimed leader of the new 'Afghanistan' on the death of Nadir Shah (*see* Map 37). Ahmad, who regarded himself as heir to Nadir's eastern domains, exploited the simultaneous Safavid and Mughal collapse to conquer Khurasan and to pursue his ambition to re-establish a Muslim empire in India, which he invaded several times, sacking Delhi and Agra in 1757 and defeating the Maratha armies at Panipat in 1761. His Indian conquests extended over parts of the Punjab, Kashmir, Sind and Baluchistan but after his death feuding among his inept heirs saw a retreat, and they were driven out by the Marathas and Sikhs.

Indeed, non-Muslims took increasing control of India in the wake of the Mughal downfall. In particular the Maratha Hindus, who had earlier pursued a troublesome insurgency against Awrangzib (*see* Map 34), were quick to exploit the subsequent power vacuum. Throughout the eighteenth century until their surrender to the British in 1818, the Marathas progressively expanded their influence from their original Deccan homeland deep into west, north, central and east India, with political power eventually resting in a loose 'pentarchy' of the five principal Maratha families. After a century of revolt in the Punjab, the Sikhs under their gifted leader Ranjit Singh secured Lahore in 1799, formally founding the Sikh Empire.

Over much the same period, the British generally succeeded both in eliminating the influence of their European rivals and in assuming political control (by conquest and treaty) of most of the subcontinent, which they would achieve by the mid-nineteenth century (*see* Map 36). A century after the death of Awrangzib, only two significant Indian Muslim states remained, Awadh and Hyderabad. This marked an almost unparalleled process of defeat and loss of Muslim power to non-Muslims and to Europeans, a pattern which would be repeated in other parts of the Islamic world in the rest of the nineteenth century (*see* Map 43).

Map 36

Islamic Revival and Reform in India under British Rule c.1820–c.1910

IN THE COURSE OF THE LONG DECLINE of the Mughal Empire, the British began to consolidate their exclusive control over India, confining their French and Portuguese rivals to a few small enclaves on the coast. In the late eighteenth and early nineteenth centuries the East India Company exercised direct rule over most of the subcontinent, a process which continued with the conquest of Sind in 1840–42 and of the Punjab in 1850. Well before the Government of India Act in 1858 (which transferred the administration of India from the East India Company to the Crown), some parts of India had come under direct rule by British officials, while others, including the Muslim princely states of Awadh and Hyderabad, remained nominally under the control of their 'traditional rulers', although the latter were obliged to accept the presence of British advisers (Residents) at their courts. The deposition of the ruler of Awadh and the subsequent annexation of the kingdom by the British in 1856 was one of the underlying factors behind the Indian revolt of 1857.

The intrusive nature of British rule, and its highly centralised system of bureaucratic control, was irksome to Muslims and Hindus alike. The British justified this ideologically in terms of putting an end to 'Mughal despotism', and arresting the 'decline' into which India had allegedly fallen at the hands of the dynasty. The revolt of 1857 was the culmination of a series of mounting grievances among all the communities. Both Muslims and Hindus feared being obliged to convert to Christianity; sepoys in the Indian Army resented being made to serve far away from their homes; British efforts to create land ownership resulted in the destabilisation of rural society, and all classes of the population resented the hostility and condescension to which the British subjected them. The revolt began at Meerut, from where the sepoy mutineers marched on a surprisingly ill-defended Delhi and set up the Mughal emperor as their leader. Thereafter widespread risings erupted until British forces regained control. In 1858 the last Mughal was deposed, bringing 650 years of Muslim rule in India to an end.

However, the Islamic community (*umma*) in India continued to develop and grow. In the first modern census conducted in 1871, the Muslims of the subcontinent numbered some 40 million, or 21 per cent of a total population of 194 million; in 1901 the proportion was about 22 per cent of 284 million. The areas with the highest density of Muslims at the beginning of the twentieth century correspond to the modern states of Pakistan and Bangladesh.

Throughout the subcontinent, educated Muslims were profoundly affected by the reverberations of various reform and/or intellectual movements which appeared in the rest of the Islamic world at the time, ranging from Wahhabism (*see* Map 38) to Islamic modernism. The origin of almost all manifestations of such tendencies in India can be traced back to Shah Wali Allah (1702–60), a member of the Naqshbandi Sufi order. He was one of the first modern Muslim thinkers to stress the importance of *ijtihad*, the application of reason and human judgement to Islamic texts, and of purging Sufism of saint worship and visits to holy shrines, practices which came to be regarded as

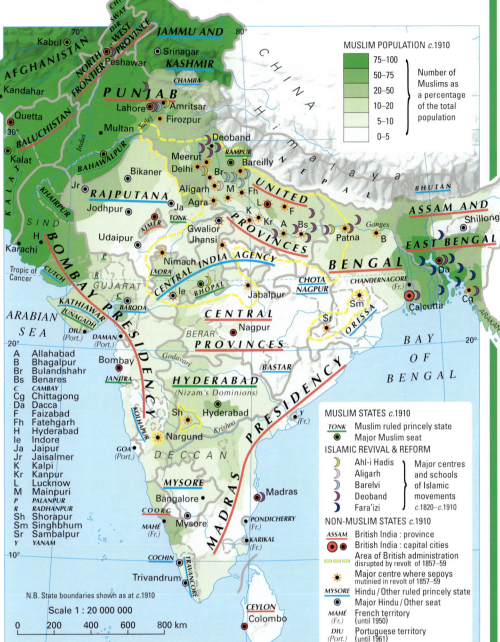

'un-Islamic' by many members of the next generation of reformers. Although modern scholarship has challenged the notion that *ijtihad* had ceased to be practised among Sunnis as long ago as the end of the ninth century, Shah Wali Allah and other reformers such as his near contemporary the Syrian 'Abd al-Ghani al-Nabulusi (1641–1731) were known for their attempts to engage actively with the world in their day, and above all to make Islam more vibrant, meaningful and 'relevant' for their contemporaries.

Aspects of Shah Wali Allah's teachings were taken up by Sayyid Ahmad Barelvi (1786–1831) the founder of the Barelvi or Mujahidin movement, which was both anti-Sikh and anti-British, seeking to 'free Hindustan from Christian rule', and another relatively militant reformer, Shariat Allah (1781–1840), the Bengali founder of the Fara'izi movement (from Arabic *fara'id*, the duties of a Muslim) which mobilised Bengali cultivators against Hindu landlords and British commercial interests. An important institution promoting Islamic

reform of a different kind (focussing on the rigorous training of *'ulama'*) was the theological college of Deoband, founded in 1867, which was both anti-Sufi and anti-British. Also influential through its *'ulama'*, the Ahl-i Hadis (followers of the *hadith*, or traditions of the Prophet) fostered a revival in north India in the 1860s, although they were non-political.

In contrast, the Aligarh movement founded by Sir Sayyid Ahmad Khan (1817–98), who had worked for the East India Company, believed that the fortunes of Muslims would be served best by an educational system that encouraged the sons of prominent families to embrace European learning and social values and thus to be able to interact with members of the British administration on their own terms. Similarly, the aim of the Muslim League, founded in Dacca in 1906, was the advancement of the interests of Muslims by the elites, especially in the context of the Morley-Minto reforms of 1909, which inaugurated Muslim-only electorates for provincial councils as well as seats reserved specifically for Muslims.

Map 37

Islam and Imperialism in Iran, Afghanistan, Central Asia and China c.1750–c.1920

MUCH OF THE ISLAMIC WORLD experienced a period of political decay in the latter half of the eighteenth century. In Asia, the Ottoman Empire was gradually losing control over many of its Arab provinces; a succession of highly unstable rulers came to power for brief periods in Iran; the Russian Empire was extending its control over the Kazakh steppe, setting the stage for its conquest of the Muslim khanates of Central Asia in the mid-nineteenth century, and was poised for similar conquests in the Caucasus, while the Mughal Empire continued its steady decline. However, it should be emphasised that most of these processes were internal to the Islamic world, since apart from the Russian advances, and British activities in India, colonial and imperial rule had still not yet affected most Muslim societies. It would not be until the nineteenth century that the more direct involvement of the imperial powers would become a major factor in the history of most parts of the Islamic world.

In Iran and Afghanistan, the power vacuum that followed the assassination of Nadir Shah permitted the formation of the first truly Afghan (Pashtun) state, headed by Ahmad Shah Abdali [Durrani] (1747–73), with its capital at Kandahar. Ahmad Shah exploited the simultaneous Safavid and Mughal collapse to conquer Khurasan, the Punjab and northwestern India, where he defeated the Marathas at Panipat in 1761 (*see* Map 35). After his death, a succession of less able heirs and the subsequent rise of the Qajars led to the reduction of Afghan territory to the area between Kabul and Herat, the core of the modern state; in addition, the capital was transferred from Kandahar to Kabul in the mid-1770s. In the meantime, Muhammad Karim Khan Zand, who came from Luristan, ruled most of the rest of Iran mainly from Shiraz for some thirty years, nominally as regent for Isma'il Safavi III, but his death in 1779 led to a period of political decentralisation that ended with the succession of the Qajars under their formidable founder, Agha Muhammad (1779–97). As descendants of the *qızılbaş* forces which had supported the Safavids (but without that group's religious legitimacy), the Qajars were Turkmen tribesmen from Gurgan and Mazandaran, who made Tehran their capital and managed to unite Iran under their often tenuous rule well into the twentieth century (1794–1925).

In the late eighteenth and early nineteenth centuries, Russia's advances into the Caucasus led to its acquiring territory formerly under Iranian suzerainty. Thus between 1801 and the Iranian/Russian Treaty of Turkmanchai in 1828, Georgia, eastern Armenia and northern Azerbaijan were annexed by Russia (as well as some smaller principalities in the western Caucasus formerly under Ottoman rule; *see* Map 38). Although it would acquire large swathes of Muslim territory east of the Caspian, Russia generally respected the Iranian frontier in that region, and although Iran would never have been able to defend itself against a determined Russian attack, the competing interests of Britain and Russia, and their desire to see that neither got the upper hand, meant that Iranian territorial integrity was not directly threatened for the rest of the nineteenth century.

For much of the period that followed, which in some sense came to an end with the Anglo-Russian partition of Iran in 1907, the Russians and the British struggled to gain control of or influence over the area lying between the expanding Russian Empire in Central Asia and British India. The 'First Afghan War' (1839–42) was launched in response to an attempt on the part of Shah Muhammad of Iran (1834–48) to occupy Herat with Russian encouragement. In response, the British organised a military expedition to restore Shah Shuja', who had ruled Afghanistan between 1803 and 1809, to the throne. Distance from its base and opposition from powerful Afghan tribes made it impossible for the force to sustain Shuja', who was ousted once more in favour of Dust Muhammad, who had ruled in Herat since 1826. Dust Muhammad extended his authority over the whole of Afghanistan by the end of the war, and remained in control of the state until his death in 1863. At the same time, the British were consolidating their position in India by annexing Sind in 1840–42 and the Punjab in 1850. Given that the Afghans did not come to the aid of the Muslims in India during the revolt of 1857 (*see* Map 36) this northwest frontier seemed to be defensible.

In general, Afghan mistrust of the Russians throughout the nineteenth century, along with the rather limited inducements that they had to offer, maintained a degree of stability in Afghanistan for several decades. This came to an end in the aftermath of the Congress of Berlin in 1878, when British officials in London, India, Iran and Central Asia agreed on a 'forward policy', and once more attempted to impose their will on Afghanistan. Under the treaty that followed the 'Second Afghan War' (1878–80), the British stationed a permanent diplomatic representative in Kabul, and took control of Afghan foreign policy. This level of involvement continued until after the First World War, when the then amir, Aman Allah (1919–29), attempted to reduce British influence. After a brief conflict in May/June 1919 (the 'Third Afghan War') the British gave up control of Afghan foreign policy, and the country became fully independent. Aman Allah's attempts to modernise the country by introducing a swathe of reforms antagonised conservative Muslim opinion, and he was obliged to abdicate in 1929.

Iran was also an arena for Anglo-Russian struggles for influence, although here economic spoils were also at stake. In order to fund their activities, the Qajar rulers, especially Nasir al-Din (1848–96) and his son Muzaffar al-Din (1896–1907), sold economic concessions to foreigners, an activity that aroused considerable opposition from the Shi'i clergy. The creation of the [British] Imperial Bank of Persia in 1885 (part of the Reuter concession) was followed in 1890 by Nasir al-Din's sale of a concession for the production, sale and export of tobacco to a British subject. This became the object of a national campaign of protest, led by merchant interests, in which, if somewhat reluctantly, the *'ulama'* became involved, and the shah was eventually obliged to cancel it. Muzaffar al-Din contracted several loans with Russia (partly to finance public works projects, but also his own

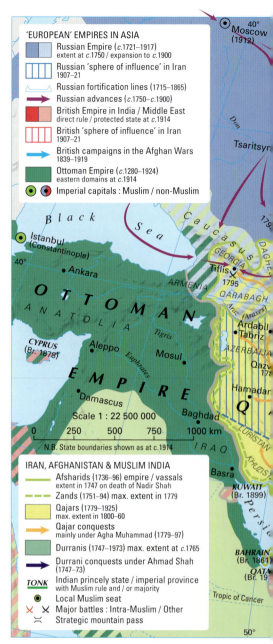

'EUROPEAN' EMPIRES IN ASIA
- Russian Empire (c.1721–1917) extent at c.1750 / expansion to c.1900
- Russian 'sphere of influence' in Iran 1907–21
- Russian fortification lines (1715–1865)
- Russian advances (c.1750–c.1900)
- British Empire in India / Middle East direct rule / protected state at c.1914
- British 'sphere of influence' in Iran 1907–21
- British campaigns in the Afghan Wars 1839–1919
- Ottoman Empire (c.1280–1924) eastern domains at c.1914
- Imperial capitals : Muslim / non-Muslim

Scale 1 : 22 500 000
0   250   500   750   1000 km
N.B. State boundaries shown as at c.1914

IRAN, AFGHANISTAN & MUSLIM INDIA
- Afsharids (1736–96) empire / vassals extent in 1747 on death of Nadir Shah
- Zands (1751–94) max. extent in 1779
- Qajars (1779–1925) max. extent in 1800–60
- Qajar conquests mainly under Agha Muhammad (1779–97)
- Durranis (1747–1973) max. extent at c.1765
- Durrani conquests under Ahmad Shah (1747–73)
- TONK Indian princely state / imperial province with Muslim rule and / or majority
- Local Muslim seat
- Major battles : Intra-Muslim / Other
- Strategic mountain pass

visits to Europe) and also sold the exclusive rights over Iranian oil to William Knox D'Arcy in 1901 for £20,000 and a 16 per cent share of any future profits. In 1908, substantial oil deposits were discovered in Khuzistan; the British government bought a majority shareholding in the Anglo-Persian Oil Company, later British Petroleum, BP, early in 1914.

Partly as a consequence of their involvement in the movement against the tobacco concession, and generally because of their opposition to European influence, the clergy became an important component of a countrywide protest known as the Constitutional Revolution (1905–11), which aimed to limit the powers of the crown. This took the form of calls for a *majlis*, parliament, which met for the first time in 1906. The *majlis* drafted a constitution, which Muzaffar al-Din accepted on his deathbed, one of whose provisions (though subsequently ignored) was that all laws should be scrutinised by a committee of clerics who would assess their compatibility with the *shar'ia*. His son Muhammad 'Ali (1907–09)

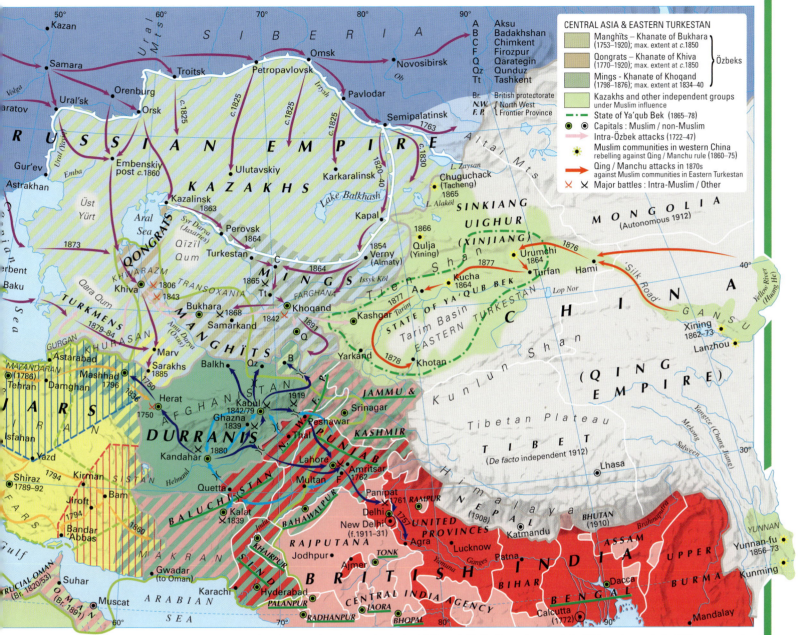

was profoundly opposed to these developments, and enlisted the aid of the Russian-led Cossack Brigade, which closed down the *majlis* and arrested and executed several politicians in 1908. The reformers had been deeply disappointed by Britain, whom they thought would back them, but who instead concluded an agreement with Russia dividing the country into Russian and British spheres of influence in the north and south in August 1907. Russian troops invaded Iran in 1911; a period of anarchy ensued which only came to an end with the rise to power of Reza Khan (later Reza Shah Pahlavi, 1925–41) who presided over the deposition of Ahmad, the last of the Qajars, in 1925. Clerical influence in politics remained dormant for several decades until its forceful re-emergence in the 1960s and 1970s.

The history of Central Asia during this period is characterised by the extension of Russian control over the Kazakh steppe, and by constant conflict among the three Özbek khanates of Bukhara, Khiva and Khoqand, which were eventually incorporated

into the Russian Empire in the 1860s and 1870s. By the late eighteenth century, Chingizid descent had ceased to be an essential qualification for rule, and the three khanates were led by dynasties of Özbek tribal origin, with frequent appeals to 'Islamic' titulature. Thus the Khanate of Khoqand in Farghana came into being in the early eighteenth century and was taken over by the ruling family of the Ming tribe. 'Umar Khan (1809–22) adopted the title of *Amir al-Muslimin*; in his time the Khanate included Tashkent and the southern part of the Kazakh steppe. In due course the Russians invaded, annexing Khoqand to the Governorate-General of Turkestan in 1876, after which it ceased to exist as a separate entity (*see* Map 44). In Bukhara, the Manghït ruler Shah Murad (1785–1800) had assumed the title of *Amir al-Mu'minin*; the Khanate extended over most of Transoxania, with the Oxus forming the border with Afghanistan. In 1868, the Russians inflicted a decisive defeat on the forces of Muzaffar al-Din Khan (1860–86), and stringent peace terms were

imposed. In Khiva, the capital of Khwarazm, the Qongrat rulers, who generally styled themselves 'khan', had discontinued the practice of appointing Chingizid puppets by the early nineteenth century. In 1873 a Russian army invaded and the Khanate became a Russian protectorate.

In Eastern Turkestan (western China) there were several Muslim rebellions against Manchu rule in the course of the nineteenth century, led mostly by Naqshbandi and other Sufi teachers, often with support of the khans of Khoqand. Ya'qub Bek, a military commander from Khoqand, took Kashgar in 1865 and eventually gained control of the Tarim Basin. Although Ya'qub's independence was recognised in treaties signed with both Russia and Britain, his state collapsed with the Qing/Manchu reconquest of Eastern Turkestan in 1878, and later became part of the 'New Province' of Sinkiang Uighur, established in 1884. The rebellions of Chinese Muslims in the provinces of Gansu and Yunnan were also suppressed by Qing forces.

Map 38

The Ottoman Empire and the Sa'udi-Wahhabi State c.1700–c.1830

ALTHOUGH THE NOTION OF 'DECLINE' has fallen out of favour among historians of the Ottoman Empire, the eighteenth and early nineteenth centuries do represent a period of steady territorial loss, if punctuated by occasional reassertions of Ottoman military strength. In the east, Nadir Shah's armies forced the Ottomans out of Azerbaijan and Qarabagh in the 1730s (*see* Map 32); in the west, the period saw the rise first of Austria and then of Russia as major powers, claiming, in the process, many of the Ottomans' most valuable European possessions. Hungary, Podolia and Transylvania had already been lost to Austria in 1699 (*see* Map 31); under the Treaty of Passarowitz (1718) Austria gained the Banat of Temeşvar, much of Serbia and part of Wallachia, although the latter two territories were returned to Ottoman rule in 1739. In 1775, Austria took the Bukovina, part of Moldavia. Perhaps most significantly, the Ottomans lost their protectorate over the strategic port of Dubrovnik (*see* Map 31) to Napoleon's armies in 1806. A rebellion in Serbia succeeded in wresting a measure of self-rule from the Ottomans in 1817, with full autonomy in 1830 (and independence in 1878).

After their decisive naval defeat at the Battle of Çeşme in 1770, the Ottomans were dealt an even more crushing blow by Russia under the terms of the Treaty of Küçük Kaynarca in 1774, which required them to give Russia two outlets on the Black Sea and free passage through the Dardanelles for its merchant vessels. Russia also obtained the right to protect the Orthodox Christians of the Empire, who formed the overwhelming majority of the non-Muslim population. The Khanate of the Crimea became independent, although its Tatar subjects were allowed to acknowledge the authority of the sultan-caliph. It was eventually annexed by Russia in 1783, and neighbouring Jedisan in 1792. Further east, Russia took over several small Ottoman protectorates in the western Caucasus (Abkhazia, Akhaltsikhe, Guria, Imeteria, Mingrelia and Svanetia) between 1803 and 1833, while most of the rest of the Caucasus came under Russian rule in the course of the century. Finally, under the Treaties of Bucharest (1812) and Edirne (1829), following yet more Russo-Turkish Wars, control of eastern Moldavia (Bessarabia) and the mouths of the Danube was ceded to Russia.

Apart from, or perhaps because of, these constant wars and territorial losses, the Empire lost control over much of its core territory in the latter part of the eighteenth century. Rural revolts were endemic in much of eastern Anatolia, while Mamluks or other local warlords were effectively in control of Egypt, Iraq, Palestine, Syria, and quasi-independent dynasties, although officially Ottoman vassals, were ruling in Algiers, Tunis and Tripoli (*see* Map 40). Imperial tax revenues declined, while expenditures, including war indemnities, soared. New taxes were imposed, and there was a surge in domestic borrowing. The Janissaries, the principal defenders of the Empire in their heyday, no longer formed a competent or viable military force, and became an increasingly unstable element in the capital and many provincial cities. Concerned observers advocated military

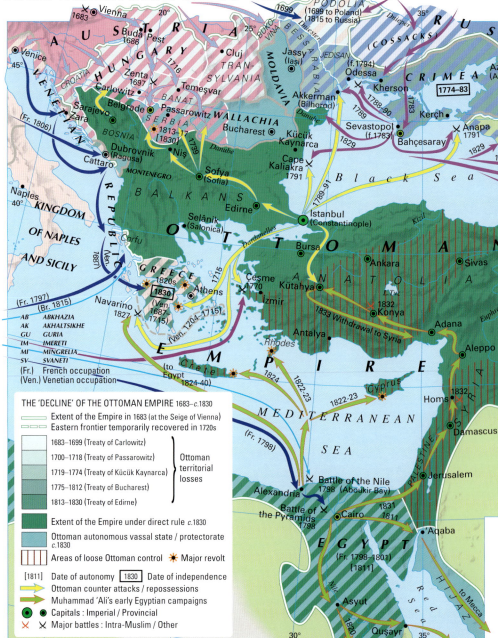

THE 'DECLINE' OF THE OTTOMAN EMPIRE 1683–c.1830
- —— Extent of the Empire in 1683 (at the Seige of Vienna)
- --- Eastern frontier temporarily recovered in 1720s
- 1683–1699 (Treaty of Carlowitz)
- 1700–1718 (Treaty of Passarowitz) } Ottoman
- 1719–1774 (Treaty of Kücük Kaynarca) } territorial
- 1775–1812 (Treaty of Bucharest) } losses
- 1813–1830 (Treaty of Edirne)
- Extent of the Empire under direct rule c.1830
- Ottoman autonomous vassal state / protectorate c.1830
- Areas of loose Ottoman control   ✳ Major revolt
- [1811] Date of autonomy   [1830] Date of independence
- ⟶ Ottoman counter attacks / repossessions
- ⟶ Muhammad 'Ali's early Egyptian campaigns
- ⦿ ● Capitals : Imperial / Provincial
- ✕ ✕ Major battles : Intra-Muslim / Other

reform, but this was fraught with difficulty, since it would run counter to the vested interests of the ruling elites. Many commentators urged the Ottoman state to emulate European practice, both in the military and in the bureaucracy, and such urgings would come to fruition in the middle decades of the nineteenth century. Indeed, there had been a long flirtation with European culture, beginning in the 'Tulip Period', between 1718 and 1730, during which the first printing press was briefly established in Istanbul. A complicated love/hate relationship persisted between the Ottomans and their European contemporaries for the rest of the lifetime of the Empire, reflecting the simultaneous polarities of 'tradition' and 'modernity', as well as the rueful admiration for the coloniser on the part of the colonised.

In July 1798, seeking to hinder British access to India, Napoleon Bonaparte launched an invasion of Egypt, then under only nominal Ottoman control. Although the French navy was defeated a few

weeks later by the British under Admiral Nelson, the invasion was significant in a number of ways. First, Napoleon brought a team of scientists and social scientists with him, who carried out intensive fieldwork in a variety of disciplines, culminating in the encyclopedic 37-volume *Description de l'Égypte* published between 1809 and 1827, one of the foundations of nineteenth century 'orientalist' scholarship. Second, the French army defeated the Mamluk army in July 1798, creating something of a power vacuum that was eventually filled by the Albanian adventurer, Muhammad 'Ali Pasha, who had come to Egypt with an Ottoman force sent to drive out the French. By 1805, he had obtained recognition as governor of Egypt both from local notables and (if reluctantly) from the Ottoman state, thus creating a monarchy that reigned until 1953. Over the following decades, the policies of Muhammad 'Ali (1805–48) and his successors would lead to Egypt's complete independence from the Empire, but eventually to British colonisation and control.

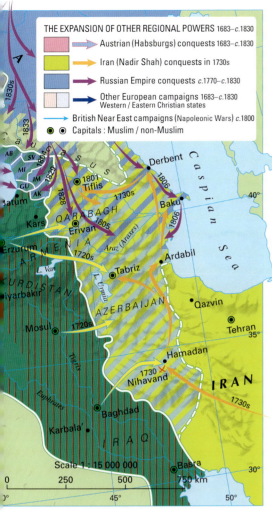

THE EXPANSION OF OTHER REGIONAL POWERS 1683–c.1830

- Austrian (Habsburgs) conquests 1683–c.1830
- Iran (Nadir Shah) conquests in 1730s
- Russian Empire conquests c.1770–c.1830
- Other European campaigns 1683–c.1830 Western / Eastern Christian states
- British Near East campaigns (Napoleonic Wars) c.1800
- ◉ ◉ Capitals : Muslim / non-Muslim

of Russia, the Greeks' most vociferous supporter. In many ways, this was a major milestone; faced with a serious provincial revolt, the Ottoman state was obliged to concede 'national independence', the first in what turned out to be a series of similar developments throughout the Balkans.

As in other remote parts of the Empire, the Ottomans' control over or presence in the Arabian Peninsula in the early modern period was very limited, particularly after their expulsion from Yemen by the Zaydi imams of San'a' in the 1630s. Providing secure access for the pilgrimage to Mecca was a vital element of Ottoman legitimacy, effected through the Sharifs of Mecca, who ruled the Hijaz, while the pilgrim caravans from Cairo and Damascus were accompanied either by Ottoman army units or by tribal forces paid by the Ottomans. In the mid-eighteenth century the relative stability of these arrangements was interrupted by the rise of Wahhabism, one of the earliest and most influential Islamic reform movements. Muhammad ibn 'Abd al-Wahhab (1703–92) preached an austere form of Hanbalism, emphasizing *tawhid*, the essential unity of God, and the sinfulness of *shirk*, the practice of attributing partners to God. In practice this was an attack on the Sufi orders, on Shi'ism, and on 'popular Islam.' Activities such as visiting the tombs of saints or invoking their assistance were denounced as *bid'a*, innovation, meriting severe punishment. 'Abd al-Wahhab also advocated *jihad* against those who did not accept his principles, and insisted on the payment of *zakat*, tax, to the leader of the community.

These ideas were transformed into a dynamic political ideology after their enthusiastic adoption by Muhammad ibn Sa'ud (1735–65), then amir of Dir'iya, a small oasis town near Riyadh. The Sa'ud family lacked both wealth and a significant tribal pedigree, but Muhammad seems to have realised the potential of an alliance between himself and 'Abd al-Wahhab; the preacher would endorse the warrior as leader of the community, and legitimise his raids (or *jihad*)

against other communities, while controlling the religious message. Together, the founders embarked on a campaign of territorial expansion and consolidation through raids into central and eastern Arabia, as far as al-Hasa and Qatif. The sons and grandsons of Muhammad ibn Sa'ud and Muhammad ibn 'Abd al-Wahhab continued the process: in 1801 Sa'udi-Wahhabi forces ventured out of the Peninsula, invading Iraq and Syria, raiding and plundering the Shi'i shrine city of Karbala'. Subsequently they occupied Mecca, and defaced the graves of the Companions of the Prophet in Medina in 1805. These military campaigns caused the migration of many tribes out of the Peninsula, mostly to southern Iraq, where many of them converted to Shi'ism.

Such activities naturally represented a grave attack on Ottoman legitimacy, and also on the authority of the Sharifs of Mecca. Given the remoteness of the Hijaz, and the parlous state of the Empire's defences, Mahmud II (1808–39) was obliged to call for the dispatch of Egyptian troops to the Najd under the command of Muhammad 'Ali's son Ibrahim Pasha, who conducted a series of successful campaigns between 1811 and 1818. Dir'iya and its fortifications were destroyed in September 1818, and 'Abdullah ibn Sa'ud (1814–18) was captured and subsequently executed in Istanbul. For a time, this put paid to Sa'udi-Wahhabi expansion; Egyptian troops withdrew to the Hijaz, and the situation in Najd was further complicated by struggles for the leadership within the Sa'ud family. There was a second Egyptian occupation between 1838 and 1843, occasioned by the Sa'udis' refusal to pay tribute to the Ottomans' Sharifian representatives in the Hijaz. Relative peace returned during the second reign of Faysal ibn Turki (1834–38: 1843–65), and a major (and permanent) revival of the dynasty's fortunes would take place, with British help, at the beginning of the twentieth century (*see* Map 39).

By 1812 the remaining Mamluks had been defeated, and Muhammad 'Ali set about reforming both the bureaucracy and the army, recruiting slaves from the Sudan and then conscripting Egyptian peasants. By the end of his reign he had the largest military and naval force in the eastern Mediterranean, and a modern administration, both to support the army and navy, and to run Egypt's internal affairs. In order to improve military and administrative efficiency, promising young men were sent to study at European universities and military academies, and foreign advisors were invited to Egypt, practices which paralleled those of the Ottoman Empire at the time.

In the first decades of his reign Muhammad 'Ali behaved as a loyal vassal of the Sultan, leading a series of campaigns on the Porte's behalf: in the Arabian Peninsula against the Wahhabis; in the Sudan, which he brought under Egyptian control; if less successfully, in Greece during the struggle for independence in the 1820s, and, less 'loyally', in Syria, which his forces occupied between 1831 and 1840 (*see* Map 39). In 1830, a few years after the Egyptian-Ottoman naval defeat at Navarino in 1827, Greece (although confined at that stage to Attica, the Peloponnese, and the nearer Aegean islands) became independent, with the somewhat grudging assistance of the principal European powers, who were increasingly fearful of the rising ambitions (*vis-à-vis* the Ottoman Empire)

The Arabian Peninsula (at half the main map scale)

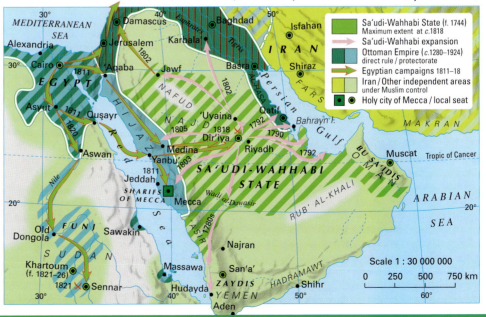

Sa'udi-Wahhabi State (f. 1744) Maximum extent at c.1818
Sa'udi-Wahhabi expansion
Ottoman Empire (c.1280–1924) direct rule / protectorate
Egyptian campaigns 1811–18
Iran / Other independent areas under Muslim control
■ ◉ Holy city of Mecca / local seat

Scale 1 : 30 000 000
0 250 500 750 km

© EIPL

65

Map 39

The Ottoman Empire and the Sa'udi State c.1830–c.1914

FOR MUCH OF THE NINETEENTH CENTURY the Ottomans held extensive and economically valuable territories in southeastern Europe, and remained a major power in the eastern Mediterranean. In an attempt to implement the major military reforms that had eluded his predecessors, Sultan Mahmud II (1808–39) ordered his 'new army' (*nizam-i cedid*) to attack the barracks of the Janissary corps in Istanbul in June 1826, which led to the elimination of the corps in the city and eventually to its dissolution as an Empire-wide military institution. After this, it became clear first, that effective reform of the Ottoman military would require a modern-educated officer corps, and second, that other measures would be necessary to bring about far-reaching change in the Empire. The next few decades saw the enactment of a series of reforms, collectively known as the *tanzimat*, 'reordering', which were designed to improve the central administration, education, law, provincial government and the status of religious minorities. This process culminated in the promulgation of the Ottoman Constitution in 1876, and the first session of the Ottoman Parliament.

Almost inevitably, the aims of the *tanzimat* were more lofty than most of its achievements, although the legal and educational reforms and the constitutional and parliamentary structures would form an enduring legacy for the modern Turkish republic. In addition, the Land Law of 1858 formed the basis of much of the pre-reform land regimes of most contemporary Arab states, and the *mecelle*, a compendium of civil law issued between 1869 and 1876, still remains in force in some parts of the Arab world. By the beginning of the twentieth century, these developments had led to 'more than half a million Ottoman civil servants [managing] activities commonly associated with nation states, from the administration of hospitals to the construction and maintenance of essential infrastructure.'

Perhaps the most controversial parts of the *tanzimat* had to do with matters of personal status. The first of the reforming decrees, the *Hatt-i Şerif* of Gülhane or Rose Chamber Edict (November 1839), approximated to a 'social contract', setting out the rights, as well the duties, of imperial subjects. It guarantees security of life and honour, regular and predictable taxation, and fixed terms of military service. Most importantly, it says: 'These imperial concessions extend to all our subjects, to whatever religion or sect they may belong.' This may seem unexceptionable, but the Ottoman Empire was a Muslim empire in which the social status of the Muslims had hitherto been dominant. Until the major territorial losses after the Russo-Turkish War of 1877–78, the Empire's non-Muslim population formed about 40 per cent of the total.

Religious liberty was further emphasized in the *Hatt-i Hümayun*, Imperial Reform Edict, of 1856. Lawsuits between those of different faiths were to be referred to 'mixed tribunals'; this seems to indicate the somewhat misguided influence of the European powers, since non-Muslims had been using the *shar'ia* courts to sue both Muslims and each other with success since records were first kept in the fifteenth century. All imperial subjects, without distinction, were to be accepted into civil and military

schools; the *jizya*, or head tax on non-Muslims, had already been abolished, and non-Muslims were now in theory obliged to do military service, usually commuted with a fee (*bedel-i askeriye*). Finally, the various non-Muslim communities (*millet*-s) were supposed to reorganize themselves in the general direction of giving lay members more influence.

The timing of the 1856 decree is crucial: it was issued a few weeks before the signature of the Treaty of Paris which ended the Crimean War, presumably in an effort to show the Europeans that the Ottoman state was capable of protecting the interests of its non-Muslim populations. The Crimean War was one of many interventions on the part of various powers to break up the Ottoman Empire or exercise influence over part of it. One of the results of this was the unification of Moldavia and Wallachia as an Ottoman protectorate in 1859. Thus for a while the Treaty of Paris preserved the status quo, until the Russo-Turkish War of 1877–78, which was followed

by the Treaty of Berlin. This time, Bulgaria, Montenegro, Romania and Serbia became, or would shortly become, fully independent states; Batum and Kars in eastern Anatolia were annexed by Russia; Greece, then confined to Attica and the Peloponnese, would acquire Thessaly in 1881 and the territory that forms the north of the modern state during the the Balkan Wars (1912/1913). Bosnia-Herzegovina was annexed by the Austro-Hungarian Empire in 1909, and by 1913, the predominately Muslim province of Albania had secured its independence. Hence, on the eve of the First World War, the Ottoman Empire had lost all its territories in the Balkans except eastern Thrace, which remains part of the Turkish Republic. As a result of all these conflicts, several million Balkan Muslims were either killed or forced to flee to the Asiatic part of the Empire; in Crete, the Muslim population, 43 per cent of the total in 1832, fell to 8 per cent by 1910.

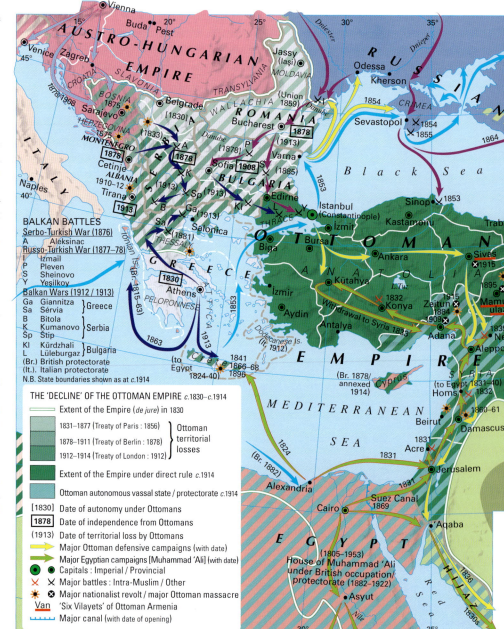

BALKAN BATTLES
Serbo-Turkish War (1876)
A   Aleksinac
Russo-Turkish War (1877–78)
I   Izmaïl
P   Pleven
S   Sheinovo
Y   Yeşilköy
Balkan Wars (1912 / 1913)
Ga   Giannitza } Greece
Sa   Sérvia
B   Bitola
K   Kumanovo } Serbia
Şp   Štip
Kl   Kürdzhali } Bulgaria
L   Lüleburgaz
(Br.) British protectorate
(It.) Italian protectorate
N.B. State boundaries shown as at c.1914

THE 'DECLINE' OF THE OTTOMAN EMPIRE c.1830–c.1914
Extent of the Empire (*de jure*) in 1830
1831–1877 (Treaty of Paris : 1856) } Ottoman
1878–1911 (Treaty of Berlin : 1878) } territorial
1912–1914 (Treaty of London : 1912) } losses
Extent of the Empire under direct rule c.1914
Ottoman autonomous vassal state / protectorate c.1914
[1830] Date of autonomy under Ottomans
[1878] Date of independence from Ottomans
(1913) Date of territorial loss by Ottomans
Major Ottoman defensive campaigns (with date)
Major Egyptian campaigns [Muhammad 'Ali] (with date)
Capitals : Imperial / Provincial
Major battles : Intra-Muslim / Other
Major nationalist revolt / major Ottoman massacre
Van 'Six Vilayets' of Ottoman Armenia
Major canal (with date of opening)

- Austro-Hungarian Empire advances
- Russian Empire advances southwards
- British Empire advances in Middle East
- Other European nation states and campaigns
  New Balkan / Western Christian
- Iran / Other independent Muslim groups
- Capitals : Muslim / non-Muslim

an Armenian majority (the closest, Van, had about 35 per cent); second, calls in the *Hatt-i Hümayun* for the reorganization of the affairs of the community had led to a gradual worsening of relations between the Patriarchate (which had always felt dependent on the good will of the Ottoman authorities), and the laity, who became increasingly critical of the Patriarch's lack of independence. Finally, 'foreign' missionary work among the Armenians, who were mostly Orthodox, resulted in the formation of a break-away Armenian Catholic *millet* in 1831 and a Protestant *millet* in 1846, which greatly damaged the unity of the community. The general failure of the Ottomans to accede to Armenian nationalist demands, and the violent reaction of the Armenian revolutionaries, led to horrific incidents in Anatolia between 1894 and 1896, and again during the First World War, resulting in the genocide of between 1 and 1.5 million Armenian civilians at the hands of the Ottoman Army and Kurdish irregular forces (the Hamidiya cavalry).

The outbreak of the 1877–78 Russo-Turkish War had encouraged Sultan 'Abd al-Hamid II (1876–1909) to prorogue both parliament and the constitution, which meant that the main goal of his opponents became the restoration of both institutions. Various movements were founded to counter 'Hamidian despotism', of which the most effective were the Committee of Union and Progress, founded in 1889 and the Young Turks, a less formal grouping, who merged together in 1906. On 23 July 1908, rebellious Ottoman troops marched on Istanbul from their barracks in Salonica; the next day, 'Abd al-Hamid announced the restoration of the constitution. He was not to survive for long: a conservative counter-revolution took place in April 1909, and it was widely believed that he had encouraged it. He was deposed and put under a form of house arrest until his death in 1918. For much of his reign he had pursued a policy of Pan-Islamism in an attempt to appeal to world Muslim sentiment to unite against

the encroachments of the European powers, re-asserting the idea of the caliphate with himself as leader of all Muslims. In spite of the secularity of the Committee of Union and Progress, which had taken over in 1909, it did not hesitate to declare a *jihad* on the outbreak of the First World War in 1914, which was enthusiastically supported by the Shi'i clerical leadership in Karbala' and Najaf.

In the second half of the nineteenth century the fortunes of the Sa'ud family had fallen to a low ebb, partly as a result of internal quarrels and betrayals, and partly because of the decline in the economy of Najd caused by the diversion of much of the overland trade to steamships in the Gulf and the Red Sea after the opening of the Suez Canal in 1869. By the 1890s the Sa'uds had lost control of the interior of the Peninsula to their principal rivals, the Rashids of Ha'il, and had taken refuge with the Amir of Kuwait. Ottoman control of the region remained tenuous, although members of both the Rashid and Sa'ud families were appointed governors of Najd at various times, while the Sharifs of Mecca continued to rule the Hijaz on the Ottomans' behalf until Sharif Husayn (1908–25) declared it an independent kingdom in 1916. In 1902, 'Abd al-'Aziz ibn Sa'ud (1902–53) captured Riyadh from the Rashids, took over the rest of Najd, and began a series of conquests that would end in 1932 with the creation of what is now Sa'udi Arabia. This was facilitated by three factors: the *Ikhwan*, an irregular army of Wahhabi zealots; the tacit assistance of the British, who did not want a power vacuum in the Peninsula (and succeeded in ensuring Ibn Sa'ud's neutrality in the First World War), and the fall of the Ottoman Empire in 1918. In the southwest of the Peninsula, the British established a coaling station at Aden in 1839, while the Ottomans initiated a second occupation of Yemen, eventually retaking San'a' in 1872. Under the Treaty of Da''n in 1904, the Ottomans and the British established a *de facto* border between Ottoman Yemen and what would become the Aden Protectorate.

These developments in eastern and southeastern Europe reflected a broader trend in the second half of the nineteenth century (which would appear somewhat later in the Arab provinces), the rise of ethno-linguistically based nationalist movements. These movements may or may not have been authentic expressions of separatist feeling, but they provided an effective means for the European powers, especially Russia and Austria, to enter the fray on behalf of various 'oppressed minorities'. Thus Russia encouraged Bulgarian and Romanian nationalism, and once these states were created, citizenship became based on religion, language, and 'ethnicity' rather than on domicile. The new states began to engage in what is now called 'ethnic cleansing', either by expelling their Muslim populations or by making life so difficult for them that they could no longer live there. The Austrian annexation of Bosnia-Herzegovina had similar, if less drastic, results (since most of its Muslim population did not leave).

Perhaps the most notorious of these movements was Armenian nationalism, encouraged by Russia, whose own fairly substantial Armenian population in the Caucasus was augmented after 1878 by the annexation of Batum and Kars. An Armenian National Assembly had been set up in 1863, but the Armenian independence movement was dogged by three seemingly insuperable problems. First, none of the so-called 'Six Vilayets' where most Ottoman Armenians resided had anything approaching

The Arabian Peninsula (at half the main map scale)

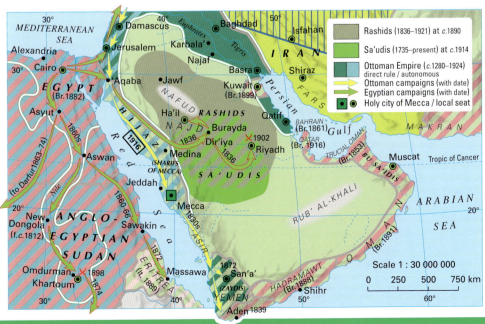

- Rashids (1836–1921) at c.1890
- Sa'udis (1735–present) at c.1914
- Ottoman Empire (c.1280–1924) direct rule / autonomous
- Ottoman campaigns (with date)
- Egyptian campaigns (with date)
- Holy city of Mecca / local seat

Map 40

Islamic Reform Movements in North and West Africa c.1650–c.1900

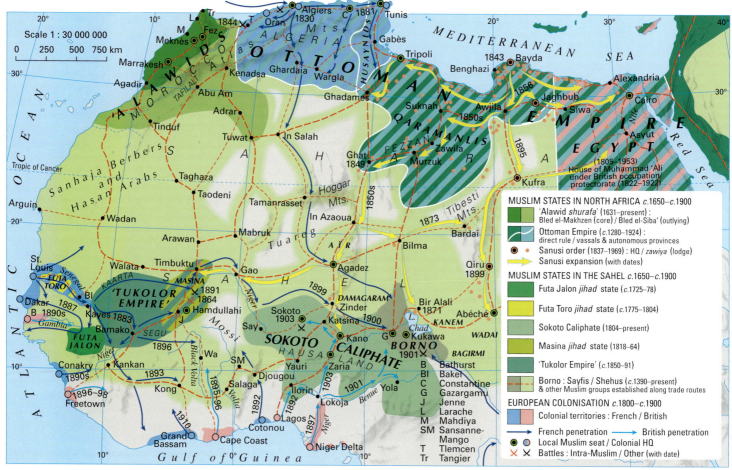

ALTHOUGH IT BROUGHT IMMENSE WEALTH to the Moroccan treasury, the Sa'did conquest of Songhay in 1591 (*see* Map 33) was too ambitious to survive for long. In Morocco itself, quarrels over the succession split Sa'did power between Fez and Marrakesh. The breach was repaired by Mawlay al-Rashid (1666–72) after the rise of the 'Alawites, *shurafa'* from Tafilalt. During the long reigns of his successors Isma'il (1672–1727) and Ahmad (1727–57) the dynasty consolidated itself by keeping the Ottomans at bay, and by expelling the Spanish from Mahdiya and Larache, and the English from Tangier. However, disastrous wars with France in 1844 and Spain in 1859–60 incurred massive indemnities, and the dynasty was only 'saved' by the imposition of a French protectorate in 1912, under which it was decided to maintain the monarchy as the principal instrument of colonial rule.

In Tunisia, the decline of Ottoman power had permitted the Husaynid dynasty to achieve *de facto* independence in 1705, which the French allowed to continue after their occupation of Tunis in 1881. Algeria, which lacked the more cohesive state structures of Tunisia and Morocco, remained under loose Ottoman suzerainty until the French invasion in 1830, which was followed by a period of brutal conquest, repression and cooptation. In 1870 it became an integral part of France, and by 1900 some 750,000 Europeans had settled in Algeria, driving most of the rural population off the cultivable land. In what is now Libya, a local dynasty, the Qaramanlis, seized power between 1711 and 1835, when Ottoman rule was reimposed until the Italian

invasion in 1911–12. Libya was also the home of the Sanusi order, a major Islamic reform movement with mahdist or millenarian undertones, whose *zawiya*-s, lodges, were scattered across the Sahara.

A number of movements arose in the Sahel in the eighteenth and nineteenth centuries which led to the greater diffusion of Islam and to its consolidation both as a system of belief and as a means of rule – that is, to the eventual formation of 'centralised Islamic states'. These developments took place before any of the more profound effects of European colonialism had been felt in West Africa. The main motivation of the leaders, who were mostly from the Qadiri Sufi order and from the mixed pastoral and sedentary ethnic group known as Fulanis (Fulbe), seems to have been a combination of wishing to install 'true' Islam by eliminating animism and what they considered as only nominal Islam, and by creating a political and social order based on Islamic principles.

The earliest of the Fulani 'jihad states' were Futa Jalon, established in the Guinea highlands around 1725 after a rebellion of the Muslims against their non-Muslim neighbours, and Futa Toro, founded around 1775 on the south bank of the Senegal. Both 'states' had Islamic schools and law courts, and became major trading centres. By far the most influential of these polities was the Sokoto Caliphate, founded by the charismatic Shaykh 'Uthman dan Fodio. He had conducted a campaign against the chiefs of Gobir in the 1780s in an attempt to get rid of un-Islamic institutions and practices, but the chiefs resented any attack on their privileges. He realised that more extreme

measures would be necessary, and launched a '*jihad* of the sword' in 1804, which ended with the establishment of a caliphate over much of Hausaland, as well as furthering the slow decline of neighbouring Borno. He saw himself as the *mujaddid*, 'renewer' (of Islam) in his time, claiming that the founder of the Qadiriya order, Shaykh 'Abd al-Qadir al-Gilani (1077–1166), appeared to him in dreams. British forces took Sokoto in 1903, but maintained the structure of the caliphate as part of a policy of indirect rule. The sultan remains one of the principal religious leaders of Nigerian Muslims, and the position is still in the hands of dan Fodio's family.

Around 1810, Ahmadu Lobbo, also a Qadiri *shaykh*, and originally a disciple of 'Uthman, broke away and set up his own thoroughgoing *jihad* state of Masina, centred on Hamdullahi.

The next wave of *jihad*-s took place only a few decades later. In the 1850s, al-Hajj 'Umar, a member of the new Tijaniya Sufi order, overran the vast upper Niger region, conquering non-Muslim Kaarta and Segu as well as engaging in intense conflict with the *jihad* state of Masina. Although the latter was incorporated into what the French called the 'Tukolor Empire' in 1864, little consolidation ensued, and 'Umar's son and successor Ahmad was defeated by the French in 1891. One of 'Umar's lasting legacies was the widespread implantation of the Tijaniya order in what became French West Africa. In general, the sense of belonging to a 'wider Islamic world' governed by the principles of Sunni orthodoxy had been firmly established throughout the Sahel by 1900 (*see* Map 43).

Map 41

The Spread and Development of Islam in Eastern Africa c.1500–c.1900

ISLAM CAME TO THE HORN OF AFRICA, the East African coast (*Zanj*) and what is now the Sudan at different times and from different directions. Muslim migration to Ethiopia began during the lifetime of the Prophet Muhammad, although for centuries it was confined to the Red Sea coast; today, Muslims account for about a third of Ethiopia's 90 million. Between the seventh and ninth centuries Islam came to what is now Eritrea, Djibouti and Somalia, although the conversion of almost all the population of the three states (now about 17 million) also owes much to the activities of the Sufi orders in the nineteenth century. In contrast, Islam came to 'eastern Sudan' (essentially the modern state) from Egypt, especially during the Mamluk period (*see* Maps 22 and 23). Beginning in the late eighth century, merchants from the Red Sea and Persian Gulf regions introduced Islam to the East African coast. In particular, large numbers of Hadramis (from south Arabia) had migrated there by the sixteenth century. The synthesis between local language and customs and the Islam of the immigrants gradually found expression in the urban Swahili culture of the area. Along the coast, as far south as the Comoros and Madagascar (*Qumr*), a string of 'Muslim port cities,' including Mogadishu, Barawa, Pate, Lamu, Malindi, Mombasa, Pemba, Zanzibar, Kilwa and Sofala, came to form part of a trading network stretching across the Indian Ocean (*see* Map 20).

In the early sixteenth century the Portuguese took over took most of the coastal cities, which were largely undefended, and also seized Muscat in Oman. By the 1540s, they were sufficiently well established in the Horn of Africa to help the Christian Ethiopians defeat a *jihad* led by Ahmad Grañ, Sultan of Harar (1506–43). However, they lacked the men and ships necessary to impose a monopoly on Indian Ocean trade and were ultimately expelled from the Persian Gulf, Zanzibar and Mombasa by the Ya'rubid rulers of Oman in the second half of the seventeenth century. By the mid-eighteenth century, the Bu Sa'idi dynasty (which still rules Oman) had replaced the Ya'rubids in Oman and East Africa.

Sa'id ibn Sultan, perhaps the ablest member of the dynasty, ruled in Muscat after 1827 and in Zanzibar between 1840 and 1856, imposing Omani rule (and, to some extent, a more 'mainstream' version of Islam) over the East African coast from Mogadishu to Kilwa. Zanzibar was the centre of a flourishing trade in slaves and ivory from the African interior, and in cloves, grown on large plantations on the island. Arab and Swahili merchants brought Islam to the interior of what is now Tanzania along the trade routes from Kilwa and Dar-es-Salaam. After Sa'id's death, one line of his successors ruled Oman from Muscat, while another son and his descendants ruled in Zanzibar. Sa'id's younger son, Barghash (Zanzibar 1870–88), was an energetic moderniser, renowned for having bought 'Arab civilisation' to the region, reflected in the adoption of Omani robes and Arab *nisba*-s, last names. He also encouraged the institutionalisation of a more universal (or 'higher') form of Islam, which was propagated by *shurafa'*, often

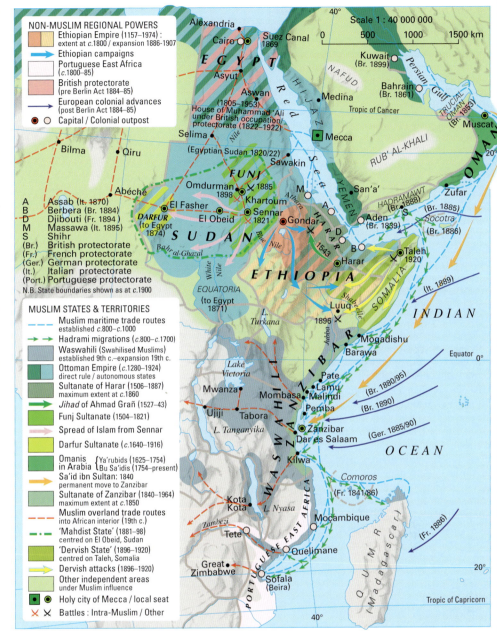

members of the 'Alawiya or Qadiriya orders who had migrated from the Arabian Peninsula. In 1890, largely because of German and Italian activity in the region, a British protectorate was established over Zanzibar, which greatly diminished the power and prestige of the sultanate.

Further north, Somalia was divided between Britain and Italy in 1891; this occasioned the foundation of an anti-colonial 'dervish state' under Sayyid Muhammad 'Abd Allah al-Hasan (1856–1920), a member of the recently founded Salihiya order. His state managed to resist British, Italian and Ethiopian forces for over twenty years.

In 1504, herders from the Blue Nile region had founded the Funj sultanate, with its capital at Sennar. Its rulers eventually converted to Islam; Sennar became a major centre of learning, and was crucial in encouraging the spread of Islam in the region, especially to Darfur, where it was adopted as the court and state religion in the late seventeenth century. In the eighteenth century,

civil wars, and the breakdown of the system of marriage alliances on which the political structure of the state depended, made the sultanate extremely vulnerable, and its forces were defeated by Muhammad 'Ali of Egypt in 1821 (*see* Map 39). Egyptian control extended widely across the area that forms the modern state, generally weakening the powers of local political and religious elites.

Sudanese opposition to Egyptian rule was expressed through the reinvigorated or newly founded Sufi orders. In 1881 Shaykh Muhammad Ahmad (1848–85) declared himself the *Mahdi*, or 'awaited saviour', forbidding 'un-Islamic' local practices and encouraging the adoption of the *shar'ia*. His army defeated General Gordon at Khartoum in 1885, and on his death some six months later, his lieutenant, the Khalifa 'Abdullahi ibn Muhammad, no doubt influenced by events elsewhere in the Islamic world (*see* Map 43), declared the foundation of an 'Islamic state', which lasted until its defeat in 1898 by an Anglo-Egyptian force at Omdurman.

Map 42

The Development of Muslim States in Southeast Asia c.1600–c.1900

THE INITIAL PHASE OF ISLAMISATION in the Indonesian Archipelago and the Malay Peninsula has already been described (*see* Map 30). Among the more salient features of the subsequent development of Islam and Islamic political and religious institutions in this region were forms of concentrated local political consolidation and 'empire-building'; conflicts with and between the various European powers over control of the spice trade; the failure of local Muslim rulers to expel the Portuguese and the Dutch; the gradual weakening of all the regional dynasties through conflicts with the colonial powers, members of their own families and regional rivals; support for, and opposition to, movements of 'Islamic reform' which mostly sought to impose 'orthodoxy' on the region, and the beginnings of anti-colonial movements which would come to fruition in the twentieth century.

In many ways, Sultan Agung's conquest of Surabaya in 1625 (*see* Map 30) marked the apogee both of his own power and of the Empire of Mataram. Subsequently Agung emerged the loser in a series of clashes with the Dutch, especially after his unsuccessful siege of Batavia in 1629. He also faced opposition from other Islamic religious centres, although he seems to have effected some kind of reconciliation with them by the time of his pilgrimage to the shrine of Tembayat in 1633. He also married one of his sons and one of his sisters into the family of the last ruler of Surabaya, thereby strengthening the legitimacy of his own dynasty. A few years after incorporating Giri and its shrine into the domains of Mataram in 1636, Agung received the title of Sultan 'Abdullah Muhammad Mawlana Matarani from the *Sharif* of Mecca; he is called king-priest (*prabu pandita*) in some Javanese chronicles.

Under his successors Amangkurat I (1645–77) and Amangkurat II (1677–1703) the Empire of Mataram faltered and then crumbled. This was due to a number of factors, including Amangkurat I's practice of killing off large numbers of potential rivals from among the Javanese nobility (both religious and temporal), his draconian economic policies, and his subservience to the VOC. Eventually such actions combined to provoke a widespread rebellion instigated by disaffected members of the nobility, which led to the destruction of the forces of Mataram at Gogodog in 1676. At this stage, in spite of protests from some of his courtiers against 'cooperation with Christians' – and similar sentiments were being expressed in the 1680s by the Minangkabau leader Ahmad Shah ibn Iskandar – the elderly sultan appealed to the VOC, whose intervention proved decisive in containing the rebellion. After his father's death in 1677, Amangkurat II, whose treasury was almost empty, was obliged to rely even more heavily on the support of the VOC in eliminating his rivals. The Dutch came to control most of western Java, eventually dividing it into two small kingdoms, Jogjakarta and Surakarta, which lasted from 1755 until their incorporation into the Republic of Indonesia in 1949.

N.B. State boundaries shown as at *c.*1900

MUSLIM EMPIRES & SULTANATES *c.*1600–*c.*1900

- Mataram (*c.*1575–1755) & successors Jogjakarta / Surakarta (1755–1949)
- Banten (1527–1918)
- Aceh (*c.*1496–1903)
- Johor-Riau (*c.*1528–present) & successors
- Jambi (*c.*1600–1904)
- Palembang (*c.*1659–present)
- Ternate (*c.*1470–present) & successors
- Tidore (*c.*1460–1904)
- Gowa-Makassar (1605–1906) & successors
- Brunei (*c.*1520–present) & sub-divisions
- Other independent Muslim groups and areas influenced by Islam
- Spheres of trade / influence (empires at apogee)
- Islamic holy shrine in Java / Muslim seat
- Rebellion / *jihad* against reform / colonial rule
- Major conflicts : Intra-Muslim / Other

Kh Kedah
Kn Kelantan
NS Negri Sembilan
Pk Perlak
Sr Selangor
Tu Trengganu

Scale 1 : 5 500 000
0   50   100   150   200   250 km

As has already been described (*see* Map 30), the arrival of Islam in western Java and southern Sumatra, and the foundation of the sultanate of Banten, has semi-mythical overtones similar to those associated with the early years of the 'Empire of Mataram'. In the late seventeenth century, the long reign of Sultan Ageng (1651–82) was a period of considerable prosperity, during which long-distance trade flourished and irrigated agriculture, particularly rice and coconut cultivation, expanded considerably. Such success inevitably engendered increasing covetousness on the part of the VOC, which was able to take advantage of the conflict developing between the sultan and his crown prince. Ageng was supported by one of the leading Islamic teachers of Indonesia, Shaykh Yusuf of Makassar (1626–99), a member of the Naqshbandi and Khalwati *tariqa*-s, and was at one stage most likely in a position to act decisively against growing VOC involvement in the affairs of Mataram. However, Ageng's son, Sultan Hajji (1682–87) effectively capitulated to the VOC, which proceeded to drive him out of Banten, and the other European (i.e. non-Dutch) traders out of Java.

The sultanate of Aceh developed into a serious rival of the Portuguese after their seizure of Malacca in 1511, although neither side emerged as a clear winner. In general, Aceh's considerable military potential was blunted by constant internal conflict and long-running disputes with Johor. Aceh enjoyed a brief period of supremacy under Sultan Iskandar Muda (1607–36) until the decisive defeat of his expedition to Malacca by the Portuguese in 1629. An endemic problem of the sultanate, which long remained a major exporter of pepper, nutmeg, and cloves (the latter mostly trans-shipped from eastern Indonesia), seems to have been its tenuous influence over its rural hinterland, and its consequent inability to control or rely on a regular agricultural surplus. Although four strong-minded queens (sultanas) ruled between 1641 and 1688, largely managing to keeping the Dutch at bay, intra-elite quarrels and a succession of weak rulers

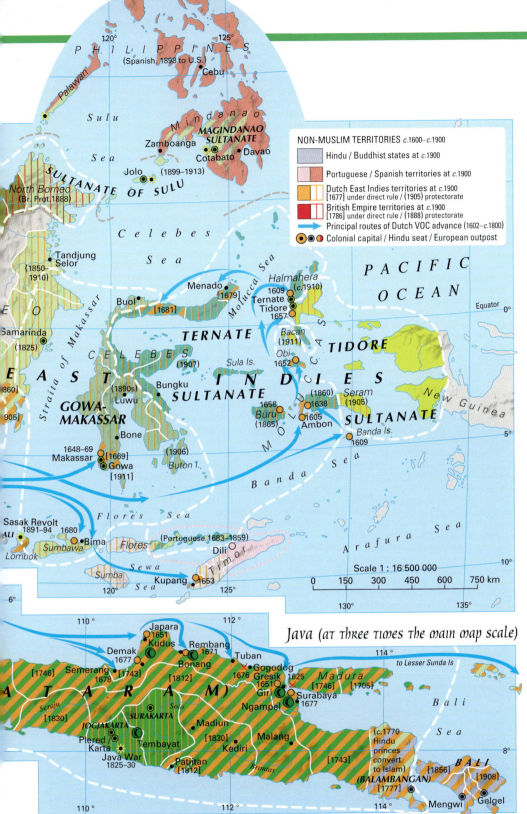

Java (at three times the main map scale)

In the eighteenth and nineteenth centuries, Islamic practices and institutions in Southeast Asia were being profoundly affected by movements in other parts of the Islamic world advocating 'reform', the rise in importance of the various Sufi orders, and by anti-colonial manifestations against the British, and the Dutch, who instituted direct colonial rule (to replace that of the VOC) in the early nineteenth century. The British had established themselves in southwestern Sumatra in the 1710s, in Penang in 1786, and subsequently in the rest of the Malay Peninsula: Anglo-Dutch rivalry was regulated by the Treaty of London of 1824. Some decades later, the sultanate of Brunei, torn by internal strife, ceded Sarawak, first to a British adventurer, Sir James Brooke, in 1841, and then in 1888 to the British government, together with the rest of Brunei and the North Borneo territory of the sultanate of Sulu.

The first major rebellion/*jihad* against the Dutch and their local allies took place in central Java around Jogjakarta in 1825–30. Its leader, Prince Dipanagara, styled himself 'caliph of the Prophet,' and many of his followers saw him as a *mahdi*. The Dutch had also become involved in the Padri 'civil wars' in Minangkabau in Sumatra between 1803 and 1838, initiated by local teachers of *fiqh* and subsequently by a number of returning *hajji*-s who had been influenced by Wahhabism and Salafism. Both the *faqih*-s and the 'Wahhabis' were determined to do away with customary law and wanted to institutionalise the *shar'ia*. They were opposed by those with strong vested interests in the *status quo*, who turned to the Dutch for support against manifestations of 'Muslim fanaticism', which included killing the populations of whole villages who would not accept the new teachings. The war ended with the imposition of direct Dutch rule in Minangkabau, but although those who advanced 'true Islam' were defeated, their prestige was greatly enhanced. There were similar conflicts in Aceh and Banten, while in Lombok the Sasaks fought a Dutch-Hindu alliance.

All in all, contacts with the wider Islamic world intensified with the development of steam navigation in the latter part of the nineteenth century. This enabled larger numbers of Muslims to make the pilgrimage to Mecca, and made possible the diffusion of newspapers, pamphlets and journals from publishing houses in Egypt and the Middle East and from within Indonesia itself. While what was then known as Salafism, equivalent at the time to 'modernist reform', was probably the main beneficiary of these processes of internationalisation, there was also a wider diffusion of the Sufi orders throughout the region. The orders and their leaders played notable roles in the Banjarmasin war of 1859–63, the Aceh war of 1873–1913, and the Banten rebellion of 1888. Finally, in the latter part of the nineteenth century, many Muslim leaders in Southeast Asia appealed to the Ottomans for assistance and/or moral support in their struggles against the Dutch and the British, particularly during the sultanate of 'Abd al-Hamid II (1876–1909). This was partly because of 'Abd al-Hamid's support for Pan-Islamism, but it was also symbolic of a widespread belief on the part of contemporaries in the fundamental unity of the Islamic world.

in the eighteenth and nineteenth centuries meant that Aceh's authority remained confined to northern Sumatra. Nevertheless it remained a formidable economic power, producing more than half the world's supply of pepper in the 1820s.

After the decline of Aceh, the principal Muslim powers in western Southeast Asia between the mid-seventeenth and early nineteenth centuries were Johor-Riau, straddling the Straits of Malacca, and the 'pepper sultanates' of Palembang and Jambi, which vied for control of southern Sumatra. Both the latter were significant exporters to China and to Europe, and both were targeted by the VOC, anxious to secure a trade monopoly. Sultans 'Abd al-Rahman and Badr al-Din of Palembang (1662–1706, 1724–57) presided over a period of

considerable prosperity, managing simultaneously to evade the monopolistic demands of the VOC and to enjoy its protection. In contrast Jambi was locked in succession struggles, and its authority rarely extended to the upriver areas of the sultanate where most of the pepper was produced. In the early 1700s the VOC's powers to insist were beginning to decline; this seems to have particularly benefitted the port of Riau, a significant centre for the export of pepper and tin, which enjoyed a brief if mercurial rise in prosperity (and independence from the VOC) under Raja Muda Mahmud (1708–18). Meanwhile in the Moluccas and Celebes, the VOC's plans to control the important clove and nutmeg trade were frustrated by powerful sultanates in Ternate, Tidore and Gowa-Makassar.

THE ISLAMIC WORLD c.1750–1914

- Muslim states established by 'Islamic renewal'
- Muslim states established by anti-colonial resistance
- Regions affected by widespread 'Islamic renewal'
- Other areas under Muslim control / influence
- ⊛ Local *jihad* / anti-colonial resistance
- ⊚ Centre of 'Islamic renewal' / Other Muslim seat
- ⊙ Ottoman imperial and caliphal capital
- ▣ Holy city of Mecca
- [42] Cross reference map number for further details

AT VARIOUS TIMES in the eighteenth and nineteenth centuries, a wave of socio-religious movements swept over much of the Islamic world, from North and West Africa to China and from Russia to Southeast Asia. Some of them were vehicles for 'Islamic renewal', while others, particularly in the nineteenth century, were expressions of anti-colonial resistance. Many of the later movements came to combine both elements: thus the Sanusi order (*see* Map 40), founded by Muhammad ibn 'Ali al-Sanusi (1787–1859), began as a movement of Islamic reform and renewal, but took on more 'political' overtones as its *zawiya*-s (religious lodges) became centres of opposition to the French and Italian colonial presence in north and west Africa.

Various explanations have been given for the appearance of such phenomena in the second half of the eighteenth century. These include: the growing weakness, and the concomitant loss of legitimacy, of the three leading Muslim empires – the Ottoman, the Safavid and the Mughal – and a profound desire on the part of some contemporaries to reverse this decline, as well as the increasingly intense encroachment of the European powers upon the Islamic world. Other factors are the dogmatic and/or politically subservient nature of some of the leading Islamic teaching institutions, and, very significantly, the 'discovery', or perhaps the reinvention, on the part of some Muslim leaders and scholars, of a pristine Islam based entirely on the Qur'an and the *sunna*. Stripped of all the accretions thrown up in the intervening centuries, this was held up as the sole path that these leaders and reformers required their subjects, and those whom they conquered, to follow.

Earlier scholarship tended to view movements of Islamic revival as having a common genealogy, but more recent research has shown that the projects of the various founders were often very diverse, and represented quite different strands of Islamic thought. In addition, the fact that the phenomenon known as 'Wahhabism' (or more recently as 'Salafism') has become so all-pervasive in the Western media has led to a tendency to over-generalise its significance in its own day. In fact, many of the reform movements that came into existence in the second half of the eighteenth century had very different origins and trajectories.

Thus the Indian reformer Shah Wali Allah (d. 1760: *see* Map 36) was profoundly affected by the consequences of the slow collapse of Mughal power (since the death of Awrangzib in 1707) and the concomitant rise in the fortunes of the non-Muslim communities, particularly the Sikhs and Hindus. He believed that it was vital to continue to practice *ijtihad*, and advocated a reformed Sufism purged of its more popular manifestations, but he did not condemn visiting saints' tombs or seeking the *baraka* of holy men. The contrast between his more

catholic approach and the 'puritanical' notions of his near contemporary, Ibn 'Abd al-Wahhab (d. 1792: *see* Map 38), and more generally with Wahhabism's 'exclusive claim to doctrinal truth', could not be starker.

The movement led by 'Uthman dan Fodio in West Africa (*see* Map 40) represents another strand of Islamic reform. His reforming ideals clashed with those of a powerful neighbouring ruler; dan Fodio's victory in the war that followed led to the foundation of a new state, the Sokoto Caliphate, whose purpose was to pursue proper Islamic practice, to eliminate animism and to create a regime of social justice underwritten by an educated application of Islamic law. He called himself a *mujaddid*, renewer, of Islam; he also identified himself with the Sufi tradition, as did many other reformers in the nineteenth century. In the 1830s and 1840s, the Amir 'Abd al-Qadir al-Jaza'iri (1808–83), a Sufi scholar and military leader, led a long campaign against the French in North Africa, initiating more than half a century of religious-based opposition to colonial rule.

In Sumatra, the Padri movement in Minangkabau in the first decades of the nineteenth century had some resemblance to dan Fodio's *jihad*, but also

Map 43

Religious Reform and Resistance to Colonialism in the Islamic World c.1750–1914

EUROPEAN COLONISATION AS AT 1914

- British Empire & spheres of influence
- Dutch East Indies
- French colonies & spheres of influence
- Italian / Other Western colonies
- Russian Empire & spheres of influence
- Imperial capital
- Other capitals : colonial / state

N.B. State boundaries shown as at 1914

Scale 1 : 45 000 000
0   500   1000   1500 km

(Br.) British
(Du.) Dutch
(Fr.) French
(Ger.) German
(It.) Italian
(O.E.) Ottoman
(Port.) Portuguese
(Sp.) Spanish
(Rus.) Russian
(U.S.) American

C   Chandernagore
D   Daman
K   Karikal
KL Kuala Lumpur
M   Mahé
P   Pondicherry
Y   Yanam

AHL-I HADIS
(1860s) [36]

of Muslims achieving *madaniyya*, civilisation, and *taraqqi*, progress, through education, to enable them to participate fully in modern society and government. Muslim deputies were elected to the Duma between 1906 and 1912, which seems to indicate a fair degree of integration into Tsarist Russian society.

In those parts of the Caucasus where the Russians had advanced at the expense of both the Ottoman Empire and Iran (*see* Maps 38 / 39) in the early 1800s the story was rather different. Although deputies from the Caucasus were also elected to the Duma, the Naqshbandi order put up strong resistance to the imposition of Russian rule in some areas, especially under Imam Shamil (1797–1871) who fought strenuously against the Russians until his capture and exile in 1859. On the whole, the experience of the Muslims in the Russian state was characterised more by assimilation than by resistance; Islamic reform manifested itself partly in attacks against rigid and dogmatic *'ulama'* but more visibly in the propagation of forms of Islamic modernism.

One of the most prolonged instances of Islamic opposition to foreign rule was the Mahdist state in the Sudan, which lasted some seventeen years (*see* Map 41). In 1881 Shaykh Muhammad Ahmad (1848–85), a member of the Sammaniya Sufi order, declared himself the *Mahdi*, or awaited saviour, and formed a large tribal army, which he called the *Ansar*, after the Prophet Muhammad's 'helpers' at Medina. In 1883 and 1885, his army defeated two British forces sent against him. The Mahdi died of natural causes in 1885, and was succeeded by his lieutenant, the Khalifa 'Abdullahi ibn Muhammad. Eventually, the British sent a stronger force to the Sudan, and defeated the Mahdists at Omdurman in 1898.

In India (*see* Map 36), Islamic resistance took several forms. The founder of the Barelvi movement, Sayyid Ahmad (1786–1831) began as a preacher of reform, spreading his message across northern India. In the late 1820s he established an Muslim state on the North West Frontier, and died in battle against the Sikhs. Sayyid Ahmad generally supported a reformed Sufism: in contrast, the Fara'izi movement in Bengal was anti-Sufi and pro-Wahhabi, although it eschewed violence. The rebellion of 1857 acted as a major watershed, as it was followed by the absorption of several formerly independent states into the territory of the British Raj. Some Muslims leaders advocated coming to terms with the British; another reaction was the foundation of the Deoband *madrasa* in 1867, which emphasised knowledge of the Qur'an and forbade visits to saints' tombs. The Deobandis believed in the personal responsibility of the individual, and encouraged Muslim women to make their homes 'bastion[s] of Islamic values'. Thus the range of responses in India was far from uniform, mirroring the wide variety of religious experience elsewhere in the Islamic world.

This map does not pretend to present an exhaustive picture of the many reform and anti-colonial movements that came into being across the Islamic world during this period. In time, the strengthening of these movements, and the gradual decline of the imperial powers, would lead to the formation of many new states in Africa and Asia in the course of the twentieth century.

contained elements of 'scripturalism'. Throughout the eighteenth century, the region had been plagued by internal strife (*see* Map 42) that often involved the abduction of men and cattle, and by conflicts that had arisen largely from the introduction of cash crops such as cassia and coffee by the Dutch. The original 'Padris' were three returning *hajji*-s (referred to disparagingly by the Dutch as *padris*, from the Spanish *padre*, priest) who attempted to prohibit cock fighting, drinking and gambling on their return from Mecca in 1803. They were also opposed to customary law (*'adat*) especially the practice of matrilineal succession, which they held up as being in contradiction to the *shar'ia*. Dutch military intervention eventually brought the 'Padri wars' to an end. Dutch rule, especially Dutch attempts to abolish 'feudalism', proved extremely divisive: thus in the 1820s, the charismatic Prince Dipanagara (1785–1855), an aristocrat and 'holy man' claiming to be the *ratu adil* or 'just king', fought a series of unsuccessful campaigns in Java against the Dutch and their local allies. The long drawn out Aceh war in north Sumatra between 1873 and 1913 was originally led by the *'ulama'* against the Dutch, who gradually

succeeded in winning over the local nobility. In addition large numbers of 'Indonesians' from Java and Ambon fought alongside Dutch forces in Sumatra.

A more diffuse picture emerges from Russia and Central Asia, perhaps because different Muslim communities came under Russian control at different times. Thus the Volga Tatars had come under Russian rule in 1552 (*see* Map 32); the Crimea was annexed in 1783, parts of the Caucasus at different times between the 1800s and the 1860s, the Kazakh steppe in the 1820s and 1830s, and Bukhara, Khiva and Khoqand between 1864 and 1876 (*see* Map 37). In 1897 there were 14 million Muslims under Russian rule, 11 per cent of the population. As elsewhere, there were conflicts between reformers and the conservative *'ulama'* of Bukhara and Samarkand over matters of belief and practice, such as the desirability of practising *ijtihad*.

A feature of both the Arab East and Central Asia in the late 1800s was the reformers' advocacy of 'Islamic modernism,' which involved embracing, rather than rejecting, modernity. Central Asian jadidism, pioneered especially by Isma'il Gasprinskii (1851–1914) was concerned with the desirability

The Islamic World since c.1900

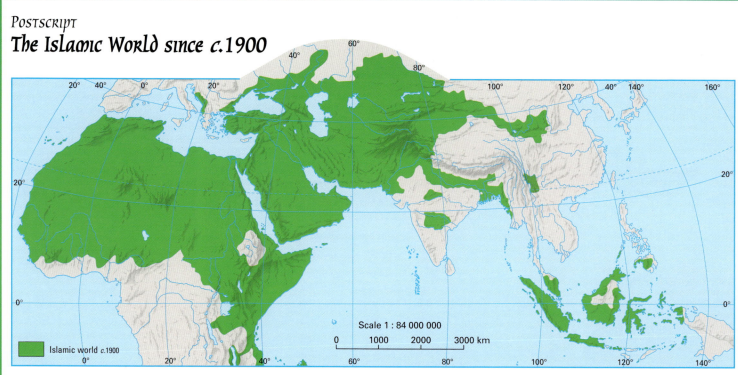

Islamic world *c*.1900

Scale 1 : 84 000 000

0   1000   2000   3000 km

THE MAPS IN THIS ATLAS cover the history of the Islamic world from the origins of Islam to the early 20th century. At this end point, even before the cataclysm of the First World War, it becomes no longer possible to map historical events in Asia and Africa in terms of the 'Islamic history' that the Atlas has been designed to illustrate. In addition, by 1914, control over a substantial part of the Islamic world had been in European hands for a century or more, as shown in Map 43.

The period after the First World War saw the disintegration of the 'land empires' of Austria-Hungary, Germany, the Ottomans, the Qajars and Russia, followed by the emergence of new national states formed mostly on the basis of language and/or ethnicity. In addition, as the twentieth century progressed, control of most of the previously or newly acquired colonial world in Asia and Africa gradually passed out of the hands of the European imperial powers, to the extent that 'full-blown' colonialism had largely disappeared by about 1970. In the course of both processes, many 'new states' came into being with majority Muslim populations.

In the inter-war period most of the Arab states of the *Mashriq* were created as semi-colonial entities out of the former Ottoman Arab provinces, under the tutelage of Britain or France. Republican Turkey emerged after the Treaty of Lausanne in July 1923, and its first president proceeded to abolish the caliphate in March 1924. During the 1920s, following the establishment of the Soviet Union, a series of semi-independent Muslim states came into being in the Caucasus and Central Asia (almost all of which became fully independent after the dissolution of the Soviet Union in 1991).

After the Second World War the pace of de-colonisation began to accelerate. Thus India (and Pakistan, which was carved out of it) became independent in 1947; the Dutch withdrew from Indonesia in 1949; the British left Egypt, Iraq and Palestine at various points in the 1940s and 1950s, Nigeria in 1960, and Malaya in 1963. France left Lebanon in 1943, Syria in 1946,

Morocco and Tunisia in 1956, what are now Mali, Mauritania, Côte d'Ivoire and other West African states in 1960, and its settler state of Algeria after eight years of civil war in 1962.

Also, as early as the 1950s (and earlier still in France) a significant tide of migration to the West from these decolonised Muslim states had begun, as is recorded on the 'Spread of Islam through the Ages' map on the front endpaper. As a result of this widespread migration there are now substantial Muslim minorities in Britain who orginate from the Indian subcontinent: in France and Spain from North Africa, in Germany from Turkey, and in the Netherlands from Indonesia. Although small scale migration to the Americas, particularly from Greater Syria, had begun in the 19th century, a sea change took place in the US after the passage of the Hart-Celler Immigration and Nationality Act in 1965, which abolished criteria for immigration to US based on nation of origin and race. This facilitated the growth of a professional Muslim middle class in many US cities, as well as a move towards the propagation of more orthodox versions of Islam than those disseminated earlier by African-American Muslim groups, and 'orthodoxy' came to gain widespread acceptance.

Many of the former colonies are now majority Muslim states, as can be seen in 'The Islamic World in the 21st Century' map on the back endpaper. Many are members of various international Islamic organisations, such as the Muslim World League or the Organisation of the Islamic Conference (founded in 1962 and 1969 respectively). But the modern histories of these states are local and national histories, just as the histories of modern Argentina or Slovenia relate primarily to the history of Latin America and Europe, rather than to the history of some eponymous 'Christian world'. In general the notion of a monolithic 'Islamic world' has largely disappeared except in the minds of those Western political scientists intent on regarding the contemporary 'Islamic' and 'Christian' worlds as for ever locked in a 'clash of civilisations'.

It may be useful to make some mention of the term 'Islamic state'. While Medina at the time of the Prophet can be described as an 'Islamic polity', based upon the Constitutions of Medina (*see* Map 3), most scholars agree that the concept of 'state' did not exist in the classical period, and that its modern form does not antedate the early 20th century. Thus the Ottoman state regarded it as its duty to defend its own borders, and generally to provide the backdrop against which the good Islamic life might be lived, but it did not intrude into the lives of its subjects on matters of religion in any way comparable to, say, the religious policing of Tudor England, let alone the Spanish Inquisition.

In addition, there is no agreement among Muslim theologians either as to how such a state might or should be set up, or indeed whether its existence would be 'lawful' at all. The modern notion of the Islamic state is usually attributed to the Pakistani theologian Abu'l-'Ala Mawdudi (1903–79). He took part in anti-British colonial agitation as a young man, especially after the abolition of the caliphate in 1924, and later founded a political party, *Jamaat-i Islami*, whose objective was the establishment of an Islamic state based on the principles of *shar'ia* law. In contrast, the distinguished Indonesian scholar Nurcholish Madjid (1939–2005) believed that any use of Islam for political ends violates its basic monotheism (*tawhid*) by mixing the notion of the unity of God with worldly politics.

The fact is that in the modern world, 'Islam' is only a part of the lives of a billion Muslims, and as our maps have shown, 'Islamic tradition' varies widely from place to place. Just as it is not especially useful to think of a one-size-fits-all entity called 'Christian civilisation' as providing some sort of explanatory background for the modern histories of Argentina or Slovenia, it is equally misleading to assume the continuing existence of an unchanging entity called the *Dar al-Islam* to explicate the histories of Afghanistan or Mali. In both cases, a myriad other factors – economic, ethnic, geopolitical, international, political and social, to name only the most obvious, need to be taken into account.

APPENDICES

Chronology of Islamic and World History
(76–95)

This chronology details the major historical events occuring across the Islamic world from pre-Islamic times to the present day with a comparative timeline for the Rest of the World.

Glossary : Islamic and Other Terms
(96–97)

This glossary provides supplementary explanations and definitions of the Islamic and other non-English terms used in the Atlas.

Glossary : Place Names
(98–99)

This glossary indicates the linguistic origins of those place names that appear on the maps in their generally accepted English nameforms and lists the changes in place names over time.

Bibliography
(100–104)

This bibliography of the atlases, books and other sources consulted in the process of compiling the maps and writing the texts for this Atlas also provides useful pointers for further reading and study.

Index
(105–112)

This index lists the principal subjects and names referred to in the map texts, sub-divided into separate indexes of (a) themes: (b) personal / group names: (c) place names.

The Islamic World in the 21st Century
(Back Endpaper)

This map presents a demographic and political survey of the Islamic world today, as well as indicating the locations of fifty of the most notable sites of Muslim heritage.

Chronology 500 BCE–500 CE

CENTRAL ISLAMIC LANDS	NORTH AND WEST AFRICA AND THE IBERIAN PENINSULA	ASIA MINOR AND THE BALKANS
*c.*500 BCE Darius I of Persia completes canal connecting River Nile to the Red Sea	*c.*500 BCE Iron-making techniques spread to sub-Saharan Africa *c.*500 Apogee of Nok culture in Jos Plateau region of Nigeria; renowned for its terracotta statues	490 Battle of Marathon; Persian attack on Athens defeated 480 Battle of Salamis; Greeks defeat Persians 479–338 Period of classical Greek culture 447 Parthenon begun in Athens 431–04 Peloponnesian War between Athens and Sparta 323 BCE Death of Alexander the Great
*c.*312 Petra established as Nabatean capital 312 Seleucid dynasty founded in Syria; devises first continuous historical dating system 330–04 Ptolemy I, Macedonian Governor of Egypt founds independent dynasty *c.*290 Foundation of Library of Alexandria		
*c.*150 Apogee of Nabatean trading empire in northern Arabia	264–41 First Punic War; Rome attacks Carthage 218–01 Second Punic War; Hannibal of Carthage attacks Rome 206 Rome gains control of Hispania 149–46 Third Punic War; Rome destroys Carthage and founds province of Africa *c.*100 BCE Camel introduced to the Sahara	
64–50 Roman conquest of Syria under Pompey the Great; Roman army reaches Yemen 30 Death of Anthony and Cleopatra; Egypt becomes a Roman province *c.*1 BCE Birth of Jesus of Nazareth in Bethlehem *c.*33 CE Jesus Christ crucified in Jerusalem		
70 Romans destroy the Jewish Temple in Jerusalem	44 CE Mauretania (Morocco and Algeria) annexed by Rome	46–57 CE Missionary journeys of St Paul
116 Roman Emperor Trajan completes conquest of Mesopotamia 132 Jewish rebellion against Rome leads to 'diaspora' of Jews		
		312 Conversion of Constantine to Christianity 325 Council of Nicaea defines Christian doctrine 330 Constantinople becomes capital of Eastern Roman Empire 378 Visigoths kill Roman emperor at Adrianople *c.*385 Under Theodosius Christianity becomes the official religion of the Roman Empire 395 Division of Roman Empire into Eastern and Western polities; foundation of Byzantine Empire
*c.*350–*c.*500 Christianity established as a major religion in the eastern Mediterranean region after surviving many decades of the 'Great Persecution'; five patriarchates (major church districts) under guidance of a patriarch (church leader) founded at Alexandria, Antioch, Constantinople, Jerusalem and Rome	409 Visigoths overrun Hispania 426 Augustine of Hippo completes *City of God* 429 Vandal kingdom in North Africa	
		451 Council of Chalcedon issues a further major statement on Christian doctrine intended to stem heretical views

RUSSIA, CENTRAL ASIA, IRAN, AFGHANISTAN AND INDIA	EASTERN AFRICA, INDIAN OCEAN, SOUTHEAST ASIA AND CHINA	REST OF THE WORLD
*c.*500 BCE Apogee of Achaemenid Persia under Darius I who ruled over a vast empire that stretched from the Nile to the Indus	*c.*500 BCE Aryan Sinhalese peoples reach Ceylon	*c.*500 BCE Foundation of Zapotec capital, Monte Albán in Mexico
		*c.*486 Birth of Buddha
	479 Death of Confucius	
		390 Sack of Rome by Gauls
334–27 Alexander the Great (of Macedon) conquests in Asia Minor, Egypt, Persia and India 322 Foundation of Mauryan empire (India)	*c.*350 Expansion of the Meroe kingdom (Nubia)	
		290 Rome completes conquest of central Italy
265 Ashoka, Mauryan emperor, converts to Buddhism 247 Foundation of Parthian dynasty (Persia)		264–41 First Punic War; Rome gains control of Sicily from Carthage
	206 Shih Huang-ti, of Qin dynasty (221–06), unites China 202 BCE Former Han dynasty reunites China	218–01 Second Punic War; Rome invaded by Hannibal of Carthage
		149 Greece under Roman domination
		89 All inhabitants of Italy granted Roman citizenship
*c.*112 BCE First use of 'Silk Road' across Central Asia as trade route linking China and the Near East		58–51 Julius Caesar conquers Gaul 49 Julius Caesar crosses the Rubicon; begins march on Rome 47–45 Civil war in Rome; Julius Caesar becomes sole leader 46 Julius Caesar introduces the Julian calendar
		27 BCE Roman republic becomes an empire
		43 CE Roman invasion of Britain
	*c.*50 CE Expansion of kingdom of Aksum (Ethiopia)	64 Nero persecutes Christians in Rome
*c.*60–100 CE Apogee of Kushana Empire in northern India 97 Chinese ambassador Kan Ting visits Persia		79 Vesuvius eruption buries Herculaneum / Pompeii
		117 Apogee of Roman Empire
		165 Smallpox epidemic ravages Roman Empire
		238 Gothic incursions into Roman Empire begin
224 Foundation of Sasanian dynasty (Persia)	280 China unified under Western Jin dynasty	*c.*300 Rise of Mayan civilisation in Mesoamerica
320 Foundation of Gupta Empire (India)		313 Edict of Milan; toleration proclaimed for the practice of all religions in the Roman Empire
*c.*350 Huns invade Persia and India	333 King of Aksum adopts Christianity as offical religion	*c.*385 Under Theodosius Christianity becomes the official religion of the Roman Empire
	*c.*400 Aksum destroys Meroe kingdom	*c.*400 Settlement of Hawaiian islands 404 Latin version of the Bible completed 406 Visigoths overrun Gaul 410 Visigoths invade Italy, leading to the end of Roman Empire in the West (*c.*476)
	420 Overthrow of Eastern Jin dynasty (265–420)	449 Angles, Saxons and Jutes begin invasions of Britain
		493 Ostrogoths take power in Italy 497 Franks convert to Christianity
480 Overthrow of Gupta empire (India)	*c.*500 Christianity spreads to Nubia from Egypt	

© EIPL

Chronology 500–750

CENTRAL ISLAMIC LANDS	NORTH AND WEST AFRICA AND THE IBERIAN PENINSULA	ASIA MINOR AND THE BALKANS
	509 Battle of Vouillé; Franks defeat Visigoths, who retreat to the Iberian Peninsula	
520s Axumite conquest of Yemen	**527–65** Byzantine conquest of most of southern Europe and North Africa (until Arab conquests in 7th and 8th centuries)	**527–65** Justinian's reign as Byzantine Emperor
570 [Year of the Elephant] Ethiopian attack on Mecca; birth of the Prophet Muhammad		
602–29 Last great Byzantine / Persian war		**610 / 620** Sasanian attacks on Constantinople repulsed
610 Prophet Muhammad receives first Qur'anic revelations		
620 Sasanian attacks on Egypt and Syria		**628** Emperor Heraclius' siege of Ctesiphon
622 The Prophet Muhammad's *hijra* from Mecca to Medina		
632 Death of the Prophet Muhammad		
632–61 The rightly guided caliphs (Abu Bakr, 'Umar, 'Uthman, 'Ali) lead the caliphate		
636 Arab armies defeat Sasanian Empire at Battle of Qadisiya		**650** Slavs complete their conquest of the Balkans
637 / 642 Arab conquest of Syria and Egypt		
661 Battle of Siffin; arbitration between 'Ali and Mu'awiya		**681** Establishment of first Bulgarian empire
661–750 Umayyad Caliphate	**670** Foundation of Kairouan	
692 Completion of The Dome of the Rock in Jerusalem during the reign of 'Abd al-Malik (685–705)	*c*.**700** Rise of empire of Ghana	
	703 al-Zaytuna Mosque founded in Tunis by Umayyads	
706–15 Great Mosque of Damascus built by Umayyad caliph al-Walid I	**711** Tariq ibn Ziyad's army crosses from North Africa to the Iberian Peninsula	
	711–13 Arab capture of Córdoba, Toledo, Seville and Mérida	**717–18** Umayyad siege of Constantinople
750 Establishment of 'Abbasid dynasty; defeat of Umayyads	**732** Muslim army halted near Poitiers	**730–87** Height of Iconoclast controversy

RUSSIA, CENTRAL ASIA, IRAN, AFGHANISTAN AND INDIA	EASTERN AFRICA, INDIAN OCEAN, SOUTHEAST ASIA AND CHINA	REST OF THE WORLD
		*c.*524 Boethius completes the *Consolations of Philosophy*
		529 St Benedict of Nursia founds monastery at Monte Cassino
		538 / 552 Introduction of Buddhism to Japan
	543 The Chinese dictionary Yupian is completed by Gu Yewang	
554 Collapse of Gupta Empire		568 Foundation of Lombard kingdom in Italy
	581–618 Sui dynasty in China	597 Papacy sends mission led by Augustine of Canterbury to begin conversion of Kent
		*c.*600 Apogee of Mayan civilisation in Mesoamerica; construction of Teotihuacan in central valley of Mexico; Monte Albán outside Oaxaca
	605 Institution of examinations for entry into the Chinese imperial bureaucracy	
	609 Grand Canal of China completed	
	618–907 T'ang dynasty in China	
	635 First (Nestorian) Christian missionaries arrive in China	
645 Muslim armies reach Khurasan and Fars	650 Sa'd ibn Abi Waqqas, a Companion of the Prophet, is the first Muslim official to visit China	
		664 Synod of Whitby; victory of Roman over Celtic Christianity in Britain
	*c.*700–*c.*1000 Decline of Ethiopian kingdom of Aksum	
705–15 Muslim rule established in Transoxania, Farghana and Indus Valley		
	*c.*730 Printing in China	731 Completion of Bede's *Ecclesiastical History of the English People*

Chronology 750–1000

CENTRAL ISLAMIC LANDS	NORTH AND WEST AFRICA AND THE IBERIAN PENINSULA	ASIA MINOR AND THE BALKANS
754–75 Caliphate of al-Mansur		
762 Foundation of Baghdad as caliphal capital of the 'Abbasids	**756** Umayyad 'Abd al-Rahman I (756–88) becomes ruler of Muslim Iberia (*al-Andalus*)	
763–809 Caliphate of Harun al-Rashid		
765 Death of the sixth Shi'i Imam Ja'far al-Sadiq		
	788–974 Idrisid dynasty in Morocco	*c.*780 Under constant attack from Arab armies as well as those of the Avars and Bulgars, the Byzantine Empire is confined to Anatolia and the Balkans, a third of its size in its heyday in the 6th century
	800–909 Aghlabid dynasty in Ifriqiya	
	809 Foundation of Fez	
	827 Arab conquest of Sicily	
836–92 Samarra' temporary 'Abbasid capital		**840–71** Aghlabid raids reach the Dalmatian coast
		863 Creation of Cyrillic alphabet derived from the Greek, supposedly by Saint Cyril, for the writing of Russian and Slav languages
868–905 Tulunid dynasty rules in Egypt		**865** Bulgars and Slavs in the Balkans accept Christianity
Early 900s Attacks on Basra and Damascus by extremist Shi'i Qarmatian movement	**909** Fatimid conquest of Ifriqiya; foundation of al-Mahdiya	
Early 900s Chaos and anarchy in Baghdad	**909–1171** Fatimid Caliphate	
	929 'Abd al-Rahman III al-Nasir of Córdoba (r. 912–61) takes the title of caliph and *Amir al-Mu'minin*; zenith of Muslim power in *al-Andalus*	
930 Qarmatians seize the Black Stone from the Ka'ba in Mecca; returned 20 years later		
945 Buyid seize Baghdad and take control of the caliphate		
969 Conquest of Egypt by Fatimids		
972 Foundation of Cairo (*al-Qahira*)		
972–1171 Fatimid Caliphate in Cairo		
986 Buyids defeat Qarmatians		

RUSSIA, CENTRAL ASIA, IRAN, AFGHANISTAN AND INDIA	EASTERN AFRICA, INDIAN OCEAN, SOUTHEAST ASIA AND CHINA	REST OF THE WORLD
		*c.*750–*c.*900 Decline of Mayan centres in the southern Mexican lowlands
751 Battle of Talas, on the northeastern edge of Transoxania; T'ang forces defeated by Muslim armies; Chinese prisoners bring the technique of papermaking to the West	**758** Arab and Persian pirates loot and burn the Chinese seaport of Guangzhou (Khanfu-Canton), which shuts down for five decades	**751** Pippin III, King of the Franks (751–68), founds Carolingian dynasty
		771 Charlemagne becomes ruler of most of northwestern Europe
		794 Kyoto becomes capital of Japan
818 Construction of the mausoleum of the eighth Shi'i Imam Reza at Mashhad		**800** Charlemagne crowned Emperor of Western (Roman) Empire in Rome
819–999 Samanid dynasty; indigenous Persian dynasty in Greater Iran and Central Asia		
820–73 Tahirid dynasty rules in Nishapur		
861–1003 Saffarid dynasty ruled parts of eastern Iran, Sistan, Khurasan, Zabulistan and Makran from its capital at Zaranj	**851** Arab merchant Sulayman al-Tajir visits Guangzhou and describes Chinese porcelain manufacture, tea consumption, granaries and the city's mosque	
862 Vikings found Novgorod		
	870 Composition of *Kakawin Ramayana*, an Old Javanese rendering of the Sanskrit *Ramayana*, in Java during the Medang Kingdom	
882 Kiev becomes capital of Russia		*c.*890 Beginning of Japanese cultural renaissance
		*c.*900–*c.*1000 Dominance of Yucatán by Chichen Itza
		910 Foundation of Abbey of Cluny
	939 Vietnam becomes independent of China	
		955 Otto I of Germany defeats Magyars at Lechfeld
977–1186 Ghaznavid dynasty in Zabulistan and northern India		**967** Fujiwara domination of Japan begins
	979 Sung dynasty reunites China	
		987 Accession of Capetians to throne of France
*c.*990 Composition of *Shah-nameh* by Firdawsi (*c.*942–1020)		**988** Foundation of Church of (Kievan) Rus' (later Russian Orthodox Church)
		990 Early expansion of Inca Empire
997–1030 Reign of Mahmud of Ghazna; Muslim power extended to Punjab and Gujarat; concomitant reduction in Hindu power	*c.*1000 First Iron Age settlement at Zimbabwe	*c.*1000 Vikings colonise Greenland and discover North America (Vinland)

Chronology 1000–1250

CENTRAL ISLAMIC LANDS	NORTH AND WEST AFRICA AND THE IBERIAN PENINSULA	ASIA MINOR AND THE BALKANS
		1018 The Byzantines under Basil II conquer Bulgaria after a 50 year struggle
1040 Seljuks defeat Mas'ud of Ghazna at Dandanqan	**1031** End of caliphate of Córdoba; rise of *Muluk al-Tawa'if*, the 'Party Kings'	**1045** Annexation of Armenia by the Byzantine Empire
1055 Seljuks capture Baghdad; expulsion of Buyids	**1062** Almoravids (of Berber origin) found Marrakesh	**1045–c.1080** Mass migration of Armenians to Cilicia seeking refuge from attacks from Byzantines and Seljuks
Late 1000s composition of *Siyasat-nameh* or *Siyar al-Muluk*, a 'Mirror for Princes' by the Seljuk wazir Nizam al-Mulk		**1071** Seljuks defeat Byzantines at Battle of Manzikert
1072–92 Reign of Malik Shah; apogee of Great Seljuk Sultanate	**1075** Almoravids conquer the Empire of Ghana; Yusuf Ibn Tashufin controls most of Morocco	*c.***1080** Establishment of an Armenian kingdom in Cilicia with its capital first at Tarsus, and later at Sis (to 1375)
	1085 Capture of Toledo by Alfonso VI of León	**1081** Establishment of the Seljuk sultanate of Rum based on Iconium / Konya (to 1307)
	1086 Almoravids defeat Alfonso VI of León at the Battle of Zallaqa / Sagrajas	
1099 Capture of Jerusalem by Crusaders	**1090–91** Almoravids take Aledo, Almería, Córdoba, Granada and Seville from local Muslim rulers	
	1118 Saragossa captured by Alfonso of Aragon; decline of Almoravid power	
1187 Recapture of Jerusalem by Muslim forces of Salah al-Din		
	*c.***1200** Rise of the Empire of Mali	
		1204 Fourth Crusade; sack of Constantinople
		1204–61 Establishment of the Latin Empire centred on Constantinople and Athens
1217–18 Fifth Crusade; fails in attempt to recapture Jerusalem		
1227–29 Sixth Crusade; leads to negotiated restoration of Christian control of Jerusalem		
1248–50 Seventh Crusade; King Louis IX surrenders to Ayyubid forces in Egypt		

RUSSIA, CENTRAL ASIA, IRAN, AFGHANISTAN AND INDIA	EASTERN AFRICA, INDIAN OCEAN, SOUTHEAST ASIA AND CHINA	REST OF THE WORLD
1010 Completion by Firdawsi of composition of *Shah-nameh*, the Iranian national epic	*c.*1000–*c.*1220 Apogee of Khmer Empire **1010** Atlas of China completed in 1,556 chapters	*c.*1000– *c.*1200 Toltec domination of central Mexico
1020 Death of Ibn Sina (Avicenna), philosopher **1025–26** Mahmud of Ghazna destroys temple of Shiva at Somnath (Gujarat) **1029** Conquest of Rayy by Ghaznavids **1030** al-Biruni completes *Kitab ta'rikh al-Hind* (History of India)	**1038** Hsi-Hsia state formed in northwest China	**1019–55** Cnut the Great rules England, Denmark and Norway *c.*1021 Composition of *The Tale of Genji* by Murasaki Shikibu **1044** Establishment of first Burmese national state **1054** Formalisation of Great Schism between Catholic and Orthodox churches
1058 Sumra Dynasty ends Arab domination over Sind		**1066** William Duke of Normandy invades England and becomes king after the Battle of Hastings. **1067** Gregory VII becomes pope; beginning of investiture conflict between papacy and 'national states' **1071** Fall of Bari completes Norman conquest of Byzantine Italy
	*c.*1080 Apogee of Srivijaya kingdom in Sumatra and Malaya	**1086** Compilation of the Domesday Book, a survey of land and property in England **1088** Foundation of University of Bologna
1090 Hasan-i Sabah establishes fortress of Alamut in Elburz Mountains **1095** Split over succession to Fatimid / Isma'ili caliphate causes permanent schism among Isma'ilis *c.*1100 'Umar Khayyam composes *Ruba'iyat*		**1095** Preaching of First Crusade at Clermont by Pope Urban II *c.*1100 Toltecs build their capital at Tula **1117** Foundation of University of Oxford **1122** Concordat of Worms reaches compromise on investiture conflict
	1132 China's first permanent navy established, with headquarters at Dinghai	**1147–49** Second Crusade following the fall of the crusader kingdom of Edessa
1148–1215 Establishment of Ghurid dynasty in Afghanistan, Iran and Pakistan	*c.*1150 Construction begins of Hindu temple complex at Angkor Wat (Cambodia)	*c.*1150 Prominence of Toltecs in Mexico **1154** Construction of Chartres Cathedral begun **1158** Foundation of the Hanseatic League **1189–92** Third Crusade **1192** First Shogun ruler in Japan **1193** Zen Buddhist order founded in Japan
1198 Death of Averroes (Ibn Rushd)		*c.*1200 Aztecs occupy central valley of Mexico **1200–1400** Construction of Great Zimbabwe **1202–04** Fourth Crusade; diverted from attack on Egypt by Venetian paymasters to capture and take control of Constantinople
1206 Qutb al-Din Aybak founds Delhi Sultanate	**1206** Beginnings of Mongol conquests under Chingiz Khan	**1215** Foundation of Franciscan and Dominican orders **1215** Magna Carta; King John makes concessions to English barons
	*c.*1220 Emergence of first Thai kingdom	
1237–40 Mongol conquest of the Principalities of Russia, including Kiev **1242** Mongol armies reach as far west as Wiener Neustadt, just south of Vienna	**1234** Mongols destroy Jin Empire (1115–1234) in northern China	

Chronology 1250–1500

CENTRAL ISLAMIC LANDS	NORTH AND WEST AFRICA AND THE IBERIAN PENINSULA	ASIA MINOR AND THE BALKANS
1258 Hülagü sacks Baghdad and destroys 'Abbasid caliphate **1259** Death of Möngke; beginning of collapse of empire of Chingiz Khan **1260** Mamluks defeat Ilkhans at 'Ayn Jalut **1260–77** Reign of al-Zahir Baybars I, founder of Bahri Mamluk dynasty **1291** Fall of Acre to the Mamluks **1295** Ilkhan ruler Ghazan (1295–1304), grandson of Hülagü, converts to Islam **1299** Ottoman Turks begin conquest of Anatolia **1300s** Rise of House of Osman (Ottomans) **1323** Peace concluded between Mamluks and Ilkhans **1340s** (and intermittently until 1500) Black Death bubonic plague in much of Asia and Africa, particularly affecting Egypt and Syria **c.1340–c.1400** Height of Mamluk expansion of Cairo; many mosques, madrassas and palaces built **1375** Mamluk conquest of Cilician Armenia **1382** Burji Mamluks (Qïpchaqs) take over Egypt from Bahri Mamluks (Circassians) **1400–01** Timur besieges Aleppo and sacks Damascus and Baghdad **1406** Death (in Cairo) of historian Ibn Khaldun **1485–1517** Hostilities between Mamluks and Ottomans break out on the frontier in Dhu'l-Qadr **c.1500** Mamluk advances up the Nile influence Islamisation of Nubia	**1269** Marinids capture Marrakesh from the Almohads **1276** Marinids build their new capital at Fez **c.1300** Kanuri Empire moves capital from Kanem to Borno **1362–91** Reign of Muhammad V of Granada; construction of the Alhambra **1377** Death of Ibn Batuta (b.1309) **c.1400** Songhay breaks away from Mali **1415** Portugal captures Ceuta; beginning of Portuguese African empire **1492** End of the *reconquista*; fall of Granada and end of Nasrid dynasty; expulsion of Muhammad XII from Granada by the forces of Aragon and Castile **1493–1591** Apogee of Songhay Empire under 'Askiyas; Timbuktu developed as centre of Islamic learning **1499–1502** Anti-Castilian revolts in Alpujarras; forced conversion/expulsion of Muslims from Granada (and later from other parts of Spain)	**1260** Michael VIII Paleologus restores Byzantine rule in Constantinople **1354** Ottomans cross to Europe; Gallipoli captured **1362** Ottomans capture Edirne **Late 1380s** Ottoman annexation of southern Bulgaria, Macedonia and Thrace **1389** Battle of Kosovo; Ottomans defeat Serbs and gain control of Balkans **1396** Battle of Nicopolis; Ottomans defeat Hungarians **1402** Battle of Ankara; Timur defeats Ottomans **1453** Ottoman capture of Constantinople **1461** Absorption of Byzantine enclave of Trebizond into Ottoman Empire **1473** Ottomans defeat forces of Uzun Hasan (Aq Qoyunlu) at Tercan **1475** Stephen of Moldavia defeats much larger Ottoman forces at Vaslui in modern Romania

RUSSIA, CENTRAL ASIA, IRAN, AFGHANISTAN AND INDIA	EASTERN AFRICA, INDIAN OCEAN, SOUTHEAST ASIA AND CHINA	REST OF THE WORLD
1256 Hülagü secures submission of citadel of Alamut		*c.***1250** Mayapán becomes dominant Mayan political centre in Yucatán
		1252 First gold coins minted in Europe
		1260 Expulsion of Jews from England
	1264 Qubilai Khan founds Yuan dynasty	
		1272 Death of St Thomas Aquinas
	*c.***1275** Islam comes to Aceh, Sumatra	
	1275 Marco Polo arrives in China	
1293 / 1298 Golden Horde sacks Moscow	**1279** Qubilai Khan conquers Sung Empire	
1295 Siege of Delhi by Mongols	**1293–1527** Hindu-Buddhist kingdom of Majapahit is leading power in Java	
1296–1300 Delhi Sultanate extends into northern Deccan and Gujarat		**1300–1400** Italian 'trecento'; Dante, Giotto, Petrarch; beginning of the Renaissance
		1305–76 Papacy moves from Rome to Avignon
1313–41 Under Özbek, Golden Horde converts to Islam		**1314** Battle of Bannockburn; Scotland defeats England
1339 Building of the Kremlin in Moscow		**1325** Rise of Aztecs; foundation of Tenochtitlán
		1333 End of Minamoto Shogunate in Japan
	1345–46 Traveller Ibn Batuta visits Sumatra, Malacca, Vietnam and China	**1337** Beginning of Hundred Years' War between France and England (to 1455)
	1349 First Chinese settlement in Singapore	*c.***1350** Japanese cultural revival
1370–1405 Reign of Timur (capital at Samarkand)	**1368** Foundation of Ming dynasty in China	**1375** Beginning of Chimú conquest of central Andes
1370 Hindu state of Vijaynagar becomes dominant in south India		
1382 Golden Horde under Toqtamïsh sacks Moscow		
1392 Death of Persian poet Hafiz	**1394** Thais invade Cambodia; Khmer capital moved to Phnom Penh	**1394** Expulsion of Jews from France
1398 Defeat of Toqtamïsh by Timur at Terek River		**1400** Death of Chaucer (b.1343)
1398 Sack and occupation of Delhi by Timur; collapse of Delhi Sultanate	*c.***1400** Establishment of Malacca as major port	**1415** Battle of Agincourt; Henry V of England resumes attack on France
	1427 Expulsion of Chinese from Vietnam	
1438–68 Reign of Abu'l-Khayr, Shïbanid ruler of Central Asia; descendants founded khanate of Samarkand	**1433** Death of senior Chinese (Muslim) admiral Zheng He (b.1371)	
1447 Collapse of Timurid Empire		
1451 Lodi dynasty takes over Delhi Sultanate		**1455** Gutenberg prints first book in Europe using moveable type
		1466–67 Onin Civil wars in Japan
	1471 Vietnamese annexation of Champa	*c.***1470** Incas under Tupac Inca Yupanqui conquer Chimú kingdom
		1475 Burgundy at the height of its powers
1478–80 Ivan III, first Tsar of Russia, subdues Novgorod and ends Mongol control of Moscow	**1487** Bartolomeu Dias rounds Cape of Good Hope	**1492** Columbus reaches America (Caribbean)
		1493 Treaty of Tordesillas; papacy divides New World between Portugal and Spain
	1498 Vasco da Gama sails to India and back, ending Muslim monopoly of Indian Ocean trade	**1497** Cabot reaches Newfoundland

Chronology 1500–1750

CENTRAL ISLAMIC LANDS	NORTH AND WEST AFRICA AND THE IBERIAN PENINSULA	ASIA MINOR AND THE BALKANS
1514 Battle of Çaldıran; Ottomans defeat Safavids **1516** Battle of Marj Dabiq: Ottomans defeat Mamluks; Syria/Palestine conquered **1517** Ottomans defeat Mamluks outside Cairo and conquer Egypt **1538** Ottomans conquer parts of Yemen	**1516** Barbarossa brothers capture Algiers **1519** Barbarossa brothers become Ottoman vassals, bringing Algiers and Tunis into the empire **1546** Mali Empire destroyed by Songhay **1550–70** Ottoman capture of Tripoli, Oran, Jerba and Malta **1578** Battle of the Three Kings in Morocco; destruction of Portuguese power in North Africa. **1578–1603** Reign of Ahmad al-Mansur **1591** Battle of Tondibi: Saʿdids defeat Songhay **1609–14** Expulsion of *moriscos* (Muslim converts to Christianity) from Spain	**1521** Ottomans capture Belgrade **1526** Ottomans defeat Hungarians at Mohács **1537** Ottoman-French alliance against the Habsburg empire **1570** Ottomans occupy Cyprus **1571** Battle of Lepanto; a new Holy League of Habsburgs, Venetians and the papacy destroys the Ottoman fleet, ending Ottoman sea power in the Mediterranean **1606** Peace of Zsitva Torok between Ottomans and Habsburgs, generally maintained until 1660s
1630s Ottomans expelled from Yemen **1639** Treaty of Zuhab: Baghdad and Iraq returned to Ottomans; western Iran returned to Safavids		**1669** Ottomans capture Crete from Venetians **1683** Siege of Vienna by Ottomans
1703–92 Life of Muhammad ibn ʿAbd al-Wahhab; alliance with Saʿudi family **1731** Death of Shaykh ʿAbd al-Ghani al-Nabulusi (b.1641), Syrian scholar, traveller, voice of reason **1735** Beginnings of Wahhabi movement	*c.*1700 Rise of Ashanti power (Gold Coast) **1705** Husaynid dynasty of Tunis achieves *de facto* independence from Ottomans **1711–1835** Qaramanli dynasty rules Tripolitania **1725** Establishment of Futa Jalon (Islamic) state in highlands of Guinea	**1699** Treaty of Carlowitz; Ottomans lose Hungary, Bosnia-Herzegovina, Croatia, Slavonia, Transylvania, Podolia, most of Dalmatia and the Peloponnese **1718** Treaty of Passarowitz; Austria gains parts of Serbia, Temeşvar and Wallachia from Ottomans **1718–30** 'Tulip period'; Ottoman court and elite flirtation with Western culture

RUSSIA, CENTRAL ASIA, IRAN, AFGHANISTAN AND INDIA	EASTERN AFRICA, INDIAN OCEAN, SOUTHEAST ASIA AND CHINA	REST OF THE WORLD
1501 Beginning of Safavid dynasty **1506** Sultan Sikander Lodi moves the capital from Delhi to Agra **1526** Babur defeats Lodis at Battle of Panipat; beginning of Mughal rule **1552** Russian conquest and absorption of Kazan **1555** Treaty of Amasya defines border between Safavid Iran and the Ottoman Empire **1556** Accession of Akbar reinforces Mughal rule **1556** Russian annexation of Astrakhan **1571** Akbar builds new capital at Fatehpur Sikri **1573** Akbar conquers Gujarat **1582–98** Russia annexes khanate of Sibir **1585** Mughal capital moved to Lahore; annexation of Kashmir and Sind **1587–1629** Shah 'Abbas; construction of new Safavid capital at Isfahan	**1500–88** Sultanate of Demak; major power in Java **1503** Zanzibar under Portuguese rule **1511** Portuguese capture and occupy Malacca **1520s** Islam adopted in Banjarmasin (Borneo) **1527** Sultanate of Banten established in west Java **1527** Conquest and Islamisation of the major Hindu-Buddhist state of Majapahit by Raden Patah **1534** Foundation of Funj sultanate *c.***1535** Islamisation of Lombok and Makassar **1540s** Portuguese establish outposts in Horn of Africa **1557** Portuguese enclave established at Macau **1570s** Spanish conquest of Philippines **1570s** Beginnings of Empire of Mataram in Java **1584** Phra Narai creates independent Siam	*c.***1510** Trade in African slaves to Americas begins **1519** Spanish conquest of Aztec empire begins **1520–21** Magellan crosses Pacific **1531** Pizarro begins conquest of Inca Empire **1534** Henry VIII of England breaks with Rome **1543** Copernicus publishes *De revolutionibus orbium coelestium*; confirms a heliocentric universe **1543** Portuguese traders arrive in Japan **1545** Silver mines discovered in Peru and Mexico **1559** Tobacco first introduced into Europe *c.***1560** Portuguese begin sugar cultivation in Brazil *c.***1565** Potato introduced to Europe **1581** Foundation of (English) Levant Company **1581** Foundation of Dutch Republic **1588** English defeat Spanish Armada
	1602 VOC (Vereenigde Oost-Indische Compagnie) chartered; plans drawn up to control spice trade in the East Indies	**1600** Foundation of East India Company **1603** Beginning of Tokugawa Shogunate in Japan **1603** Union of English and Scottish crowns **1607** Dutch Republic becomes independent **1607** First permanent English settlement in America (Jamestown, Virginia) **1607** First opera; *La Favola d'Orfeo* by Monteverdi **1609** Telescope invented; scientific revolution in Europe begins: Kepler, Bacon, Galileo, Descartes **1616** Deaths of Shakespeare and Cervantes **1618–48** Thirty Years' War in northern Europe **1620** *Mayflower* lands in New England **1625** Dutch settle New Amsterdam
	1619 Foundation of Batavia; beginning of over three centuries of Dutch power in East Indies **1625** Sultan Agung of Mataram conquers Surabaya **1629** Portuguese defeat Sultan Iskandar Muda of Aceh's expedition to Malacca	**1636** Foundation of Harvard College
1638 Russian eastern expansion reaches Pacific	**1640s** VOC forces Portuguese out of East Indies **1641** Dutch take Malacca from Portuguese **1644** Fall of Ming dynasty; foundation of Ch'ing **1651–82** Period of prosperity in Java under the rule of Sultan Ageng	**1642–49** English Civil War **1645** Tasman discovers Tasmania / New Zealand **1656** Completion of St Peter's in Rome **1664** New Amsterdam acquired by English from Dutch (later renamed New York)
1653 Completion of Taj Mahal **1674** Foundation of (Hindu) Maratha kingdom **1689** Treaty of Nerchinsk; first Sino-Russian pact **1690** Foundation of Calcutta by English **1691** Firangi Mahal madrasa in Lucknow built **1703** Foundation of St Petersburg **1707** Death of Awrangzib; decline in Mughal power **1709** Russia defeats Sweden at Battle of Poltava **1722** Afghan invasion of Iran; capture of Isfahan **1724–1948** Nizams of Hyderabad gain independence **1738–40** Nadir Shah invades India; sacks Delhi **1747** Ahmad Khan Abdali (Durrani) founds the kingdom of Afghanistan	**1676** Destruction of army of Mataram at Gogodog **1697** Chinese occupation of Outer Mongolia **1708–18** Sultanate of Riau enjoys a period of economic prosperity and independence from the VOC under Raja Muda Mahmud. **1714–1824** British establish outposts in Sumatra	**1684** La Salle claims Louisiana for France **1685** Birth of Bach, Handel and Scarlatti **1687** Publication of Newton's *Philosophiæ Naturalis Principia Mathematica* **1707** Union of English and Scottish parliaments **1709** Abraham Darby discovers technique of producing pig iron using coke furnaces **1718** Foundation of New Orleans **1728** Bering, explorer of the Arctic, begins Russian reconnaissance of Alaska **1730** Beginnings of Methodism in England

Chronology 1750–1830

CENTRAL ISLAMIC LANDS	NORTH AND WEST AFRICA AND THE IBERIAN PENINSULA	ASIA MINOR AND THE BALKANS
		1770 Ottoman (naval) defeat by Russia at Çeşme
1774 Treaty of Küçük Kaynarca; Ottomans obliged to allow Russia two ports on the Black Sea and free passage through the Dardanelles, as well as the right to protect the Orthodox Christians of the Ottoman Empire	**1775** Foundation of Futa Toro '*jihad* state' on the south bank of the Senegal river	**1775** Austria takes Bukovina from Ottomans
1793 Selim III attempts to reform Ottoman Empire		
1798 Napoleon invades Egypt, then under only nominal Ottoman control, and defeats Mamluk army at the Battle of the Pyramids outside Cairo		
1798 French naval forces defeated at Aboukir Bay (Battle of the Nile) by British under Nelson		
1798–1801 French occupation of Egypt		
1801 Sa'udi-Wahhabi forces invade Iraq and Syria and plunder the shrine at Karbala'	**1804–1903** Sokoto caliphate, founded as a Fulani '*jihad* state,' by 'Uthman dan Fodio, extends over much of Hausaland (Bukina, northern Nigeria / Cameroon)	
1805 Sa'udi-Wahhabi forces occupy Mecca and Medina		**1806** Ottomans lose their protectorate over Dubrovnik to Napoleon
1805–48 Muhammad 'Ali *de facto* ruler of Egypt		
1809–27 Publication (in Paris) of the *Description de l'Égypte*	*c*.**1810** Ahmadu Lobbo, a Qadiri *shaykh*, and originally a disciple of 'Uthman dan Fodio, sets up his own '*jihad* state' of Masina on the upper Niger river	
		1817 Serbian rebellion against Ottomans
1818 Destruction of Sa'udi-Wahhabi stronghold at Dir'iya by troops commanded by Ibrahim Pasha, son of Muhammad 'Ali of Egypt; execution of 'Abdullah ibn Sa'ud in Istanbul		**1821–30** Greek war of independence
		1822–23 Muhammad 'Ali campaigns in Crete, Cyprus and Rhodes on the Porte's behalf
1824–40 Egyptian forces occupy Crete	**1824** First Anglo-Ashanti war	
1826 Dissolution of the Janissaries		**1827** Egyptian-Ottoman naval defeat at Navarino by British, French and Russian forces
		1830 Greece (Attica, the Peloponnese and the nearer Aegean islands) becomes independent of Ottoman Empire
	1830 French begin conquest of Algeria	

RUSSIA, CENTRAL ASIA, IRAN, AFGHANISTAN AND INDIA

1755 Alaungpaya founds Rangoon; reunites Burma
1756 Manghïts capture the Khanate of Bukhara
1756–59 French gain control of Carnatic, India
1757 Durrani Afghans sack Delhi and Agra
1757 Destruction of Junghars by Qing Empire
1757 British defeat Nawab of Bengal and his French allies at Plassey

1760 Death of Muslim reformer Shah Wali Allah
1761 Durrani Afghans defeat Marathas at Panipat
1761 British capture Pondicherry; destruction of French power in India

1779 Agha Muhammad founds Qajar dynasty
1780 Muhammadian College founded in Calcutta
1783 Russia annexes Khanate of Crimea

1796 British conquer Ceylon
1799 Defeat and death of Tippu Sultan of Mysore
1799 Sikhs under Ranjit Singh take over Lahore and found the 'Sikh Empire'
1801 Anglo-Persian Treaty; Britain offered support against Russian economic penetration and French military intervention in Persia
1803–33 Russian expansion into western Caucasus

1817 Foundation of Hindu College, Calcutta by Raja Ram Mohan Roy, David Hare and Radhakanta Deb
1818 Marathas surrender to British
*c.***1821** Shariat Allah founds Fara'izi movement; mobilises Bengali Muslim cultivators
*c.***1823** Sayyid Ahmad Barelvi founds Barelvi or Mujahidin (Islamic reform) movement
1825 Suppression of Decembrist mutiny in Russia
1828 Treaty of Turkmanchai; Iran loses Georgia, eastern Armenia, northern Azerbaijan and much of the western Caucasus to Russia
1828 Foundation of Brahmo Samaj (Hindu reform movement) in Calcutta by Raja Ram Mohan Roy and Debendranath Tagore; start of 'Bengal Renaissance'

EASTERN AFRICA, INDIAN OCEAN, SOUTHEAST ASIA AND CHINA

1751–59 China overruns Tibet and Eastern Turkestan

1755 Jogjakarta and Surakarta successor states instituted on partition of territories of Mataram

1786 British establish themselves in Penang

1793 Lord Macartney leads British mission to the Chinese court

1803–38 Padri wars in Minangkabau, Sumatra

1819 British found Singapore as free trade port
*c.***1820s** Aceh produces half the world's pepper
1821 Defeat of Funj sultanate in the Sudan by forces of Muhammad 'Ali of Egypt
1824 Treaty of London regulates Anglo-Dutch rivalry in the East Indies and Malay Peninsula
1825–30 Anti-Dutch rebellion / *jihad* in Java led by Prince Dipanagra
1827–56 Sultan Sa'id ibn Sultan Bu Sa'idi extends Omani rule to Zanzibar and the East African coast

REST OF THE WORLD

1756 Beginning of Seven Years' War

1759–60 British conquer Quebec and Montreal
*c.***1760** Beginnings of European Enlightenment
1762 John Harrison invents marine chronometer
1762 Publication of Jean-Jacques Rousseau's *Social Contract*
1763 Treaty of Paris transfers most French North American possessions to Britain
1765 James Watt invents steam engine
1768 Captain Cook begins exploration of Pacific
1769 Richard Arkwright invents water-powered spinning frame
1770–1830 Great age of European orchestral music; Haydn, Mozart, Beethoven
1776 Publication of Adam Smith's *The Wealth of Nations* and Tom Paine's *Common Sense*
1776 Declaration of American Independence
1783 Britain recognizes American independence
1788 Foundation of British colony of Australia
1789 George Washington becomes first President of the United States of America
1789 French revolution begins
1792 Proclamation of French Republic; beginning of revolutionary wars
1792 Edmund Cartwright invents steam-powered weaving loom
1796 Edward Jenner discovers smallpox vaccine
1798 Robert Malthus publishes *Essay on the Principle of Population*

1803 Louisiana Purchase doubles size of the United States of America
1805 Battle of Trafalgar; British under Nelson defeat French and Spanish fleets
1807 Abolition of serfdom in Prussia; abolition of slave trade within British Empire
1808–28 Independence movements in Portuguese and Spanish America; 13 new states created

1812 Napoleon invades Russia and suffers a catastrophic defeat outside Moscow
1815 Napoleon defeated by British and Prussian forces at Battle of Waterloo and exiled to St. Helena; Congress of Vienna dismantles Napoleonic empire
1818 Shaka founds Zulu kingdom in southeast Africa
1819 US purchases Florida from Spain

1823 United States announces Monroe Doctrine; asserts European states should not interfere with affairs of the Americas
1825 First passenger steam railway runs between Stockton and Darlington
*c.***1826** Joseph Nicéphore Niépce takes and develops first permanent photograph in Burgundy, France

Chronology 1830–1914

CENTRAL ISLAMIC LANDS	NORTH AND WEST AFRICA AND THE IBERIAN PENINSULA	ASIA MINOR AND THE BALKANS
1831–40 Occupation of Syria and Palestine by Ibrahim Pasha of Egypt	**1830s / 1840s** Sultan 'Abd al-Qadir al-Jaza'iri campaigns against French in Morocco and Algeria	**1830** Ottomans forced to concede to the growing 'national independence' movement in Balkans; Belgrade / northern Serbia given greater autonomy
1838–43 Second Egyptian occupation of Najd	**1835** Ottomans reimpose direct rule over what is now Libya	
1839 British establish a coaling station at Aden	**1837** Sayyid Muhammad ibn 'Ali al-Sanusi founds Sanusiya order, establishing *zawiya*-s from Jaghbub to Timbuktu	
1839 *Hatt-i Şerif* of Gülhane; first reforming decree of *Tanzimat* period, sets out rights and duties of Ottoman subjects		
1853–55 Crimean War	**1850s** al-Hajj 'Umar conquers the upper Niger region and implants the Tijaniya order over much of West Africa	
1856 *Hatt-i Hümayun* guarantees full religious liberty to all Ottoman subjects		
1858 Ottoman Land Law introduced; forms the basis of land regimes of Turkey and many contemporary Arab states	**1859–60** War between Morocco and Spain; Morocco forced to pay massive indemnities	**1859** Unification of Moldavia and Wallachia ('Romania') as an Ottoman protectorate
	1860 French expansion into West Africa from Senegal	
		1863 Armenian National Assembly
1869 Opening of Suez Canal		
1869–76 Compilation of the *mecelle* or Ottoman civil code	**1870** Algeria becomes part of France	
1872 Second Ottoman occupation of Yemen; Sa'na' is taken		
1875 British government buys Khedive's shares in Suez Canal		
1876 First Ottoman Constitution		
1877–78 Russo-Turkish War; Ottoman Parliament prorogued		**1878** Treaty of Berlin; Bulgaria, Montenegro and Serbia become independent of the Ottoman Empire
1878 Treaty of Berlin; Romania. Montenegro and Serbia become independent of the Ottoman Empire; Bulgaria becomes autonomous	**1881** France occupies Tunisia and rules it as a protectorate	**1881** Greece acquires Thessaly
1882 Battle of Tall al-Kabir; British defeat Egyptian nationalists and begin military occupation	**1884** Berlin Conference on partition of Africa; Germany acquires South West Africa, Togo and Cameroon	
1882 Members of Hovevei Zion found first Zionist settlement in Ottoman Palestine		
1889 Formation of Committee of Union and Progress: to counter 'Hamidian despotism'		
1890s Sa'udis lose control of central Arabia to Rashids of Ha'il and take refuge with Amir of Kuwait		
1902 'Abd al-'Aziz ibn Sa'ud captures Riyadh, expels Rashids of Ha'il	**1900** Some 750,000 Europeans now settled in Algeria	
1904 Treaty of Da''n; Ottomans and British establish *de facto* border between Ottoman Yemen and what would become the Aden Protectorate	**1900** Copper mining begins in Katanga	
	1903 British forces end Sokoto caliphate	
1908 Young Turk Revolution; restoration of the Ottoman constitution	**1905–06** Moroccan crisis; unsuccessful attempt by Germany to advance its commercial interests	**1908** Bulgaria proclaims its independence
1909 Attempted counter-revolution in Istanbul; Sultan 'Abd al-Hamid II deposed	**1911–12** Italian invasion and conquest of Libya	**1908** Austria-Hungary annexes Bosnia-Herzegovina
	1912 French protectorate imposed on Morocco	**1912 / 1913** Balkan Wars; Ottoman Empire loses all remaining territory in Europe except eastern Thrace

RUSSIA, CENTRAL ASIA, IRAN, AFGHANISTAN AND INDIA

1830s Russia begins conquest of Kazakhstan

1839–42 First Afghan war; failed British attempt to restore their protégé Shah Shuja' to the throne of Afghanistan
1843 British annex Sind
1845–49 British conquest of Kashmir and Punjab

1853 First railways and telegraph lines in India

1856 British annexation of Awadh
1857–59 Indian revolt; deposition and exile of last Mughal Emperor Bahadur Shah II
1859 Russians capture Imam Shamil, Muslim leader in northern Caucasus
1860s Foundation of Ahl-i Hadis reform movement in northern India
1861 Emancipation of Russian serfs

1864–76 Incorporation of khanates of Bukhara, Khiva and Khoqand into the Russian Empire
1865 Ya'qub Beg of Khoqand takes Kashgar
1867 Foundation of Islamic college at Deoband

1878–80 Second Afghan war
1880s Islamic reform movement founded in Crimea by Isma'il Gasprinski
1884 Eastern Turkestan becomes part of the new Chinese province of Sinkiang Uighur (Xinjiang)
1885 Foundation of Imperial Bank of Persia
1885 Foundation of Indian National Congress
1886 British annex Upper Burma
1887 French establish Indo-Chinese Union

1894–95 Russo-Japanese war; Formosa to Japan

1901 Indian Census; Muslims 22 % of population
1905 First Russian Revolution
1905–11 Constitutional revolution in Iran
1906 Foundation of Muslim League in Dacca
1907 Anglo-Russian Entente divides control of Iran
1908-09 Major oil deposits found in Iran
1909 Morley-Minto reforms; aids Muslims in India
1914 British government buys majority share holding in Anglo-Persian Oil Company (later BP)

EASTERN AFRICA, INDIAN OCEAN, SOUTHEAST ASIA AND CHINA

1839–42 First Opium War; Britain annexes Hong Kong
1841 Sultan of Brunei cedes Sarawak to a British adventurer, Sir James Brooke

1850–64 Taiping rebellion; civil war in southern China against the Manchu-led Qing Dynasty

1856–60 Second Opium War; British, French and US forces against China

1859–63 Banjarmasin war against the Dutch
1860 Treaty of Peking; China cedes maritime province to Russia

1863–93 France establishes protectorates over Cambodia, Cochin China, Annam, Tonkin, Laos

1873–1912 Aceh war against the Dutch

1881–98 Mahdist state in Sudan

1885 General Gordon's Anglo-Egyptian army defeated by Mahdist forces at Khartoum
1886 Britain and Germany partition East Africa
1888 Sarawak, Brunei and North Borneo come under British rule; Banten rebellion against Dutch
1891 British establish protectorate over Zanzibar
1896 Battle of Adowa: Ethiopians defeat Italians
1898 Fashoda crisis; climax of territorial disputes between Britain and France in East Africa
1899 Beginning of 'dervish state' in Somalia; campaigns against British, Ethiopian and Italian forces led by Muhammad 'Abd Allah al-Hasan

1907 First rubber grown commercially in Singapore
1910 Japan annexes Korea
1911 Chinese revolution; Sun Yat Sen becomes first president of new republic

REST OF THE WORLD

1832 Death of Goethe (b.1749)
1833 Factories Act (UK); first workers' rights
1833 Abolition of slavery in British Empire
1836–49 'Great Trek' of Boer colonists from Cape; foundation of Natal, Orange Free State, Transvaal
1838 First electric telegraph (UK)
1840 Britain annexes New Zealand
1840 First postage stamps (UK)
1845 United States annexes Texas
1845–49 Irish famine; large scale emigration to US
1846–48 US conquers New Mexico and California
1848 Second Republic proclaimed in France
1848 Marx and Engels issue *Communist Manifesto*
*c.*1850 Apogee of Romantic music; Berlioz, Brahms, Chopin, Liszt, Mendelssohn, Verdi, Wagner
1854 Convention of Kanagawa; Japan opens to West
1853 David Livingstone's African explorations begin
1853 Haussmann begins rebuilding of Paris
1855 Bessemer process; mass production of steel
1859 Darwin publishes *The Origin of Species*
1860 Abraham Lincoln US president; South secedes
1860 Beginning of unification of Italy
1860s Great age of European novel; Dostoyevsky, Dickens, Dumas, Flaubert, Tolstoy, Trollope, Turgenev
1861–65 American Civil War
1861 Pasteur evolves germ theory of disease
1863 Slavery abolished in US
1863 First underground railway (London)
1866 First trans-Atlantic cable laid
1867 Karl Marx publishes *Das Kapital* (Vol.1)
1867 Russia sells Alaska to United States
1867 Dominion of Canada established
1868 Japan; Togukawa Shogunate ends; Meiji returns
1869 Completion of first transcontinental railroad (US)
1870 Declaration of papal infallibility
1870 Franco-Prussian War; Germany takes Alsace-Lorraine from France
1871 Proclamation of German Empire
1871 Suppression of Paris commune
*c.*1875 Emergence of Impressionism in painting
1876–1911 Porfirio Diaz dictator of Mexico
1879 War of the Pacific (Chile, Bolivia, Peru)
1880 First Australian frozen beef arrives in London
1884 Maxim gun perfected
1885 King of Belgium acquires Congo
*c.*1885 Daimler and Benz pioneer the automobile
1888 Dunlop patents first pneumatic tyre in Belfast
1890 Dismissal of Bismarck by Kaiser Wilhelm II
1891–1905 construction of Trans-Siberian railway
1895 Röntgen, German physicist, discovers X-rays
1896 Marconi builds first radio transmitter
1897 Herzl convenes first Zionist conference in Basle
1898 Spanish-American War; US annexes Guam, Philippines and Puerto Rico
1900 Max Planck begins to evolve quantum theory
1901 Creation of Commonwealth of Australia
1903 First successful powered flight by Wright brothers
1905 Einstein publishes his *Theory of Relativity*
1910 Formation of Union of South Africa
1913 Henry Ford develops conveyor belt car assembly
1914 Opening of Panama Canal
1914 Outbreak of First World War

© EIPL

Chronology 1914–1960

CENTRAL ISLAMIC LANDS	NORTH AND WEST AFRICA AND THE IBERIAN PENINSULA	ASIA MINOR AND THE BALKANS

1914 Outbreak of First World War; British troops invade Iraq and occupy Basra

1916–18 British-sponsored Arab revolt

1917 (British) Egyptian Expeditionary Force invades Palestine and Syria; British government 'view with favour the establishment in Palestine of a national home for the Jewish people …' (Balfour Declaration)

1918 British and Arab armies occupy Damascus

1919 Egyptian 'revolution' against British occupation

1920 Anti-British revolt in Iraq; allocation of 'A' mandates at San Remo; Iraq, Palestine and Transjordan to Britain, Lebanon and Syria to France

1922 Egypt becomes semi-independent

1929 Foundation of Muslim Brotherhood in Egypt by Hasan al-Banna

1932 Iraq mandate (under British) ended; independence granted, with King Faysal as head of state

1932 Creation of Kingdom of Sa'udi Arabia under Ibn Sa'ud

1936 Outbreak of Arab revolt in Palestine against Jewish immigration

1948 Establishment of State of Israel; first Arab-Israeli war

1952 Husayn ibn Talal becomes King of Jordan at the age of 16

1952 Army seizes power in Egypt; proclamation of republic (1953); rise of Nasser

1953 US and UK-backed coup in Iran ousts elected Prime Minister Muhammad Musaddiq

1956 Suez crisis; Anglo-French-Israeli invasion of Egypt

1958 First Lebanese Civil War

1958 Revolution in Iraq ends monarchy; establishment of a republic under 'Abd al-Karim Qasim

---

1921 Battle of Annual; defeat of Spanish troops by Moroccan forces under 'Abd al-Karim

1926 Crushing of revolt of 'Abd al-Krim in Morocco

1936–39 Spanish Civil War

1941 Germans conquer Cyrenaica and advance towards Egypt

1942 Battle of El Alamein; German defeat and retreat; Anglo-American landings in Morocco and Algeria

1954 Beginning of nationalist anti-colonial revolt in Algeria

1956 Morocco and Tunisia become independent

1915–16 Armenian genocide in eastern Anatolia

1920 Mustafa Kemal (Atatürk) leads resistance to partition of Turkey

1920–22 Greco-Turkish War over post-war territorial claims; eventually Greek army expelled from Turkey

1922 Ottoman sultanate abolished by Turkish nationalists under leadership of Mustafa Kemal (later Atatürk)

1923 Turkish Republic proclaimed; capital Ankara

1924 Atatürk abolishes caliphate

1928 Roman script introduced for Turkish language

1929 Kingdom of Yugoslavia established as an independent state, formed out of former Ottoman and Austro-Hungarian provinces (known since 1922 as Kingdom of Serbs, Croats and Slovenes)

1941 Germany and Italy invade Yugoslavia

1945 Proclamation of Yugoslav Republic; Josip Broz (Tito) (1892–1980) Prime Minister 1945–63, President 1963–80

RUSSIA, CENTRAL ASIA, IRAN, AFGHANISTAN AND INDIA	EASTERN AFRICA, INDIAN OCEAN, SOUTHEAST ASIA AND CHINA	REST OF THE WORLD
1914 British government buys majority shareholding in Anglo-Persian Oil Company, later British Petroleum (BP) **1917** Russian revolution; tsar abdicates (February) Bolsheviks take over (October) **1918** Treaty of Brest-Litovsk; Russia withdraws from First World War; civil war / foreign intervention in Russia **1919** Third Afghan War; independence gained **1919** Massacre of pilgrims at Amritsar by British **1920–22** Gandhi leads non-cooperation movement **1921** Lenin (1870–1924) introduces New Economic Policy in Russia **1925–41** Reza Khan (Pahlavi) becomes Shah of Iran after deposition of Ahmad Shah Qajar **1929** Stalin (1878–1953) becomes leader of the Soviet Union **1935** Government of India Act gives autonomy to Indian provinces **1936** Stalin launches 'Great Terror' in Russia **1942** Gandhi and Indian Congress leaders arrested **1943** German Sixth Army surrenders to Russians at Stalingrad **1947** India and Pakistan partitioned and become independent **1948** Burma and Ceylon become independent	 **1920** British overthrow 'dervish state' in Somalia **1931** Japanese invade Manchuria **1934–35** Beginning of 'Long March' of Chinese Communists under Mao Tse Tung and Chou En Lai; strategic retreat by Red Army pursued by the army of the Kuomintang led by Chiang Kai-Shek **1935–36** Italy invades and takes over Ethiopia **1940–41** Italy expelled from Somalia, Eritrea and Ethiopia **1942** Japanese forces overrun Southeast Asia in a quick succession of startling victories, including the strategic capture of British Singapore **1946** Creation of Philippine Republic **1946** Vietnamese struggle against France begins **1946-49** Civil War in China ends with Communist victory; Chiang Kai Shek retreats to Taiwan **1947** Italian empire in Africa dismembered **1950** China invades Tibet **1954** Battle of Dien Bien Phu; defeat of French forces in Vietnam by Viet Minh communist-nationalist revolutionaries **1955** Bandung Conference (Indonesia); beginnings of Non-Aligned Movement **1958–61** 'Great Leap Forward' in China **1959–75** War between North and South Vietnam **1960** Beginning of Sino-Soviet dispute	**1915** Italy enters war on side of Allies **1917** US enters war on side of Allies against Central Powers (Austria, Germany, Ottoman Empire) **1918** Armistice 11 November; end of First World War **1919** Creation of League of Nations; Treaty of Versailles; German colonies redistributed **1919** Rutherford (1871–1975) splits the atom **1919** Bauhaus school of design in Germany **1919** Alcock & Brown; first flight across Atlantic **1920s–1930s** Era of great film-makers; Chaplin, Eisenstein, Ford, Griffith, Hitchcock and Disney **1921** US Emergency Quota Act restricts immigration **1922** Mussolini takes power in Italy **1923** Tuberculosis vaccine developed in France **1925** Publication of Kafka's *The Trial* and Adolf Hitler's *Mein Kampf* **1929** Wall Street crash precipitates Great Depression **1931** Collapse of German and Austrian banks **1933** Hitler becomes Chancellor of Germany **1933** US President Roosevelt introduces 'New Deal' **1936** First public television transmission (UK) **1937** Jet engine tested (UK); nylon invented (US) **1938** *Anschluss*; unification of Germany & Austria **1939** Germany occupies Czechoslovakia and Poland; German-Soviet non-Aggression Pact; Britain and France declare war on Germany **1939** Development of penicillin (UK) **1940** Germany overruns Belgium, Luxembourg, Netherlands, France, Denmark and Norway; Battle of Britain; Italy enters war on German side **1941** Germany invades Soviet Union and declares war on US; Nazis initiate their 'Final Solution' **1941** Japan attacks US Pacific Fleet at Pearl Harbor **1942** Fermi designs first nuclear reactor (US) **1943** Italy capitulates to Allies **1944** D-Day: seaborne invasion of occupied France by Allies; advances by Red Army on eastern front **1945** Yalta Conference; defeat of Germany and suicide of Hitler; end of war in Europe **1945** US drops atomic bombs on Hiroshima and Nagasaki forcing Japan to surrender; end of war **1945** United Nations established; HQ, New York **1946** Juan Perón becomes president of Argentina **1946** First electronic computer built in US **1947** Marshall Plan for economic reconstruction of Europe; beginnings of Cold War **1948** Communist takeover in Czechoslovakia and Hungary; Berlin airlift; Yugoslavia splits with USSR **1949** Creation of German Democratic Republic; formation of NATO and COMECON **1950–53** Korean War; ends in partition of peninsula **1951** End of US occupation of Japan **1951** First nuclear power station in Arco, Idaho, US **1952** Development of contraceptive pill (US) **1953** Crick & Watson explain structure of DNA (UK) **1953** Death of Stalin; crushing of revolt in East Berlin **1955** Warsaw Pact; collective defence of Soviet bloc **1956** Major civil rights protests in Alabama, US **1956** Hungarian uprising crushed by USSR **1957** First space satellite (*sputnik*) launched by USSR **1957** European Economic Community (EEC) founded **1958** Charles de Gaulle leads Fifth Republic in France **1959** Fidel Castro takes power in Cuba **1960** Sharpeville massacre in South Africa

Chronology 1960–2014

CENTRAL ISLAMIC LANDS	NORTH AND WEST AFRICA AND THE IBERIAN PENINSULA	ASIA MINOR AND THE BALKANS

CENTRAL ISLAMIC LANDS

1963 Ba'thist / Nationalist coup in Iraq against Qasim
1964 Palestine Liberation Organisation (PLO) founded by Yasir 'Arafat

1967 Six Day War: Third Arab-Israeli War; territorial losses for Egypt, Jordan, and Syria

1970 Death of President Nasser of Egypt (b.1918)
1971 Hafiz al-Asad becomes president of Syria
1973 Fourth Arab-Israeli War; OPEC triples oil price

1975–90 Lebanese Civil War (Syria invades 1976)
1977–78 Egyptian-Israeli peace talks: Camp David Accords; Egypt recognises Israel
1979 Saddam Husayn becomes President of Iraq
1980 Outbreak of Iran / Iraq War (to 1988)
1981 Assassination of President Sadat of Egypt; succeeded by Husni Mubarak
1982 Israel invades Lebanon; expulsion of PLO from Beirut; Syrian army and air force attack Hama; Israel withdraws from Sinai
1985 Israel withdraws from Lebanon

1988 First *intifadha* by Palestinians against Israel in the Occupied West Bank and Gaza; PLO recognises State of Israel

1990 Iraq invades Kuwait
1991 Gulf War; UN coalition forces led by US invade Iraq and expel Iraq from Kuwait
1993 'Oslo Accords' between Israel and Palestinians for limited Palestinian self-rule
1994 Jordan recognises Israel
1999 Death of King Husayn of Jordan; succession of King 'Abdullah II
2000 Death of President Hafiz al-Asad of Syria; succession of Bashshar al-Asad
2000 al-Aqsa *intifadha* in occupied Palestinian territories
2001 Taliban regime overthrown in Afghanistan
2003 US led coalition invades Iraq and overthrows Saddam Husayn
2004 Israel assassinates Hamas leaders Shaykh Ahmad Yasin and 'Abd al-'Aziz al-Rantisi
2006 Israeli attack on Lebanon repelled; Hamas defeats Fatah in Palestinian legislative election
2006 Trial and execution of Saddam Husayn
2007– Sectarian civil war in Iraq
2008 Israel invades Gaza
2011–13 'Arab Spring' street protests oust Mubarak (Egypt 2011); Saleh (Yemen 2012); Morsi and the Muslim Brotherhood government (Egypt 2013)
2011– Conflict in Syria has wide regional implications
2014 'Abd al-Fattah al-Sisi, former head of military intelligence, elected president of Egypt

NORTH AND WEST AFRICA AND THE IBERIAN PENINSULA

1962 Algeria becomes independent

1967 Civil war in Nigeria to 1970; failed secession of Biafra

1976 Morocco and Mauritania partition Spanish Sahara; disputed territory renamed Western Sahara

1986 US bombs Libya in retaliation for terrorist acts
1986 Spain and Portugal join EEC

1990s Prolonged conflict in Algeria after pro-Islamist elections results annulled

2002 Civil war in Côte d'Ivoire
2004 Libya agrees to abandon weapons of mass destruction
2004 Bomb attacks on Madrid commuter trains
2005 Election of Ellen Johnson Sirleaf as president of Liberia, first elected female head of state in Africa

2010–11 'Arab Spring' revolution spreads throughout North Africa; fall of incumbent regimes in Tunisa (Ben 'Ali) and Libya (Gaddafi)
2013 Islamist insurgency of Tuareg in northern Mali threatens cultural treasures of Timbuktu
2014 Boko Haram, Nigeria's militant Islamist group, kidnap hundreds of schoolgirls

ASIA MINOR AND THE BALKANS

1963 Tito becomes president of Yugoslavia (until his death in 1980)

1967 Military coup in Greece

1974 Democracy restored in Greece
1974 Turkey invades Cyprus; occupies northern part of the island, divided by Attila Line

1981 Greece joins EEC

1991 Break up of Yugoslavia; Croatia, Macedonia, and Slovenia declare independence
1992 Civil War in Bosnia-Herzegovina; siege of Sarajevo from February 1992 to April 1996

1998–99 Fighting in Kosovo; NATO Campaign against Serbia over Kosovo
1999 Slobodan Milošević (d.2006) ousted as president of Serbia

2007 Bulgaria and Romania join European Union
2008 Kosovo declares independence

2013 Croatia joins European Union

RUSSIA, CENTRAL ASIA, IRAN, AFGHANISTAN AND INDIA	EASTERN AFRICA, INDIAN OCEAN, SOUTHEAST ASIA AND CHINA	REST OF THE WORLD
	1961–73 Increasing US involvement in Vietnam	**1961** German Democratic Republic builds Berlin Wall
		1961 Yuri Gagarin (USSR), first man in space
		1961 South Africa becomes independent republic
		1962 Second Vatican Council reforms Catholic dogma
		1962 Cuban missile crisis; threat of nuclear war
	1964 China tests first atomic bomb	**1963** President Kennedy assassinated in Dallas, US
1965 Border war between India and China	**1965** President Sukarno of Indonesia overthrown by military coup	**1964** Civil Rights Act (US) inaugurates 'Great Society'
	1965 Indo-Pakistan war	**1964** Publication of *Thoughts of Chairman Mao*
	1966–76 Cultural Revolution in China	**1965** Hart-Celler Immigration and Nationality Act abolishes racial criteria for immigration to US
	1968 Viet Cong launch Tet Offensive in Vietnam	**1966** Beginnings of violence in Northern Ireland
		1968 Assassinations of leading civil rights champions Martin Luther King and Robert Kennedy
		1968 Liberalisation in Czechoslovakia halted by USSR
		1969 Neil Armstrong (US), first man to land on moon
		1970 Salvador Allende elected President of Chile
1971 Breakaway of East Pakistan from West Pakistan; formation of Bangladesh		**1971** US initiates policy of détente towards USSR and China; US abandons gold standard
		1973 Military coup in Chile; Pinochet ousts Allende
		1973 Britain, Denmark and Ireland join EEC
	1974 Emperor Haile Selassie of Ethiopia deposed by military junta	**1974** Death of Salazar; end of dictatorship in Portugal
	1975 Communists take over Cambodia, Laos and Vietnam	**1974** Resignation of President Nixon after Watergate
		1975 Death of Franco; end of dictatorship in Spain
		1976 Jimmy Carter elected US president
1979 Iranian Revolution; overthrow of Shah Muhammad Reza Pahlavi; inauguration of Islamic Republic under Ayatullah Khumayni (d.1989)	**1979** Sino-Vietnamese war; Vietnam expels Khmer Rouge government from Cambodia	**1976–82** Military junta rules in Argentina after coup
1979 Invasion of Afghanistan by USSR (until 1989)		**1979–92** Civil wars in Nicaragua and El Salvador
1981 US hostages in Iran released after 444 days		**1980** Black majority rule established in Zimbabwe
1984 Assassination of Indira Gandhi, Indian premier		**1980** Ronald Reagan elected US president
1985–91 Mikhail Gorbachev president of USSR		**1980s** Personal Computer (PC) revolution in West
1986 Major disaster at Chernobyl nuclear power plant (Ukraine, USSR); widespread radiation fallout	**1986** Fall of Ferdinand Marcos in Philippines	**1985** Democracy restored in Bolivia, Brazil, Uruguay
1988 Gorbachev introduces greater political-economic freedoms (*glasnost*) and reforms (*perestroika*) in USSR		**1987** INF treaty between US and USSR; phased elimination of intermediate nuclear weapons
1988 Benazir Bhutto restores civilian rule in Pakistan		**1987** US stock market crashes (Black Monday)
1991 Boris Yeltsin elected first president of Russian Federation; disintegration of USSR ends with 15 republics declaring full independence of Moscow (Estonia, Latvia, Lithuania, Belarus, Ukraine, Moldova, Georgia, Armenia, Azerbaijan, Turkmenistan, Uzbekistan, Tajikistan, Kyrgyzstan, Kazakhstan)	**1989** Crushing of Chinese pro-democracy movement in Tiananmen Square, Beijing	**1987** World population reaches 5 billion
		1988 Global recognition of ozone layer being depleted
		1989–90 US military intervention in Panama
		1990 Restoration of democracy in Chile
		1990 Nelson Mandela freed after 26 years in prison
1991 Autonomous Muslim republic of Chechnya declares independence from Russia		**1993** European Union founded; stronger political ties
		1994 Nelson Mandela elected as the first black president of South Africa; apartheid dismantled
1994–95 War in Chechnya; Russia destroys capital Grozny, but guerrilla warfare continues unabated		**1994** Genocide of a million Tutsis and moderate Hutus massacred by Hutu extremists in Rwanda
1997 Reformist Muhammad Khatami elected president of Iran	**1997** Britain returns Hong Kong to China	**1994** Channel Tunnel links Britain and France
2000 Vladimir Putin becomes president of Russia; hardline policy taken against Chechen rebels	**1998** al-Qa'ida terrorist bombings of US embassies in Nairobi, Kenya and Dar es Salaam, Tanzania	**1995** Oklahoma City terrorist bombing
2002 Chechen terrorists lay siege to Moscow theatre	**1998** India and Pakistan carry out nuclear tests	**1990s** Growth of World Wide Web (internet)
2004 Chechen terrorists hold 1200 hostages at a school in Beslan, North Ossetia	**1998** Resignation of President Suharto of Indonesia and gradual restoration of democracy	**1999** Launch of European single currency (Euro)
2006-07 US and European confrontation with Iran over nuclear programme	**2002** al-Qa'ida bombings in Bali and Mombasa	**2000** First successful animal cloning (UK); human genome sequenced
2009 Anti-government riots in Iran	**2004** Tsunami in Indian Ocean kills at least 150,000	**2001** al-Qa'ida attack on World Trade Centre and Pentagon causes deaths of nearly 3000 people in US
2009–14 Hamid Karzai wins second 5-year term as president of Afghanistan	**2005** Further al-Qa'ida bombings in Bali	**2003** President Bush declares 'Global War on Terror'
2010 Major terrorist attack on Moscow Metro	**2006** World's largest hydroelectric plant inaugurated at Three Gorges Dam on Yangtze River, China	**2004** Ten new states join European Union
2013 Election of Hasan Rouhani as president of Iran; beginning of resolution of Iranian nuclear issue	**2008** Olympics held in Beijing	**2005** Death of Pope John Paul II; Benedict succeeds
	2009 North Korea detonates major nuclear device	**2005** Terrorist bombings on London Underground
	2009 Defeat of Tamil Tigers in Sri Lanka	**2006** Race riots in French cities
2013 Malala Yousafzai, Pakistani schoolgirl, shot by Taliban; addresses UN in her fight for education for all		**2007** First artificial sperm cells created
		2008 Barack Obama elected first black US president
		2008–09 Major international financial crisis / recession
		2010 Earthquake in Haiti leaves 100,000 dead;
2014 US combat troops withdraw from Afghanistan	**2013** Somali-based terrorist group, al-Shabab, lay siege to the Westgate shopping mall in Nairobi, Kenya; 67 killed, over 200 injured	**2010** Obama's health care reforms become law in US
		2013 Pope Benedict resigns; Pope Francis elected
		2013 Higgs-Boson ('God') particle 'discovered'

Glossary : Islamic and Other Terms

This glossary gives supplementary explanations of the Islamic and other non-English terms used in the text of this Atlas. The terms (shown in **bold type**) are of Arabic origin unless otherwise indicated.

Abbreviations used:

Ar.	*Arabic*
incl.	including
Ja.	*Javanese*
lit.	literally
Pers.	*Persian*
pl.	plural
sing.	singular
Sp.	*Spanish*
Tc.	*Turkic*
T.	*Turkish*

NB. Arabic plurals generally are used (eg. *awqaf*), but where it makes more sense an English plural (**-s**) may be added (eg. *zawiya-*s).

adat (*Ja.*)	(non-Islamic) customary law
agha (*T.*)	military notable
ahl al-kitab	'people of the book', monotheists with written scriptures: Christians, Jews, Sabaeans and Zoroastrians
'alim (pl. *'ulama'*)	religious scholar (pl.'clergy')
amir	prince, commander
Amir al-Mu'minin	'Prince of the Believers'; honorific title of caliph
Amir al-Umara'	'Prince of Princes'; (designation of Buyid rulers)
'amma	common people
al-Andalus	Muslim-ruled Iberia (711–1492)
Ansar	Medinan helpers / supporters of the Prophet
ashraf	*see* **sharif**
'askari	military class
atabeg (*T.*)	prince, principality
ataliq (*Tc.*)	advisers, tutors, especially of children of Mongol khans
awqaf	*see* **waqf**
a'yan (pl.)	notables
baraka	blessing
bedel-i askeriye (*T.*)	payment (made by non-Muslims) in lieu of military service
chaharbagh (*Pers.*)	irrigated garden divided into four, usually by water channels
cizye (*T.*)	*see* **jizya**
da'i	missionary
Dar al-Islam	Islamic world
da'wa	religious mission (lit. "the call")
devşirme (*T.*)	levy of (mainly) Christian youths from the Balkans for service in the Ottoman army and bureaucracy
dhimmi	non-Muslim
diwan al-kharaj	exchequer
diwan al-rasa'il	chancery
fara'id	duties of a Muslim
fatwa	legal opinion rendered by religious scholar
faqih (pl. *fuqaha'*)	legal / religious scholar
fiqh	jurisprudence
hajib	(court) chamberlain
hajj	the pilgrimage to Mecca
hasham	personal bodyguard; militia
Ifranj	'Franks', Europeans
ijtihad	interpretation of religious texts
imam	religious or prayer leader (lit. "one who stands in front")
iqta'	land grant, fief
jihad	war fought against non-Muslims or 'heretics'
jizya	canonical tax paid by non-Muslims
kafir (pl. *kuffar*)	infidel(s) (= non-monotheists)
kalam	Islamic theology
Kanuni (*T.*)	'Lawgiver' / honorific title of Süleyman II (1520–66)
katib (pl. *kuttab*)	clerk(s)
khalifa (pl. *khulafa'*)	caliph; successor to the Prophet
kharaj	tax on cereal producing land
khutba	Friday prayer (in which the name of the ruler is invoked)
madina	historic / pre-colonial city
madrasa	(religious) school

mahdi	awaited saviour	*ratu adil* (*Ja.*)	'just king' in the Javanese tradition
majlis	council / parliament	*reconquista* (*Sp.*)	Christian reconquest of Spain
Mahdiyya	millenarian movement in late 19th century Sudan	*ridda* (wars)	rejection of the authority of the Prophet after his death
mamluk	slave soldiers, commanders (lit. 'owned'); dynasty in Egypt and Syria (1250–1517)	*sadah*	*see* **sayyid**
		Saqaliba	Slavs
		sayyid (pl. **sadah**)	descendants of the family of the Prophet
mashta	common pasturage		
mecelle (*T.*)	Ottoman civil law	*shar'ia*	Islamic law
millet (*T.*)	'nation'; religious sect or confession	*sharif* (pl. **ashraf**)	descendant of the Prophet
Morisco(s) (*Sp.*)	Muslim convert(s) to Christianity in *al-Andalus*, mostly expelled in the early 17th century	*shaykh*	leader (of a tribe, religious group, etc.)
		shirk	polytheism, attributing partners to God
		sira	life / biography of the Prophet
Mudéjar(es) (*Sp.*)	Muslim(s) living under Christian rule	*suq*	covered market (bazaar)
mufti	jurisconsult	*sura*	section of the Qur'an
al-Muhajirun	'the Emigrants' (with the Prophet from Mecca to Medina in 622)	*ta'ifa* (pl. **tawa'if**)	party; faction; (more modern = confession, sect)
mujaddid	'renewer' of Islam	*tanzimat* (*T.*)	series of administrative, constitutional, legal and military reforms by various Ottoman governments in the 19th century (lit. "reordering")
muluk al-tawa'if	'party kings'; political arrangements in post-Umayyad *al-Andalus*		
al-Murabitun	'the Frontier Warriors' (Almoravids)		
al-mutalaththimun	'the veiled ones'; nickname for *al-Murabitun* / Almoravids	*tariqa* (pl. **turuq**)	(Sufi) fraternity; Sufi order
		tawhid	unity, oneness of God
muwalladun	converts to Islam in *al-Andalus*	*timar*	fiefdom, land grant
na'ib	deputy (military, civilian)	*'ulama'*	*see* **'alim**
nawab (*Ar. / Pers.*)	governor, ruler	*ulus* (*T.*)	appanage; Central Asian ruler's division of territory among heirs
naqib al-ashraf	custodian of the records of the descendants of the Prophet		
		umma	community of believers / of Muslims
nizam	title of ruler	*'urf*	customary (incl. tribal) law
paria (*Sp.*)	tribute paid by *ta'ifa* kingdoms of *al-Andalus* to Christian kingdoms of Spain	*vaqf* (*T.*)	*see* **waqf**
		wali sanga (*Ja.*)	'nine saints' of Java in the 15th / 16th centuries
presidio(s) (*Sp.*)	fortified port(s) established by Spain and Portugal on Atlantic and Mediterranean coasts of North Africa in 15th / 16th centuries		
		waqf (pl. **awqaf**)	mortmain properties, religious endowments
qanun	secular statute (Ottoman)	*wazir* (pl. **wuzara'**)	minister
qadi	judge	*yeniçeri* (*T.*)	'new troops', janissaries
qızılbaş (*T.*)	Safavid foot soldiers as described by the Ottomans (lit. "red heads")	*zakat*	canonical / Islamic taxation
		zawiya	religious lodge
ra'ya	flock, subjects	*zimmi* (*T.*)	*see* **dhimmi**

Glossary : Place Names

This glossary provides a supplementary explanation of the linguistic origins of place names within the Islamic world found on the maps of this Atlas that are shown either as their generally accepted English name-forms (e.g. Cairo; Seville), or where historic variant name-forms have been recorded on successive maps (e.g. Tana>Azak>Azov). The principal entry, recording its English or current official local name-form, is shown in **bold type** and includes the contemporary location.

The following abbreviations indicate linguistic origin:

anc.	*ancient*	*Lat.*	*Latin*
Ar.	*Arabic*	*Ma.*	*Marathi*
Ben.	*Bengali*	*Pers.*	*Persian*
Ber.	*Berber*	*Port.*	*Portuguese*
Du.	*Dutch*	*Rom.*	*Romanian*
Fr.	*French*	*Rus.*	*Russian*
Geo.	*Georgian*	*Slav.*	*Slavic*
Gk.	*Greek*	*Sp.*	*Spanish*
It.	*Italian*	*Ta.*	*Tamil*
Ja.	*Javanese*	*T.*	*Turkish*

Adalia *see* **Antalya**

Adrianople *see* **Edirne**

Aila *see* **'Aqaba**

Akkirman *see* **Bilhorod**

Alanya [Turkey]: Alaiye (*T.*)

Aleppo [Syria]: Beroea (*Gk.*); Halab (*Ar.*); Halep (*T.*)

Alexandria [Egypt]: al-Iskandariyya (*Ar.*)

Algarve [Portugal]: al-Gharb (*Ar.*)

Algeciras [Spain]: al-Jazira al-Khadra (*Ar.*)

Algiers [Algeria]: al-Jaza'ir (*Ar.*); Alger (*Fr.*)

Alhama [Spain]: al-Hamma (*Ar.*)

Almería [Spain]: al-Mariya (*Ar.*)

Amid *see* **Diyarbakır**

Ankara [Turkey]: Ancyra (*Gk.*)

'Annaba [Algeria]: Hippo (*Lat.*); Buna (*Ar.*); Bône (*Fr*)

Antakya [Turkey]: Antioch (*Gk.*)

Antalya [Turkey]: Adalia (*Gk.*)

Antioch *see* **Antakya**

'Aqaba [Jordan]: Berenice (*Gk.*); Aila (*Lat.*); Ayla (*Ar.*)

Azov [Russia]: Tana (*It.*); Azak (*T.*)

Bab al-Abwab *see* **Derbent**

Batavia *see* **Jakarta**

Beirut [Lebanon]: Biruta (*anc.*); Berytus (*Lat.*); Bayrut (*Ar.*)

Bejaïa [Algeria]: Bijaya (*Ar.*); Bougie (*Fr.*)

Beroea *see* **Aleppo**

Bijaya *see* **Bejaïa**

Bilhorod [Ukraine]: Moncastro (*It.*); Akkirman (*T.*)

Bitola [Macedonia]: Manastır (*T.*)

Boğdan *see* **Moldova**

Bombay [India]: Bom Baim (*Port.*); Mumbai (*Ma.*)

Bostra *see* **Busra**

Buna *see* **'Annaba**

Busra [Syria]: Bostra (*Gk.*)

Caesarea Cappadociae *see* **Kayseri**

Caffa *see* **Feodosiya**

Cairo [Egypt]: al-Qahira (*Ar.*)

Calcutta [India]: Kolkata (*Ben.*)

Ceuta [Spanish Morocco]: Septa (*Lat.*); Sebta (*Ar.*)

Constantinople *see* **Istanbul**

Córdoba [Spain]: Kartuba (*anc.*); Qurtuba (*Ar.*)

Dabil *see* **Dvin**

Damascus [Syria]: Dimashq (*Ar.*)

Denizli [Turkey]: Laodicea (*Gk.*)

Derbent [Daghestan]: Bab al-Abwab (*Ar.*)

Diyarbakır [Turkey]: Amid (*anc.*)

Dubrovnik [Croatia]: Ragusa (*It.*)

Durazzo *see* **Dürres**

Dürres [Albania]: Dyrrachium (*Gk.*); Durazzo (*It.*)

Dvin [Armenia]: Dabil (*Ar.*)

Dyrrachium *see* **Dürres**

Ecbatana *see* **Hamadan**

Edessa *see* **Urfa**

Edirne [Turkey]: Adrianople (*Gk.*)

Eflak *see* **Wallachia**

Emesa *see* **Homs**

Erdel *see* **Transylvania**

Feodosiya [Crimea]:Theodosia (*Gk.*); Caffa (*It.*); Kefe (*T.*)

Fez [Morocco]: Fas (*Ber.*); Fas (*Ar.*); Fès (*Fr.*)

Filibe *see* **Plovdiv**

Gibraltar [British / Spain]: Jabal Tariq (*Ar.*)

Granada [Spain]: Gárnata (*anc.*); Gharnata (*Ar.*)

Guadalajara [Spain]: Wadi al-Hijara (*Ar.*)

Guadalquivir [Spain]: al-Wadi al-Kabir (*Ar.*)

Guadiana [Spain]: Wadi Ana (*Ar.*)

Gurganj *see* **Urgench**

Hamadan [Iran]: Ecbatana (*anc.*)

Hippo (Regius) *see* **'Annaba**

Homs [Syria]: Emesa (*Gk.*); Hims (*Ar.*)

Iconium *see* **Konya**

Istanbul [Turkey]: Byzantium; Constantinople (*Lat.-Gk.*)

İzmir [Turkey]: Smyrna (*Gk.*)

İzmit [Turkey]: Nicomedia (*Gk.*)

İznik [Turkey]: Nicaea (*Gk.*)

Jakarta [Indonesia]: Sunda Kalapa / Jayakarta (*Ja.*); Batavia (*Du.*)

Jassy [Romania]: Iaşi (*Rom.*)

Jeddah [Saudi Arabia]: Jidda (*Ar.*)

Jerusalem [Palestine]: al-Quds (*Ar.*)

Kayseri [Turkey]: Caesarea Cappadociae (*Lat.*)

Kairouan [Tunisia]: al-Qayrawan (*Ar.*)

Kefe *see* **Feodosiya**

Konya [Turkey]: Iconium (*Gk.*)

Larisa [Greece]: Yenişehir (*T.*)

Lisbon [Portugal]: Olissipo (*Lat.*); al-Ushbuna (*Ar.*); Lisboa (*Port.*)

Madras [India]: Chennai / Chennapattanam (*Ta.*)

Malatya [Turkey]: Melitene (*Gk.*)

Manastır *see* **Bitola**

Marrakesh [Morocco]: Marrakec (*Ber.*); Marrakush (*Ar.*)

Mecca [Saudi Arabia]: Makka (*Ar.*)

Medina [Saudi Arabia]: Yathrib (*Ar.*); al-Madinah (*Ar.*)

Meknès [Morocco]: Miknas (*Ber.*); Miknasa (*Ar.*)

Melitene *see* **Malatya**

Moldova [Romania]: Boğdan (*T.*)

Moncastro *see* **Bilhorod**

Mosul [Iraq]; al-Mawşil (*Ar.*); Musul (*T.*)

Nicaea *see* **İznik**

Nicomedia *see* **İzmit**

Niš [Serbia]: Naissus (*Gk. / Lat.*); Niş (*T.*)

Oran [Algeria]: Wahran (*Ar.*)

Plovdiv [Bulgaria]: Philippopolis (*Gk.*); Filibe (*T.*)

Ragusa *see* **Dubrovnik**

Rayy *see* **Tehran**

Rusafa [Syria]: Sergiopolis (*Gk.*)

Salonica [Greece]; Thessaloniki (*Gk.*); Selanik (*T.*)

Sarajevo [Bosnia-Herzegovina]: Saraybosna (*T.*)

Selanik *see* **Salonica**

Sergiopolis *see* **Rusafa**

Serres [Greece]: Siroz (*T.*)

Seville [Spain]: Ishbiliya (*Ar.*); Sevilla (*Sp.*)

Skopje [Macedonia]: Üsküp (*T.*)

Smyrna *see* **İzmir**

Sofia [Bulgaria]: Serdica (*Lat.*); Sredets (*Slav.*); Sofya (*T.*)

Sunda Kalapa *see* **Jakarta**

Tana *see* **Azov**

Tangier [Morocco]: Tanja (*Ber.*); Tanja (*Ar.*); Tanger (*Fr.*)

T'bilisi [Georgia]: Tpilisi (*Geo.*); Tiflis (*Rus.*)

Tehran [Iran]: Rayy (*Pers.*)

Tétouan [Morocco]: Tittawin (*Ber.*); Tittawan (*Ar.*)

Toledo [Spain]: Toletum (*Lat.*); Tulaytula (*Ar.*)

Transylvania [Romania]: Erdel (*T.*)

Trebizond [Turkey]: Trapezus (*Gk.*); Trabzon (*T.*)

Tripoli [Libya; Lebanon]: Tarabulus (*Ar.*); Trablus (*T.*)

Urfa [Turkey]: Edessa (*Gk.*)

Urgench [Uzbekistan]: Gurganj (*T.*)

Üsküp *see* **Skopje**

Wallachia [Romania]: Eflak (*T.*)

Yathrib *see* **Medina**

Yenişehir *see* **Larisa**

Zanzibar [Tanzania]: Zangibar (*Pers.*); Zanjibar (*Ar.*)

Bibliography

Atlases and Works of Reference

Ágoston, Gábor, and Bruce Alan Masters, *Encyclopedia of the Ottoman Empire*, New York, Facts on File, 2008.

Ajayi, J.F. Ade, and Michael Crowder, *Historical Atlas of Africa*, Harlow, Longman, 1985.

Barraclough, Geoffrey, and Richard Overy (eds.), *The Times History of the World*, new edition, London, Times Books, 1999.

Bosworth, Clifford Edmund, *The New Islamic Dynasties: A Chronological and Genealogical Manual*, New York and Edinburgh, Columbia University Press and Edinburgh University Press, 1996.

Bregel, Yuri, *An Historical Atlas of Central Asia*, Leiden, Brill, 2003.

Brice, William (ed.), *An Historical Atlas of Islam*, Leiden, Brill, 1981.

Chew, Allen F., *An Atlas of Russian History: eleven centuries of changing borders*, New Haven CT, Yale University Press, 1967.

Cribb, Robert, *Historical Atlas of Indonesia*, Honolulu, University of Hawai'i Press, 2000.

Darby, H.C., and Harold Fullard (eds.), *The New Cambridge Modern History, Vol. XIV–Atlas*, Cambridge, Cambridge University Press, 1970.

Deutsche Forschungsgemeinschaft, Bonn, and Institute for Scientific Co-operation, Tübingen, *Tübinger Atlas des Vorderen Orients (TAVO) = Tübingen Atlas of the Near and Middle East,* revised edition in German and English, Berlin and London, Gerlach Verlag, 1983.

Gailey, Harry A., *The History of Africa in Maps*, Chicago, Denoyer-Geppert, 1967.

Gilbert, Michael, *The Dent Atlas of Russian History*, second edition, London, Dent, 1993.

Habib, Irfan, *An Atlas of the Mughal Empire*, Delhi, Oxford University Press, 1982.

Hattstein, Markus, and Peter Delius (eds.), *Islam: Art and Architecture*, London, Könemann, 2000.

Kazhdan, Alexander, P. (ed.), *The Oxford Dictionary of Byzantium, Vols. I–III*, New York and Oxford, Oxford University Press, 1991.

Kennedy, Hugh N. (ed.), *An Historical Atlas of Islam*, second revised edition, Leiden, Brill, 2002.

Magocsi, Paul Robert, *Historical Atlas of Central Europe: from the early fifth century to the present.* second revised edition, Seattle, University of Washington Press, 2002.

Mu'nis, Husayn, *Atlas ta'rikh al-Islam* (Atlas of Islamic History), Cairo, al-Zahra li'l-I'lam al-'Arabi, 1987.

Pitcher, Donald E., *An Historical Geography of the Ottoman Empire: from earliest times to the end of the sixteenth century*, Leiden, Brill, 1972.

Pluvier, Jan M., *Historical Atlas of South-East Asia*, Leiden, Brill, 1995.

Riley-Smith, Jonathan (ed.), *The Atlas of the Crusades*, London, Times Books, 1991.

Robinson, Francis, *Atlas of the Islamic World since 1500*, New York and Oxford, Facts on File, 1982.

Roolvink, Roelof, *Historical Atlas of the Muslim Peoples*, Amsterdam, Djambatan, 1957.

Ruthven, Malise, with Azim Nanji, *Historical Atlas of Islam*, Cambridge MA, Harvard University Press, 2004.

Schwartzberg, Joseph E. (ed.), *A Historical Atlas of South Asia*, 2nd impression, New York and Oxford, Oxford University Press, 1992.

The Times Atlas of European History, second edition, London, Times Books, 1997.

The Times (Comprehensive) Atlas of the World, thirteenth edition, London, Times Books, 2011.

Books and Articles

Abu Lughod, Janet, *Before European Hegemony: the World System A.D. 1250–1350*, New York and Oxford, Oxford University Press, 1989.

Abun-Nasr, Jamil M., *A History of the Maghrib in the Islamic Period*, Cambridge, Cambridge University Press, 1987.

Ajayi, J.F. Ade, and Michael Crowder, *History of West Africa, Vol. 1*, 3rd edn., London, Longman, 1985.

Adib Mahjul, Cesar, *Muslims in the Philippines*, Quezon, University of the Philippines Press, 1999.

Allsen, Thomas T., *Culture and Conquest in Mongol Eurasia*, Cambridge, Cambridge University Press, 2001.

Amitai-Preiss, Reuven, and David O. Morgan (eds.), *The Mongol Empire and its Legacy*, Leiden, Brill, 1999.

Arak'el (of Tabriz), Vardapet, (trs. George A. Bournoutian), *Book of History (Armenia / Persia, 1602–66)* Costa Mesa, CA, Mazda Publishers, 1998.

Arié, Rachel, *L'Occident Musulman au Bas Moyen Age*, Paris, de Boccard, 1992.

_____, *Etudes sur la Civilisation de l'Espagne Musulmane*, Leiden, Brill, 1990.

Barnett, Richard B., *North India Between Empires: Awadh, the Mughals, and the British*, Berkeley and Los Angeles, University of California Press, 1980.

Birken, Andreas, *Die Provinzen des Osmanischen Reiches*, Wiesbaden, Ludwig Reichert Verlag (Beihefte zum Tübinger Atlas des Vorderen Orients, Reihe B, Geisteswissenschaften no 13), 1976.

Bosworth, C. E., *The Later Ghaznavids: Splendour and Decay. The Dynasty in Afghanistan and Northern India, 1040–1186*, Edinburgh, Edinburgh University Press, 1977.

_____, *The Ghaznavids. Their Empire in Afghanistan and Eastern Iran, 994–1040*, Edinburgh, Edinburgh University Press, 1963.

Bournoutian, George A., *Russia and the Armenians of Transcaucasia, 1797–1889, A Documentary Record*, Costa Mesa, CA, Mazda Publishers, 1998.

_____, *Khanate of Erevan under Qajar Rule, 1795–1828*, Costa Mesa, CA, Mazda Publishers, 1992.

_____, *Eastern Armenia in the Last Decades of Persian Rule 1807–1828*, Costa Mesa, CA, Mazda Publishers, 1992.

Brett, Michael, *The Rise of the Fatimids: The World of the Mediterranean and the Middle East in the Tenth Century*, Leiden, Brill, 2001.

Brower, Daniel R., and Edward J. Lazzerini (eds.), *Russia's Orient: Imperial Borderlands and Peoples, 1700–1917*, Bloomington, IN, Indiana University Press, 2001.

Brummett, Palmira, *Ottoman Seapower and Levantine Diplomacy in the Age of Discovery*, Albany, NY, State University of New York Press, 1994.

Bulliet, Richard, *Conversion to Islam in the Medieval Period; an Essay in Quantative History*, Cambridge, MA, Harvard University Press, 1979.

Busse, Heribert, *Chalif und Grosskönig: Die Buyiden im Iraq (945–1055)*, Beirut and Wiesbaden, Franz Steiner Verlag, 1969.

Cahen, Claude (trs. J. Jones-Williams), *Pre-Ottoman Turkey: a general survey of the material and spiritual culture and history c.1071–1330*, London, Sidgwick and Jackson, 1968.

Cahen, Claude (trs. P. M. Holt), *The Formation of Turkey: the Seljukid Sultanate of Rum: Eleventh to Fourteenth Century*, London, Longman, 2001.

Chaudhuri, K.N., *Asia before Europe: Economy and Civilisation of the Indian Ocean from the Rise of Islam to 750*, Cambridge, Cambridge University Press, 1990.

_____, *Trade and Civilisation of the Indian Ocean; an Economic History from the Rise of Islam to 1750*, Cambridge, Cambridge University Press, 1986.

Choueiri, Youssef M. (ed.), *A Companion to the History of the Middle East*, Oxford, Blackwell, 2005.

Cissoko, Sékéné-Mody, *Histoire de l'Afrique Occidental; moyen âge et temps modernes, VIIe siècle–1850*, Paris, Présence Africaine, 1966.

Clarence-Smith, William Gervase, 'South-East Asia and China to 1910', in Francis Robinson (ed), *The New Cambridge History of Islam: Volume 5…*, 2010, pp. 240–68.

Collins, Robert O., and James A. Burns, *A History of Sub-Saharan Africa*, Cambridge, Cambridge University Press, 2007.

Cook, Michael, *Muhammad*, Oxford, Oxford University Press, 1983.

Daftary, Farhad, *A Short History of the Isma'ilis*, Edinburgh, Edinburgh University Press, 1998.

_____, *The Isma'ilis, their History and Doctrines*, Cambridge, Cambridge University Press, 1990.

Dale, Stephen F., *The Muslim Empires of the Ottomans, Safavids and Mughals*, Cambridge, Cambridge University Press, 2010.

_____, *The Garden of the Eight Paradises: Babur and the Culture of Empire in Central Asia, Afghanistan and India*, Leiden, Brill, 2004.

Dallal, Ahmad, 'The Origins and Objectives of Islamic Revivalist Thought, 1750–1850', *Journal of the American Oriental Society*, 113, 3, 1993, pp. 341–59.

Donner, Fred McGraw, *The Early Islamic Conquests*, Princeton, NJ, Princeton University Press, 1981.

Dunn, Ross E., *Resistance in the Desert: Moroccan Responses to French Imperialism 1881–1912*, London, Croom Helm, 1977.

Egger, Vernon O., *A History of the Muslim World since 1260: the Making of a Global Community*, Upper Saddle River NJ, Prentice Hall, 2007.

_____, *A History of the Muslim World to 1405: the Making of a Civilization*, Upper Saddle River NJ, Prentice Hall, 2004.

Elisséeff, Nikita, *l'Orient Musulman au Moyen Age 622–1260*, Paris, Armand Colin, 1977.

Bibliography

Feener, R. Michael, 'New networks and new knowledge: migrations, communication and the reconfiguration of the Muslim community in the nineteenth and early twentieth centuries', in Robert Hefner (ed.), *The New Cambridge History of Islam: Volume 6...*, 2010, pp. 39–68.

—————————, 'South-East Asian localisations of Islam and participation within a global umma, *c.*1500–1800', in David O. Morgan and Anthony Reid (eds.), *The New Cambridge History of Islam: Volume 3...*, 2010, pp. 470–503.

Frye, Richard N., *The Golden Age of Persia: the Arabs in the East*, London, Weidenfeld and Nicholson, 1975.

Ghirshman, Roman, *L'Iran des origines à l'Islam*, Paris, Payot, 1951.

Goitein, S. D. (revised and edited by Jacob Lassner), *A Mediterranean Society: an Abridgement in One Volume*, Berkeley and Los Angeles, CA, University of California Press, 1999.

Gommans, Jos J.L., *The Rise of the Indo-Afghan Empire c.1710–1780*, Leiden, Brill, 1995.

Grabar, Oleg, *The Alhambra*, Cambridge MA, Harvard University Press, 1978.

Guichard, Pierre, *L'Espagne et la Sicile Musulmanes aux XIe et XIIe siècles*, Lyon, Presses Universitaires de Lyon, 1991.

Hansen, Walder, *The Peacock Throne: the Drama of Mogul India*, New York, Holt, Rinehart and Winston, 1972.

Haarmann, Ulrich (ed.), *Geschichte der Arabischen Welt*, Munich, C. H. Beck Verlag, 1994.

Hartog, Leo de, *Russia and the Golden Horde: The History of the Russian Principalities and the Golden Horde, 1221–1502*, London, I.B. Tauris, 1996.

Harvey, L.P., *Muslims in Spain, 1500–1614*, Chicago, University of Chicago Press, 2005.

—————————, *Islamic Spain, 1251 to 1500*, Chicago, University of Chicago Press, 1992.

Hassan, Yusuf Fadl, *The Arabs and the Sudan from the seventh to the early sixteenth century*, Edinburgh, Edinburgh University Press, 1967.

Hefner, Robert (ed.), *The New Cambridge History of Islam: Volume 6, Muslims and Modernity : Culture and Society since 1800*, Cambridge, Cambridge University Press, 2010.

—————————, 'South-East Asia from 1910', in Francis Robinson (ed.), *The New Cambridge History of Islam: Volume 5...*, 2010, pp. 591–622.

Hess, Andrew C., *The Forgotten Frontier, a History of the Sixteenth-Century Ibero-African Frontier*, Chicago, IL, University of Chicago Press, 1978.

Hillenbrand, Carole, *The Crusades: Islamic Perspectives*, Edinburgh, Edinburgh University Press, 1999.

Hillgarth, J.N., *The Spanish Kingdoms 1250–1516*, Vols. 1–2, Oxford, Oxford University Press, 1978.

Hiskett, Mervyn, *The Development of Islam in West Africa*, London and New York, Longman, 1984.

Holt, P.M., 'The Mamluk Institution', in Youssef M. Choueiri (ed.), *A Companion to the History of the Middle East*, Oxford, Blackwell, 2005, pp. 154–69.

Hourani, Albert, *A History of the Arab Peoples*, Cambridge, MA, Harvard University Press, 1991.

Hunwick, John, 'Songhay, Bornu and Hausaland in the sixteenth century', in J.F. Ade Ajayi and Michael Crowder (eds.), *History of West Africa, Vol. 1*, 3rd edn., London, Longman, 1985, pp. 324–56.

Imber, Colin, *The Ottoman Empire, 1300–1650*, Basingstoke, Palgrave Macmillan, 2002.

İnalcik, Halil, with Donald Quataert, *An Economic and Social History of the Ottoman Empire 1300–1914*, Cambridge, Cambridge University Press, 1994.

Irwin, Robert, *The Middle East in the Middle Ages: the Early Mamluk Sultanate 1250–1382*, Carbondale and Edwardsville, IL, Southern Illinois University Press, 1986.

Jackson, Peter, *The Delhi Sultanate: A Political and Military History*, Cambridge, Cambridge University Press, 1999.

Jelavich, Charles, and Barbara Jelavich, *The establishment of the Balkan National States, 1804–1920*, Seattle and London, University of Washington Press, 1977.

Jones, Philip James, *The Italian City State*, Oxford, Clarendon Press, 1997.

Julien, Charles-André (ed. and rev. R. Le Tourneau, trs John Petrie, ed. C.C. Stewart), *History of North Africa: Tunisia: Algeria: Morocco: From the Arab Conquest to 1830*, London, Routledge and Kegan Paul, 1970.

Kaegi, Walter E., *Byzantium and the Early Islamic Conquests*, Cambridge, Cambridge University Press, 1992.

Kennedy, Hugh, *Muslim Spain and Portugal: a Political History of al-Andalus*, London and New York, Longman, 1996.

—————————, *The Prophet and the Age of the Caliphs: The Islamic Near East from the sixth to the eleventh century*, London and New York, Longman, 1986.

Khodarkovsky, Michael, *Russia's Steppe Frontier: the Making of a Colonial Empire 1500–1800*, Bloomington, IN, Indiana University Press, 2002.

Klausner, Carla, *The Seljuk Vezirate; a Study of Civil Administration 1055–1194*, Cambridge, MA, Harvard University Press, 1973.

Laffan, Michael Francis, *Islamic nationhood and colonial Indonesia: the umma below the winds*, New York, Routledge, 2003.

Lagardère, Vincent, *Les Almoravides: le jihad Andalou (1106–1143)*, Paris, L'Harmattan, 1998.

Lapidus, Ira, *A History of Islamic Societies*, Cambridge, Cambridge University Press, 1988.

Lev, Yaacov, *Saladin in Egypt*, Leiden, Brill, 1999.

_____, *State and Society in Fatimid Egypt*, Leiden, Brill, 1991.

Levtzion, Nehemia, 'Islam in the Bilad al-Sudan to 1800', in Nehemia Levtzion and Randall L. Pouwels (eds.),
   The History of Islam in Africa, Athens, OH, Ohio University Press, 2000, pp. 63–91.

Levtzion, Nehemia, and Randall L. Pouwels (eds.), *The History of Islam in Africa*, Athens, OH,
Ohio University Press, 2000.

Levtzion, Nehemia, and Randall L. Pouwels, 'Introduction: Patterns of Islamization and Varieties of Religious Experience
   among Muslims of Africa,' in Nehemia Levtzion and Randall L. Pouwels (eds.), *The History of Islam in Africa*,
   Athens, OH, Ohio University Press, 2000, pp. 1–18.

Liaou, Angeliki, and Henry Maguire (eds.), *Byzantium: a World Civilization*, Washington DC, Dumbarton Oaks, 1992.

Lombard, Michel, (trs. Joan Spencer), *The Golden Age of Islam*, Amsterdam, Oxford and New York,
   North-Holland / American Elsevier, 1975.

Lopez, Robert S., and Irving W. Raymond, *Medieval Trade in the Mediterranean World: Illustrative Documents Translated
   with Introductions and Notes*, New York, Columbia University Press, (1955), 1990.

Mantran, Robert, *L'Expansion musulmane (VIIe-XIe siècles)*, Paris, Presses Universitaires de France, 1969.

Marshall, P.J. (ed.), *The Eighteenth Century in Indian History: Evolution or Revolution*, Delhi, Oxford University Press, 2003.

Martin, Bradford G., 'Arab Migrations to East Africa in Medieval Times', *International Journal of African
   Historical Studies*, 7, 1974, pp. 367–90.

McNeill, William H., *A World History*, 4th edition, Oxford, Oxford University Press, 1999.

Metcalf, Barbara Daly, *Islamic revival in British India: Deoband, 1860–1900*, Princeton, NJ, Princeton University Press, 1982.

Metcalf, Barbara Daly, and Thomas R. Metcalf, *A Concise History of India*, 3rd edition, Cambridge,
   Cambridge University Press, 2012.

Momen, Moojan, *An Introduction to Shi'i Islam*, New Haven, CT, Yale University Press, 1985.

Morgan, David O., *Medieval Persia 1040–1797*, London, Longman, 1988.

_____, *The Mongols*, Oxford, Basil Blackwell, 1986.

Morgan, David O., and Anthony Reid (eds.), *The New Cambridge History of Islam: Volume 3, The Eastern Islamic World,
   Eleventh to Eighteenth Centuries*, Cambridge, Cambridge University Press, 2010.

Newman, Andrew J., *Safavid Iran: Rebirth of a Persian Empire*, London, I.B. Tauris, 2009.

Ostrowksi, Donald, *Muscovy and the Mongols: Cross Cultural Influences on the Steppe Frontier, 1304–1489*, Cambridge,
   Cambridge University Press, 1998.

Peters, F. E., *Muhammad and the Origins of Islam*, Albany, NY, State University of New York Press, 1994.

Pouwels, Randall L., *Horn and Crescent: Cultural change and traditional Islam on the East African coast, 800–1900*,
   Cambridge, Cambridge University Press, 1987.

Powell, James M., *Muslims under Latin Rule 1100–1300*, Princeton, NJ, Princeton University Press, 1990.

Power, Daniel, and Naomi Standen (eds.), *Frontiers in Question: Eurasian Borderlands, 700–1700*, Basingstoke,
   Macmillan, 1999.

Raymond, André, *Grandes villes arabes à l'époque Ottomane*, Paris, Sindbad, 1985.

Reid, Anthony, 'Islam in South-East Asia and the Indian Ocean littoral, 1500–1800: expansion, polarization, synthesis',
   in David O. Morgan and Anthony Reid, *The New Cambridge History of Islam: Volume 3…*, 2010, pp. 427–69.

_____, *Charting the Shape of Early Modern Southeast Asia*, Chiang Mai, Thailand, Silkworm Books, 1999.

_____, *Southeast Asia in the Age of Commerce, 1450–1680: Volume Two: Expansion and Crisis*, New Haven, CT,
   Yale University Press, 1993.

_____, *Southeast Asia in the Age of Commerce, 1450–1680: Volume One: The Lands Below the Winds*,
   New Haven, CT, Yale University Press, 1988.

Reilly, Bernard F., *The Medieval Spains*, Cambridge, Cambridge University Press, 1993.

Riasanovsky, Nicholas V., and Mark D. Steinberg, *A History of Russia*, 7th edition, Oxford, Oxford University Press, 2005.

Richards, John F., *The Mughal Empire*, Cambridge, Cambridge University Press, 1996.

Ricklefs, M.C., *A History of Modern Indonesia*, 4th edn., Stanford, CA, Stanford University Press, 2008.

Rippin, Andrew, *Muslims: their Religious Beliefs and Practices*, 2nd edition, London and New York, Routledge, 2001.

Robb, Peter, *A History of India*, London, Basingstoke, 2002.

Robinson, David, *The Holy War of Umar Tal: the Western Sudan in the mid-nineteenth century*, Oxford,
   Clarendon Press, 1985.

Bibliography

Robinson, Francis (ed.), *The New Cambridge History of Islam: Volume 5: The Islamic World in the Age of Western Dominance*, Cambridge, Cambridge University Press, 2010.

Saad, Elias N., *Social History of Timbuktu*, Cambridge, Cambridge University Press, 1983.

Safran, Janina M., *The Second Umayyad Caliphate: the Articulation of Caliphal Legitimacy in al-Andalus*, Cambridge, MA, Harvard University Press, 2000.

Sanders, Paula A., 'The Fatimid state, 969–1171', in Carl F. Petry (ed.), *The Cambridge History of Egypt; Volume I: Islamic Egypt, 640–1517*, Cambridge, Cambridge University Press, 1998, pp. 151–74.

Saunders, J.J., *The History of the Mongol Conquests*, London, Routledge and Kegan Paul, 1971.

Schimmel, Annemarie, *The Empire of the Great Mughals: History, Art and Culture*, London, Reaktion Books, 2004.

Sivers, Peter von, 'Egypt and North Africa', in Nehemia Levtzion and Randall L. Pouwels (eds.), *The History of Islam in Africa*, Athens, OH, Ohio University Press, 2000, pp. 21–54.

Sourdel, Dominique, trs. J. Montgomery Watt, *Medieval Islam*, London, Routledge and Kegan Paul, 1979.

Stavrianos, L.S., *The World to 1500: a Global History*, Eaglewood Cliffs, NJ, Prentice Hall, 1970.

Streusand, Douglas E., *The Formation of the Mughal Empire*, Delhi, Oxford University Press, 1989.

Sugar, Peter, *Southeastern Europe under Ottoman Rule, 1354–1804*, Seattle, University of Washington Press, 1977.

Tarling, Nicholas, *Southeast Asia: a Modern History*, Melbourne, Oxford University Press, 2005.

Tate, D.J.M., *The Making of Modern South-East Asia: Volume I, The European Conquest*, Kuala Lumpur and Singapore, Oxford University Press, 1971.

Todorov, Nikolai, *The Balkan City 1400–1900*, University of Washington Press, Seattle WA and London, 1983.

Treadgold, Warren, *A Concise History of Byzantium*, Basingstoke, Palgrave, 2001.

Vryonis, Speros, *Byzantium and Europe*, New York, Harcourt Brace, 1967.

Wade, Geoff, 'Early Muslim Expansion in South-East Asia, eighth to fifteenth centuries', in David O. Morgan and Anthony Reid (eds.), *The New Cambridge History of Islam: Volume 3…*, 2010, pp. 366–408.

Walker, Paul E., 'The Isma‘ili Da‘wa and the Fatimid Caliphate', in Carl F. Petry (ed.), *The Cambridge History of Egypt; Volume I: Islamic Egypt, 640–1517*, Cambridge, Cambridge University Press, 1998, pp. 120–50.

Walz, Terence, *Trade between Egypt and Bilad as-Sudan, 1700–1820*, Cairo, Institut Français d'Archéologie Orientale du Caire, 1978.

Wasserstein, David, *The Rise and Fall of the Party Kings: Politics and Society in Islamic Spain 1002–1086*, Princeton, NJ, Princeton University Press, 1985.

Whittow, Mark, *The Making of Byzantium, 600–1025*, Berkeley and Los Angeles, University of California Press, 1996.

Wink, André, *al-Hind: the Making of the Indo-Islamic World, Volume III, Indo-Islamic Society 14th–15th Centuries*, Leiden, Brill, 2004.

_____, *al-Hind: the Making of the Indo-Islamic World, Volume II, The Slave Kings and the Islamic Conquest, 11th–13th Centuries*, Leiden, Brill, 1997.

Woods, John E., *The Aqquyunlu: Clan, Confederation, Empire*, revised edition, Salt Lake City, University of Utah Press, 1999.

Index

This index lists the principal subjects and names referred to in the map texts, which have been subdivided into three categories:

(A) **THEMES** (wars; treaties; movements; other features and events).
(B) **PERSONAL AND GROUP NAMES** (people[s]; dynasties; tribes; other ethnic groups and collectivities).
(C) **PLACE NAMES** (towns; capitals; regions; rivers; mountains; other physical features).

The arrangement is in word-by-word alphabetical order with the headwords shown in **bold type**. Supplementary explanations are given where appropriate.

In names beginning with the Arabic "**al-**", the "**al-**" has been ignored in alphabetization; thus "**al-Nasir**" appears under "**N**".

Short forms of names with "**Ibn**", as for "**Ibn Tumart**", appear under "**I**".

The numerical references are to the map numbers on which the names appear in the accompanying texts.

(A) INDEX OF THEMES

Aceh war, 1873–1913, in Sumatra against Dutch 43
'adat (customary law), in Southeast Asia, 43
Afghan Wars, 1839–42: 1878–80: 1919, 37
agriculture 19, 42
Aligarh movement, in Muslim India 36
Amasya, Treaty of, 1555, between Ottomans and Safavids 31
Amir al-Mu'minin, Commander of the Faithful 14
Amir al-Umara', Prince of the Princes 10
Anglo-Persian Oil Company 37
animist religion 3
anti-colonial resistance 42, 43
apostasy 2
appanage or 'family sovereignty' 16, 21, 25, 32
Arabic (language) 1, 4
Armenian genocide 39
Armenian patriarchate 39
Avestan scriptures 2
'Ayn Jalut, Battle of, 1260, between Mongols and Mamluks 21

Badr, Battle of, 624, between the followers of the Prophet Muhammad and the Meccans 3
Bahriya, elite force of last Ayyubid ruler, al-Salih Ayyub 22
Balkan Wars, 1912–13: 1913, 39
Barelvi reform movement in Muslim India 36, 43
Batavia, siege of, 1629: Dutch forces besieged by Javans 42
Berlin, Congress of, 1878, 37
Black Stone, part of the Ka'ba in Mecca 10
bubonic plague 22, 23
Bucharest, Treaty of, 1812, between Ottoman Empire and Russia 38

Cairo citadel 18, 23
Çaldıran, Battle of, 1514, between Ottomans and Safavids 23
camels 19
caravan trade routes 15
     see also **Silk Road: trans-Saharan trade**
Carlowitz, Treaty of, 1699, between Austrians and Ottomans 31
cassia 43
Catalan Map (1375) 15
Catholic Church 2
cavalry 25, 29
censuses 25, 31, 36
Central Asian cavalry tactics 29
Çeşme, Battle of, 1770, between Ottomans and Russians 38
Chain Tower, fortification on the Nile 18
chamberlain (*hajib*) at 'Abbasid court 5
Christian settlers in the Levant after/during the Crusades 17
Christianity
     conversion to 27, 32
     division of Christendom 2
     Nestorianism 21
     Orthodox Church 2, 5, 24, 38

city-states 33
civil law (Ottoman) 39
civil wars 7, 12, 28
Clermont, Council of, 1095: proclamation of First Crusade 17
clove trade 30, 41, 42
coffee 43
coins 19, 25
colonialism, European 36, 40, 43
Commander of the Faithful 14
Committee of Union and Progress, reform movement in late Ottoman Empire 39
commodities 19
Companions of the Prophet 3, 38
Congress of Berlin, 1878, 37
Constitutional Revolution, in Iran, 1905–11, 37
Constitutions of Medina, foundational document of the early Islamic polity 3
conversion to Islam 2, 3, 4, 5, 8, 21, 24, 30
corn 19
corsairs 31, 33
cotton 19, 20
court life / politics 5, 9
Crimean War, 1853–56 between Britain, France, the Ottoman Empire, and Russia 39
crops 19
Crusades 17, 18
cults 3
customary law (*'adat*), in Southeast Asia 43

Da"n, Treaty of, 1904 between British and Ottomans dividing Yemen 39
Dark Ages 5
dates 19
da'wa, religious mission (of Fatimids) 10
Deoband *madrasa* in Muslim India 36, 43
Description de l'Égypte, encyclopedia compiled after the Napoleonic expedition of 1798, 38
devşirme, levy of Christian/Muslim boy recruits for the Ottoman army and bureaucracy 25
disease 22, 23
Dome of the Rock, the 'Noble Sanctuary' in Jerusalem, 4
Dutch East India Company (VOC) 30, 31, 34, 42

earthquakes 20
East India Company (English / British) 31, 34, 35, 36
economic recession 11
Edirne, Treaty of, 1829, between Ottomans and Russians 38
education 36, 39, 43
'ethnic cleansing' in Balkans 39

family sovereignty 16
     see also **appanage**
Fara'izi movement, in Muslim India 36, 43
farming 19, 42
'fiefdoms' 25
Fifth Crusade 18
Firangi Mahal *madrasa*, in Lucknow, India 34
First Crusade 17

First World War, 1914–18, 39
food supply 19, 20, 31
fortifications 27
'forward policy' in British India 37
Fourth Crusade 18
Friday prayer 9
Friday sermon 18
fruit 19

gold 14, 19, 20, 33
grain 19
Great Schism between Catholic and Orthodox churches 2
Greek (Orthodox) Church 2
Greek philosophy 6

hadith, 'tradition literature' 6, 11
hajib, chamberlain, at 'Abbasid court 5
Hanbali *madhhab*, Sunni school of Islamic law 38
Hatt-i Hümayun, Imperial Reform Edict, 1856, 39
Hatt-i Şerif of Gülhane, Rose Chamber Edict, 1839, 39
Hattin, Battle of, 1187, between Crusaders and Ayyubids 18
hijra, the Prophet's migration from Mecca to Medina in September 622, 3
Hinduism 29
holy war *see* **crusades**; *jihad*
horses 19
hospitals 11

icons 5
ijtihad, interpretation of religious texts 36, 43
Ikhwan, Wahhabi zealots 39
Imperial Bank of Persia 37
Imperial Reform Edict, issued by Ottomans in 1856, 39
Indian Ocean trade 20, 41
Indian revolt of 1857, 36, 43
iqta', land grant 12
iron 19
Islam
     advent of 2
     conversion to 2, 3, 4, 5, 8, 21, 22, 30
     Central Asia 24, 32, 37, 43
     East Africa 41, 43
     India 9, 16, 20, 28, 29, 34, 35, 36, 43
     Islamic law 3, 30, 37, 39, 42
     messianism 10
     modernism 43
     North Africa 14, 33, 43
     origins 2
     reform 36, 38, 40, 42, 43
     Russia, 25, 32, 37, 43
     Southeast Asia 30, 42, 43
     taxation 38
     theology 6, 29
     'trading diaspora' 15
     West Africa 15, 33, 43
     see also **Isma'ilism; Shi'ism; Sunni Islam**

Index

(B) INDEX OF PERSONAL AND GROUP NAMES

Index

Index

Index

Index

Index

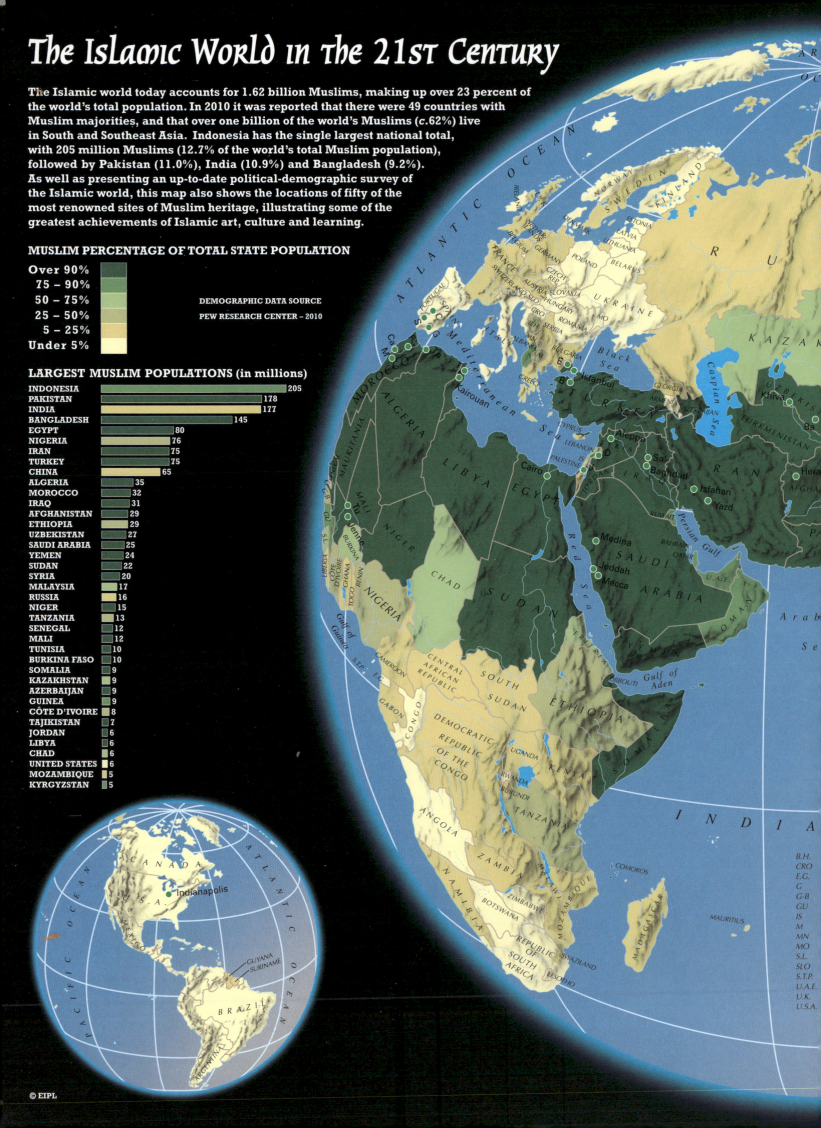

The Islamic World in the 21st Century

The Islamic world today accounts for 1.62 billion Muslims, making up over 23 percent of the world's total population. In 2010 it was reported that there were 49 countries with Muslim majorities, and that over one billion of the world's Muslims (*c.*62%) live in South and Southeast Asia. Indonesia has the single largest national total, with 205 million Muslims (12.7% of the world's total Muslim population), followed by Pakistan (11.0%), India (10.9%) and Bangladesh (9.2%). As well as presenting an up-to-date political-demographic survey of the Islamic world, this map also shows the locations of fifty of the most renowned sites of Muslim heritage, illustrating some of the greatest achievements of Islamic art, culture and learning.

MUSLIM PERCENTAGE OF TOTAL STATE POPULATION

- Over 90%
- 75 – 90%
- 50 – 75%
- 25 – 50%
- 5 – 25%
- Under 5%

DEMOGRAPHIC DATA SOURCE
PEW RESEARCH CENTER – 2010

LARGEST MUSLIM POPULATIONS (in millions)

Country	Population
INDONESIA	205
PAKISTAN	178
INDIA	177
BANGLADESH	145
EGYPT	80
NIGERIA	76
IRAN	75
TURKEY	75
CHINA	65
ALGERIA	35
MOROCCO	32
IRAQ	31
AFGHANISTAN	29
ETHIOPIA	29
UZBEKISTAN	27
SAUDI ARABIA	25
YEMEN	24
SUDAN	22
SYRIA	20
MALAYSIA	17
RUSSIA	16
NIGER	15
TANZANIA	13
SENEGAL	12
MALI	12
TUNISIA	10
BURKINA FASO	10
SOMALIA	9
KAZAKHSTAN	9
AZERBAIJAN	9
GUINEA	9
CÔTE D'IVOIRE	8
TAJIKISTAN	7
JORDAN	6
LIBYA	6
CHAD	6
UNITED STATES	6
MOZAMBIQUE	5
KYRGYZSTAN	5